Cinema, Politics and Society in America

Cinema, Politics and Society in America

edited by
Philip Davies and Brian Neve

St. Martin's Press
New York

First published in the United States of America in 1981

All rights reserved. For information write:
St. Martin's Press, Inc.,
175 Fifth Avenue,
New York, NY 10010

Library of Congress Card Catalog Number 81–52234

ISBN 0–312–13901–2

Photoset in Garamond by
Northern Phototypesetting Co., Bolton
Printed in Great Britain

Contents

Acknowledgements

The editors wish to acknowledge the help provided by the American Politics Group of the Political Studies Association in the form of a grant during the planning stages of this volume. Julie Lawson and Julie Richardson typed fast and accurately in Bath, while in Manchester Rosamund Davies not only provided secretarial assistance, but hosted visiting authors, managed the house and baby Andrew while the editors created domestic chaos, and was generous with suggestions, encouragement and support. Thanks are also due to the staff of Manchester University Press, especially John Banks, for constructive help at all stages of production.

Philip Davies and Brian Neve

Introduction

The papers in this book draw in particular on a number of recent developments in the study of American film and the American film industry: a revived interest in the social significance of the recurring themes and images of American film, and a growing body of work on the political and economic history of the American film industry. The last decade has seen increased interest in the study of feature films in order better to understand the political and social climates of particular times, and changes in these climates over time. There seems little doubt about the potential of this approach although film specialists may well be sceptical about analyses which isolate individual films from relevant questions of film tradition, genre and authorship. While the social and political context of production is at times essential to an adequate reading of film, there is certainly a danger of explicating film as if its meaning were entirely unproblematic, and of using catch-all phrases such as 'reflect' and 'mirror' without adequate thought as to the processes involved. Whatever the discipline on which such study is based, the most successful work is likely to add to knowledge of social, political and industrial factors involved in a film's production, while also attempting to deal with the films on their own terms. The lines of influence between film and society are by no means easy to draw, and it is difficult – on the basis of aggregate studies of popular culture and its relationship to social forces – to arbitrate between conceptions of Hollywood as essentially manipulative, and those which see stars and themes as direct responses to popular wishes and desires. The interactions become even more complex when bankers, politicians and censors are brought into the analysis.

Christopher Frayling examines the Western from a social perspective by way of a critique of the varying attempts made to put the Western genre, and its changes over time, into a wider cultural and social context. Rejecting those approaches which see the Western in terms of American 'foundation myths' and the conflicts attendant on the coming of 'civilisation' to the West, Frayling argues that Will Wright's study *Sixguns and Society* provides the basis for more fruitful work by seeking to explain – with reference to changes in the social structure of twentieth-century America – key shifts in the plots of film Westerns. Wright uses key texts of social analysis as touchstones of the socio-economic structure, but uses the concepts of myth and narrative structure in a much more rigorous way than before. As Frayling points out, Wright is weakest in his lack of interest in the changing industrial structure of the American film industry; changing themes may reflect the changing industry structure and the establishment of television as the staple provider of mass genre entertainment. Certainly there are problems – not only in the assessment of film profits – in comparing films of the period described in Michael Wood's study of *America in the Movies* with those of the 1970s and 1980s.[1]

Robert Reiner also finds Wright's work to be heuristic, but not entirely suitable for his survey of cops in American film. Reiner analyses the 'vigilante spirit' of the 1930s G-Man cycle, and the role of private eyes and detectives in postwar *film noir* and neo-documentary. But his most extensive examination is of the films of the period since the mid-1960s which he sees as revolving around the tensions of 'law versus order and professional versus bureaucracy'. Here again there are traces of a 'vigilante spirit' in characteristic films of the period; Clint Eastwood's film persona is to the right, and yet he remains a counter-cultural star, a fact that says something of the weakening of 1960s liberalism in the years that followed.

Studies of individual films from a 'film and history' or 'film and society' perspective attempt to explicate intentions, the mix of contributions and financial and other pressures, and contemporary interpretations and reactions.[2] As well as the dangers of undervaluing the visual content of film, and of ignoring the techniques of film scholarship, there may in this approach be excessive reliance on key social science texts as representing the reality of particular periods. Brian Neve seeks to provide social context to *On the Waterfront*, while not disputing the primacy of the film. He claims no methodology able to reveal its essential meaning, or to determine the reactions of its contemporary audience, although box-office figures can certainly indicate something of a film's social impact. A 'reading' of the film is suggested; but a 'reading' is precisely what it is, not a revealed truth.

Eric Mottram's allusive style – in accumulating images – matches that of the movies themselves, and his contribution raises to consciousness a series of rarely acknowledged images and motifs in American film. Leonard Quart contributes a discussion of the revival of working-class themes in the American cinema of the 1970s. He draws attention to the apparent influence of *On the Waterfront* on this revival; apart from more obvious examples, *White Line Fever* (directed and co-written by Jonathan Kaplan in 1975) seems to echo some of the themes of the earlier film. In relation to the 1950s, a number of studies have suggested the impact of social life – from 'grey flannel' conformity to H-bomb anxiety – on the films of the period. The effect is measured in part by Michael Wood in his analysis of the increasing strain involved in reproducing the happy-go-lucky Gene Kelly musicals as the 1950s progressed. A film such as *The Invasion of the Body Snatchers* (Don Siegel, 1956) – as analysed by Stuart Samuels is almost too full of social meaning, while the concern with civic indifference – for example in Phil Karlson's *The Phenix City Story*, in 1955, as well as in *On the Waterfront* – also has social implications for the period.[3] The writing of documentary histories of individual films, the study of the development of the key genres of American film, and the analysis of aspects of American life as portrayed by Hollywood – all these approaches, amongst others, may provide for an eventual narrowing down of the pluralistic agenda of relationships between film and society that Michael Wood has drawn up, and which is quoted by Christopher Frayling in his discussion of the Western. Wood has put the problem as follows: 'I mean, what *are* those meanings I talk about in my book. They seem to me to be *there*; but if no one connected with the making of the film thought of them, and no one in the audience at the time saw them, what exactly does *there* mean?'[4]

The industrial structure of Hollywood provides an economic and commercial environment with its own particular consequences for the movies. From its beginnings in many small companies to its present form as a multinational enterprise, the American film industry has always had to balance normal commercial practice against the peculiar nature of its own product. The success of the industry depends on selling a relatively short-lived product in an unpredictable market. Film-makers have tried to impose as much order as possible on this difficult situation, primarily by repeated attempts to institute some form of economic centralisation. As Richard Maltby points out in his discussion of the studio system, moves towards cartel practices were evident as early as 1908 with the formation of the Motion Picture Patents Company (MPPC). During the early years of film entertainment in the United States the important patents on cameras, projectors, film and other essential materials were held by different, competing companies, of which Edison and Biograph were the most significant. These two companies, and others such as Vitagraph and Pathe, attempted to gain greater industrial control by instituting a series of patent suits and counter-suits which eventually numbered over five hundred.[5]

The formation of the Motion Picture Patents Company signified a truce in this expensive legal wrangle whereby the patents of ten companies involved in manufacture and distribution of motion pictures were pooled. The MPPC also organised the General Film Company which bought out smaller distributors or forced them out of business. Together with the MPPC's monopoly on the use of Eastman film stock and control over projector patents, this tightened its domination of production, distribution and exhibition of movies. These developments were stimulated by the belief that monopoly would ensure reliable profits and industrial stability, but the drive to monopoly never met with complete success. Although by 1912 the MPPC controlled more than half the exhibition outlets and much of the production side of the industry, that still left room for independent production and exhibition – even some of the MPPC's own employees were tempted into the independent side of the industry. The end of this early movement to economic centralisation in the film industry came in 1918 when the federal courts accepted the United States government's case that the practices of the company violated the Sherman Anti-Trust Act.[6]

The demise of the MPPC did not halt the drive towards the safety offered by centralised control in the film industry. Independents amalgamated, expanded and became vertically integrated; in the aftermath of the 1918 anti-trust decision major film companies were formed which prospered with the development of the studio system. Co-operation between the leading companies – Paramount, Loew's Inc. (MGM), Twentieth Century–Fox, Warner Brothers, RKO, Columbia, Universal and United Artists – reduced competition, stabilised the market and allowed the companies to control all stages of the industry without resorting to discredited attempts to establish a formal monopoly. The ability to exert effective national control over the product had in its turn consequences for the form that product took. Maltby argues that the wish to maintain a reliable profit discouraged experimentation and created a tendency towards a standardised product. In an industry where control of production was in a few hands, and where films produced outside the major studio system stood little chance of finding a distributor, any trend towards standardisation was liable to be a powerful guiding force.

If the film industry had been timid in its choice and treatment of subjects this cannot be attributed solely to limitations imposed directly by market forces. Some sections of the American public acknowledged the potential social and political power of movies at a very early stage in the industry's development. Even the earliest Kinetoscope films attracted censorious comment, and by 1922 Donald Ramsey Young was able to report approvingly on a wide variety of censorship bodies.[7]

In Chicago the licensing of films for exhibition was a power accorded to
the Department of Police, while some States followed Pennsylvania's
1911 lead in setting up Boards of Censors. Legal backing for censorship
was provided by the Supreme Court in the 1915 case of Mutual Film
Corporation *v.* Industrial Commission of Ohio, a decision that was used
to justify censorship even of newsreels.[8]

Non-governmental bodies were also watching the movies carefully.
Young mentions the efforts of the General Federation of Women's
Clubs, the Ministerial Association of Lancaster, Pennsylvania, and the
Women's Co-operative Alliance of Minneapolis. These and many other
civic groups voiced the growing middle-class concern about the social
power of the film industry. The efforts of these groups were spurred by
views such as Young's that '. . . the number of pictures tending to have a
harmful effect on motion picture patrons [is estimated] at 20 per cent'.
His fears were not restricted to the contents of the films since he
contended that 'there is an undoubted effect on standards of conduct
resulting from the fact that the audience, often young boys and girls, are
packed in narrow seats, close together, in a darkened room'.[9]

By the time Young's dissertation supporting censorship was
published, impetus for the censorship lobby had been provided by
scandal in Hollywood. Roscoe (Fatty) Arbuckle was charged with the
manslaughter of actress Virginia Rappe; film director William Desmond
Taylor was murdered; actor Wallace Reid died of narcotics addiction:
the worst suspicions of Hollywood debauchery and immorality seemed
to be confirmed. Arbuckle's films were immediately banned in New
York, Chicago, Los Angeles and many other cities, and in spite of his
eventual acquittal his career was destroyed. More generally these
scandals set off such a spate of State and local censorship activity that in
1922 the film industry moved to institute its own regulatory body, the
Motion Picture Producers and Distributors of America (MPPDA). Will
Hays, then US Postmaster General, was invited to become the first
President of MPPDA.

The first regulatory effort of the Hays Office was the 1924
'Formula', whereby the office reviewed plays and novels which were to

be adapted to the screen. A more general attempt at regulation was the 1929 'Don'ts and Be Carefuls', a list of subjects which were to be handled with care and discretion. The next step was the Production Code of 1930, a complex set of guidelines for film-makers. However each of these regulatory instruments was easily evaded, and it was not until the formation of the Catholic League of Decency, with its very effective campaign of boycotting movies it considered offensive, that the MPPDA created effective machinery to enforce the code. Once again, the industry showed that in the face of adversity timidity was considered the best response.[10]

In dealing with the themes of the cinema of the 1930s, Philip Melling discusses Andrew Bergman's interpretation of 'Depression America and its films'.[11] Bergman argues that a study of the successful films and film cycles of the 1930s can reveal many of the popular feelings and assumptions of the time, and that the films of the period 'showed that individual initiative still bred success, that the federal government was a benevolent watchman, that we were a classless, melting pot nation'. He argues that in choosing between alternatives – all of which reflect contemporary social attitudes in some way – the public triggers a reinforcing response from Hollywood which articulates the currently dominant social myths of the nation. Philip Melling questions whether the relationship between political events and events in the popular culture was as dynamic as Bergman suggests. Seeing mainly an *evasion* of politics in the Hollywood film of the period, Melling questions whether the 'tensions and assumptions' of the time can be found in the intellectual histories of the films. He draws attention to the limited popularity of the Warner Brothers 'topicals' in the 1930s; this, and the great financial success of 'escapist' films, is confirmed – however impressionistically – by reading the lists of top money-making films for that decade.[12] Instead Melling stresses the continuity of 1920s film themes – particularly the 'enduring appeal of self-sufficient individualism' – and argues that it was the incongruity between these themes and the meagre opportunities available in Depression America that led to the prominence of scapegoats in the cinema of the mid and late 1930s.

As has been pointed out, the ex-'poverty row' studios of Warner Brothers and Columbia seemed to be more independent of New York control in the 1930s, and their product to some extent reflects this greater independence.[13] The strong social element in Warner Brothers productions, and the pro-New Deal attitude (continued into the war years) probably owes something to Jack Warner's close friendship with Franklin D. Roosevelt. Elsewhere in Hollywood, in their resistance to the guilds and their virulent campaign against Upton Sinclair's bid for the Governorship of California in 1934, the moguls of the 1930s generally struck a public posture firmly to the right. A Warner Brothers 'topical' such as *Marked Woman* (Lloyd Bacon, 1937) clearly reflects contemporary class politics; the co-scriptwriter, Robert Rossen, joined the Communist Party in 1937 and contributed a series of scripts for Warners in the late 1930s and early 1940s which reflected an emerging (albeit a minority) Popular Front culture. For example, Rossen's script for *The Sea Wolf* – with Edward G. Robinson, John Garfield and Ida Lupino, and one of the top money-making films of 1941 – was anti-fascist while also celebrating the humanity of the rank and file. Leonard Quart has discussed elsewhere the themes shared in the period 1935–45 by the American Communist Party and the cinema of (among others) Frank Capra and John Ford.[14]

A sociology of Hollywood during this period would be of interest not only in explaining the distinctiveness of the Warner Brothers studio but also in tracking the interchanges between New York (and in particular the radical theatres there) and Hollywood. Richard Maltby, in his contribution on the Congressional investigations, discusses the continuity of personnel involved in socially-oriented films of the 1940s, while Brian Neve touches on the impact of the Group Theatre on Hollywood and on the continuing influence of the New York theatrical world (and later of television) on American cinema. Speaking more broadly, Alexander Walker has argued as follows: 'A fascinating study still waits to be made of the politics of the film capital: not the industry–studio politics, but the radical-reactionary brand which probably came west with the politically conscious talents recruited for the talkies and also with the growth of the totalitarian studio system and its answering response from the craft unions'.[15]

In his paper on Hollywood in the 1940s Ralph Willett discusses the wartime alliance between the American government and the film industry; the 'foreign policy' of Warner Brothers, in particular, had for some time closely followed that of Roosevelt, while other studios and directors worked on propaganda projects for the Administration. Willett goes on to examine the period of American *film noir*, and the related question of the role of women in the films of the mid and late 1940s. He argues that *film noir* 'shows what happens when the individual tries to be exceptional, tries daringly for experience beyond the timid, middle-class world of order, family and deferred gratification'.

Its unity based on style as much as theme, *film noir* — from its semi-romantic beginnings to its psychotic climax — figures largely in studies that attempt to assess the significance for American culture of the recurring themes and images of American film. Barbara Deming argues that the 'heroes and heroines who are most popular at any particular period are precisely those who, with a certain added style, with a certain distinction, act out the predicament from which the movie-dream then cunningly extricates us'. Thus she finds heroes constantly doubting the cause before committing themselves to it. In the loneliness and doubt of the heroes of the period — archetypically Humphrey Bogart in *Casablanca* — Michael Wood sees a dream of freedom and a fear of social obligation at the heart of American culture. Philip Slater, referring to the films of more recent decades, makes the connection another way by arguing that audiences are attracted to generous and altruistic behaviour on the screen while resolutely 'pursuing loneliness' in their everyday life. This ambivalence between generosity, and its undoubted attractiveness, and the eternal American compulsion to finish first, has also been related to the noted 'moralism' in American foreign policy. Why should the United States fight overseas except reluctantly, and with an altruistic objective? From the cold-war crusade to the 'helping the Vietnamese to help themselves' rationalisations of the 1960s, Americans have found self-interest, and national interest, hard concepts to own up to. The bleak, corrupt world of *film noir* proper – in the late 1940s and early 1950s – is certainly more subversive and durable than that of the social problem film of the same time. As Paul Schrader has argued, the rise of McCarthy and Eisenhower showed that Americans were eager to see a 'more bourgeois view of themselves', and 'Any attempt at social criticism had to be cloaked in ludicrous affirmations of the American way of life.'[16]

Even after 1945 the Hollywood Communist Party retained the loyalty of a number of successful scriptwriters. They felt that films such as *Home of the Brave* (1949), *Crossfire* (1947) and *Pinky* (1949) were an important step forward, especially on the question of race – one of the Communist Party's key domestic issues.[17] Independent companies such as Enterprise Studios also indicated a possible model for future, collaborative production. While this company's collapse predated the blacklist era, the films that John Garfield and Bob Roberts contributed to Enterprise – *Body and Soul* (1947) and *Force of Evil* (1948), both scripted by Abraham Polonsky – illustrate the self-critical strain in postwar American cinema that was not to survive the Congressional investigations.[18] The Popular Front culture limped on in (for example) *Gentleman's Agreement*: the explicit Americanism and implicit socialism are merged as ideologies. With the emerging cold war – and President Truman's mobilisation of Congressional and public opinion behind America's active international role – such an association became untenable, and Americanism had to be reassociated with an explicit anticommunism.

Richard Maltby also sees the paranoid atmosphere of *film noir*, in particular the creation of the archetype of the espionage agent, as contributing to the Congressional backlash of 1947. Maltby generally sees the 1947 investigations as a battleground for two paranoid world views, but he also draws attention to more tangible political conflicts. As Maltby suggests, Hollywood, following its recognised and legitimised wartime role, assumed that 'its responsible contribution to the war effort would be converted to a responsible contribution to postwar political debate'. In its efforts to discredit the Roosevelt administration (with which Hollywood had closely associated itself in the war years) and embarrass its successor, the House Committee on Un-American Activities challenged this assumption. While the paranoia was evident – certainly on the Committee's side – and while the social-problem films of the post war period now look less than outspoken, one should not rule out real disputes about the role of popular culture and the control of the massively successful Hollywood machine of 1946.

On 5 October 1945 there was a picket line of more than a thousand formed in front of the Warner Brothers studio gates in Burbank. Looking on, J. L. Warner is said to have declared that he was 'through making pictures about "the little man" '. Richard Maltby discusses how Federal politics descended on Hollywood in 1947, and he is right to stress the impact of John Howard Lawson's testimony in provoking the retreat of Hollywood liberals, leaving the witnesses exposed to the anti-communist purge. The First Amendment strategy was collectively agreed on by the 'unfriendly witnesses', but Edward Dmytryk has said that as soon as he heard Lawson's presentation (with its charge that the Committee, and not the witnesses, were on trial) he knew that the cause was lost.[19] Having said this, in retrospect it is difficult now to see the stand by the Hollywood Ten as anything other than a principled resistance to the Committee and its allies. The Congressional investigations of 1947 and the early 1950s effectively halted Hollywood's interest in social questions, and left in their wake bitter recriminations between friendly and unfriendly witnesses. Few of those blacklisted felt fully able to endorse Dalton Trumbo's magnanimous summary of the affair in 1970: 'It would do no good to search for villains or heroes or saints or devils because there were none; there were only victims'.[20]

Ralph Willett's essay discusses some of the consequences of government involvement in filmmaking during the Second World War. Through the Bureau of Motion Pictures the federal government's Office of War

Information (OWI) persuaded a compliant Hollywood to make a substantial pro-Allies effort. Ironically, compliance with these propaganda demands did not necessarily guarantee continued favour with the federal government. The House Committee on Un-American Activities was later to view with suspicion films that showed Russia in a favourable light, and that treated sympathetically the problems of America's black or Jewish minorities – themes that the OWI had encouraged. The federal government also established the Information Media Guaranty Program which, starting in 1948, gave a subsidy on foreign currency earned by the exportation of films, providing the exported films reflected the best elements of American life.[21] While it may have been inconsistent about just what these best elements were, the government never wavered from the belief that film had a significant propaganda role at home and abroad.

By the 1940s the industrial practices of the film industry were again causing official concern that competition was being stifled. This led, in 1948, to another Supreme Court decision (United States *v.* Paramount Pictures 334 US 131) ordering an end to some practices whereby the major studios maintained control of every stage in the industry from production to exhibition. Most significantly the studios were ordered to sell off their lucrative cinema chains. As both Maltby and Davies point out, simultaneously with this new economic order came a vigorous political attack on the industry from Congressional investigators, and a substantial fall in audience figures. Audiences had fallen before; the industry had been investigated before, and each of these problems had been overcome. However, shorn of their theatre chains the major studios no longer had available the massive regular income that came from exhibition. Without this economic cushion the ability to weather the new storm seemed limited.

The industry up to the 1950s has been accused of catering too much to a broad, uniform definition of public taste, stifling the talents that could have been used with the adoption of a more pluralistic approach.[22] As audiences continued to fall and traditional attractions did not reverse the trend, an atmosphere of desparate experimentation developed in the early 1950s. If Hollywood's market aim had been too generalised before, now there began the discovery of specialised, commercially viable markets within the movie-going audience. At the same time the strictures of the MPPDA Production Code were being breached – once these rules were not contributing to a stable, healthy market they became expendable in the search for new audiences. A declining role for censorship was also indicated by the Court's comments in the Paramount case that 'We have no doubt that moving pictures, the newspapers and radio, are included in the press whose freedom is guaranteed by the First Amendment', and extended in 1952 when the Court struck down a New York State censorship statute.[23]

Conventional genres could not contain the new approaches to film. A more personal style of film-making, which some directors had achieved within the studio system, became more generally accepted within the industry. The traditional fear of controversy and novelty took second place to the growing fear of economic collapse. Themes which had always played a minor role in the film industry became the subject of substantial investments (see Mary Ellison on 'Blacks in American film', and Eric Mottram's 'Blood on the Nash Ambassador: cars in American film'); while subjects which had always been among the mainstays of Hollywood's output gained new directions (see Christopher Frayling on 'The Western'; Robert Reiner's 'Keystone to Kojak: the Hollywood cop'; and Leonard Quart and Albert Auster, 'The working class goes to Hollywood'). Some of these themes found small, reliable audiences, which suggested that a regular profit could be made with the possibility that adjustments to the product could widen the audience appeal.

Outside the studio system some independent producers were successfully marketing low-budget action-packed movies aimed at suburban drive-ins and other non-first-run cinemas. Chief among these independent producers was Roger Corman who, first at American International Pictures, then with his own New World Pictures, became expert at the cheap production and rapid turnover of exploitation movies. His method was aimed at producing 'The Greatest Ten Day Picture of the Decade', a self-parodying accolade Corman himself gave to *Hollywood Boulevard*. By always having two film units and two directors operating on the same location, and often with the same actors, he ensured as little waste of resources as possible. Faltering plots and banal scripts were rescued by a stress on movement, action, visual impact, sex and violence – and by skillful film editing.

Corman also helped train a new generation of film-makers. An element of his cost-cutting was to find promising film students and offer them work. Openings in the film industry have always been few, so the work experience was more important to these students than the pay. Therefore labour costs could be kept very low while talented young film-makers had the opportunity to learn every facet of the industry. By the late 1960s some of these skilled newcomers were making their mark. The phenomenal success of *Easy Rider* (1969) in particular gave the major production companies pause for thought. The film was produced by a company including Corman protegés Jack Nicholson and Peter Fonda, and contained the Corman formula of action, movement and violence held together with a pinch of social statement. Its success confirmed the studio executives in their growing willingness to accommodate new talent and new themes.

The major studios' attempt to corner the 'youth market' (prompted by *Easy Rider*), and other profitable minority sectors, often met with little success. Many such themes remained the province of small companies catering to the cult taste of midnight movie audiences. However, as Davies points out, Hollywood's period of frantic experimentation had allowed new personnel to become established in the industry. Independent companies were putting together the majority of film packages; finance came from major companies which were now often just part of the 'leisure services' branch of some conglomerate business; and film school graduates and trainees from small companies such as American International were showing their talents in major productions. This new film-making combination has thrived.

The contemporary health of American film production does not signal a massive return of the lost audience of the 1950s. Rather a revised economic structure has allowed the redevelopment of old protective practices. Television has an appetite for programming that has long made it a market for films, and developments such as the widespread ownership of colour sets, and the expansion of cable television systems, have enlarged this market.[24] Also increasingly significant are international sales. While always important to Hollywood, the decline of many national film industries – and the inability of others to compete with the scale of American film investment – has increased the United States' hegemony of the screen. American film takes up over half of the world's screen time, and American companies virtually monopolise international film distribution.[25] Furthermore the Paramount decision does not apply to television or to international business, allowing an almost inevitable drift towards the monopolistic practices which characterised previous periods of economic stability.

This new economic stability has been accompanied by a re-emergence of staid ways. The heavily advertised, pre-sold blockbuster with plenty of tie-in products now attracts vast financing. Some of the talented 1960s newcomers to Hollywood have become a new establishment. This generation of film-makers has been accused of knowing 'everything about film, and nothing about life',[26] an impression that such films as *Star Wars*, *Close Encounters of the Third Kind* (1977), *Obsession* (1976) and *1941* (1979) tend to support. But film has not been reduced to superficiality and special effects. For example, *The China Syndrome* (1979) tackles the serious problem of the threat posed by nuclear power plants; and *Apocalypse Now* (1979) portrays vividly the horrors of war; and some small projects can still be put together – but in general substantial commercial backing shies away from controversial films. The new economic order has provided major investors with a relatively firm long-term pay-off but one which relies on an international television and cinema audience. To maintain interest without giving offence in such a large market may lead increasingly to films of powerful visual form, but little content.

Despite the almost complete abolition of censorship, Hollywood is no nearer to any explicit concern with politics or political ideas. Films about institutional or (in the 1960s) street politics have been more numerous than might be supposed,[27] but have usually concerned issues of individual morality rather than questions of programme or ideology. From *Advise and Consent* (1962) and *The Best Man* (1964) to *The Candidate* (1972) and *The Seduction of Joe Tynan* (1979) the corruptions of power and power-seeking are dominant themes. Just as politicians must become celebrities in order to gain power, so celebrities are half way to becoming politicians; indeed, in a country lacking a debate about public philosphies, style may be everything. From John Wayne, courted by Governor Wallace to be his running mate in 1968, through Jane Fonda, to Ronald Reagan's successful bid for the Presidency in 1980, the interconnections between Hollywood and media politics have been considerable. With the decline of party politics, the Presidential system is even more vulnerable to celebrity. Eisenhower's style represented 1950s middle-America just as James Dean came to represent an emerging youth culture. John Kennedy became a celebrity in the White House by pursuing a 'heroic', Hollywood-type, Presidential style; *John Ford's Cuban Missile Crisis* was a successful underground play of the 1960s. Such tendencies, however impressionistic, seem to fit Christopher Lasch's model of an emerging 'culture of narcisism' in America.[28] Following Watergate, 'faction', in the shape of the crusading journalists of *All the President's Men* (1976) and the White House aides of *Washington Behind Closed Doors* (1977), became 'box office'. Only in the troubled metaphors of *Night Moves* (1975), *The Parallax View* (1974), *Coma* (1978) and other films is there some reflection of the sense of pessimism and of impenetrable power – beyond the reach of any individual hero to resolve – that came to America in the wake of the political traumas and disappointments of the 1970s.

Notes

1   Will Wright, *Sixguns and Society: a Structural Study of the Western* (Berkeley, Calif., 1975); Michael Wood, *America in the Movies* (New York, 1975). See also John H. Lenihan, *Showdown: Confronting*

Modern America in the Western Film (Urbana, Ill., 1980).

2   John E. O'Connor and Martin A. Jackson, *American History/American Film: Interpreting the Hollywood Image* (New York, 1979).

3   Stuart Samuels, 'The Age of Conspiracy and Conformity: "Invasion of the Body Snatchers" (1956)' in O'Connor and Jackson, *American History/American Film*, pp. 204–17.

4   We take the liberty of quoting a letter by Michael Wood to Brian Neve, 4 October 1978.

5   James Monaco, *How to Read a Film* (New York, 1977), pp. 199–201; J. T. Allen, 'The Decay of the Motion Picture Patents Company', in *The American Film Industry*, ed. Tino Balio (Madison, Wis., 1976), pp. 119–34.

6   United States *v.* The Motion Picture Patents Company (1918).

7   Donald Ramsey Young, *Motion Pictures: a Study in Social Legislation* (Philadelphia, Pa., 1922).

8   Mutual Film Corporation *v.* Industrial Commission of Ohio 236 US 230 (1915).

9   Young, *Motion Pictures*, pp. 6, 83.

10 Cobbett Steinberg, *Reel Facts* (New York, 1978), pp. 456ff.

11 Andrew Bergman, *We're in the Money: Depression America and its Films* (New York, 1971).

12 Steinberg, *Reel Facts*, pp. 339–41.

13 Edward Buscombe, 'Walsh and Warner Brothers', in *Raoul Walsh*, ed. Phil Hardy (Colchester, 1974), pp. 51–61.

14 Leonard Quart, 'Frank Capra and the Popular Front', *Cineaste*, vol. VIII, No. 1 (summer 1977), pp. 4–7.

15 Alexander Walker, *Stardom: the Hollywood Phenomenon* (Harmondsworth, 1974), p. 300.

16 Paul Schrader, 'Notes on film noir', *Film Comment*, vol. 8, No. 1 (spring 1972), pp. 8–13; Barbara Deming, *Running Away from Myself: a Dream Portrait of America Drawn From the Films of the 40s* (New York, 1969); Michael Wood, *America in the Movies*; Philip Slater, *The Pursuit of Loneliness* (Harmondsworth, 1971), p. 8.

17 Larry Ceplair and Steven Englund, *The Inquisition in Hollywood: Politics in the Film Community 1930–60* (New York, 1980), p. 73.

18 Allen Eyles, 'Films of Enterprise', *Focus on Film*, No. 35 (April 1980), pp. 13–27.

19 Gordon Kahn, *Hollywood on Trial* (New York, 1948), p. 11; Edward Dmytryk, soundtrack of *Hollywood on Trial* (film, directed by David

Helpern, USA, 1976).

20   Quoted in Victor S. Navasky, 'The Hollywood Ten Recalled: To Name
     or Not to Name', *New York Times Magazine* (25 March 1973), p.
     111. See the debate between Lou and Mickey in Arthur Miller, *After
     the Fall* (Harmondsworth, 1968), pp. 40–5.

21   T. H. Guback, 'Film as International Business', *Journal of
     Communication*, vol. XXIV (winter 1974), p. 94.

22   See I. C. Jarvie, *Movies and Society* (New York, 1970), pp. 276–8.

23   Burstyn *v.* Wilson 343 US 495 (1952).

24   US Bureau of the Census, *Statistical Abstract of the United States: 1979*
     (100th edition) (Washington, D.C., 1979), pp. 585, 587.

25   T. H. Guback, 'Film as International Business'.

26   James Monaco, *American Film Now* (New York, 1979), p. 51.

27   Andrew Sarris, *Politics and Cinema* (New York, 1978), p. 17.

28   Christopher Lasch, *The Culture of Narcissism: American Life in an Age of
     Diminishing Expectations* (New York, 1978). Also see James David
     Barber, *The Pulse of Politics: Electing Presidents in the Media Age* (New
     York, 1980).

P. H. Melling

The mind of the mob:
Hollywood and popular culture
in the 1930s

The belief that 'in any period of stress there are certain tensions which permeate a society and affect the majority of its functioning members, artists and moviemakers included' has led Andrew Bergman, in his study of American cinema in the 1930s, to suggest that moviemakers of this period did not intuit the yearnings of a 'natural unconscious, but felt the same tensions everyone else did and wanted to represent them in various ways'.[1] Bergman's argument rests on the assumption that popular culture in a period of stress is the product of events in the political culture, that 'tensions' expressed through the popular culture are 'tensions' transferred from politics to art. Although the argument is ingeniously applied throughout the book I am not altogether sure that the assumption on which it rests is a correct one: that the 1930s was a period in which popular throught and the culture which expresses it were shaped by events in politics and economics between 1929 and 1941. It may be true that, as Bergman asserts, 'Sixty million persons did not escape into a void each week', since people 'do not escape into something they cannot relate to'.[2] But it is not necessarily true also that what people did 'relate to' was determined by shifts which took place in their political consciousness. The 'tensions' of the 1930s may have been inflamed by the Crash in 1929 but they were not wholly activated by the Crash or resolved on the occasion of Roosevelt's inauguration. It is debatable whether we can assume that a loss of faith in legitimate institutions from 1929 to 1933 was simply manifested in a cinema of despair. Nor is it certain that a cinema of despair prior to 1933 was subsequently displaced by a cinema of social consciousness which reflected an increase in public confidence in the benevolence and accountability of the federal government. The response to Frank Capra in 1934 or the response to the 'G-Men' was not necessarily of a piece with that response to Franklin D. Roosevelt. Nor should it be seen as proof or evidence of a reduction in 'tension' occasioned by a style of consensus politics. Although we might have sympathy with Bergman's desire to repudiate the language of mystical critics like Siegfried Kracauer (for whom a cinema of 'stress' is a cinema of 'intuition')[3] and those crypto-Puritans on the left and right who attack mass art as a form of barbarism (as a reductive influence on both cultural standards and proletarian ideals), the mechanical reasoning implicit in his argument seems inadequate to deal with that evasion of politics in Hollywood films of the 1930s.

Critics of 1930s popular culture have laid a false trail by concentrating too greatly on the symbolic significance of events which occurred in 1929 and 1933. A too-common suggestion is that if popular thought has its origin in politics and its outlet in film then 'the intellectual history of the films' will provide us with 'the richest of sources for studying . . . the tensions and assumptions of the period'.[4] It is difficult to accept this line of reasoning since the relationship between political events and events in popular culture in the 1930s was much less dynamic than critics have assumed. Hollywood paid little or no attention for example to those 'assumptions' which characterised the debates of writers on the left in the early 1930s. Nor in later years did it show any willingness to assess the aims of the Popular Front although 'the war in Spain' as Leslie Fiedler makes abundantly clear 'was the chief event of the Thirties for most of us [writers and intellectuals]'.[5] If the 1930s was an age of apocalyptic faith for writers and intellectuals then it was also the casualty of a failed apocalypse. Spain occurred and Hollywood ignored it; so did Roosevelt. In the most distinguished literature of the 1930s, popular cinema and popular politics were seen to distract the public from the real issues. Movements on the left, argues Fiedler, were the victims both of meliorism and of obsessions fostered by consumer industries. Marxism emerged as one of the great lost causes of the 1930s, its image ruined by the Moscow show trials and the Hitler–Stalin pact. Spain too became an indecisive defeat in a 'marginal' engagement, an event of symbolic promise but not realised fact; what Fiedler records in a sentimental quest for purity in the 1930s as part of 'the other memory'.

A common argument of those on the left who survived the 1930s is that the radical energies of the American public were somehow diverted by the organised deceit of Hollywood and Roosevelt. A conspiracy, it is said, can be seen to exist in the support which Jack Warner gave to Roosevelt and in the capitalist paternalism of Warner Brothers 'topicals'. Thus *Heroes for Sale* (1933), *Wild Boys of the Road* (1933) and *Angels with Dirty Faces* (1938) are seen as being fraudulent since they corrupt public need with a soft-centred programme which encourages the muting of class anxieties and stresses the need for victims to endure within a pseudo-reformist social structure. The assumption here is that the public was deceived where the intellectual was betrayed. But it is doubtful whether the film-watching public was deeply offended by the lack of interest of Hollywood in the aims and energies of the Popular Front or deceived by the lip service it paid to radicalism. Political doctrine was not required from Hollywood cinema by fans in the 1930s. Nor was it required in large doses from American politicians who used the mass media to promote their image. An exercise in style, not a display of doctrine, was what the people wanted from personality figures. Hence the success of Roosevelt who, on his radio chat shows, appealed to the people not with dull involved statements of party policy but through theatrical methods. The political style of a successful politician like Roosevelt smoothly complemented the prevailing style in advertising industries and the popular culture. Roosevelt possessed the ability to entertain in a way that expressed his feeling for occasion and his intimate knowledge of the common man's needs. It was not the ideology of liberalism that made Roosevelt such an appealing figure – a liberalism which, when articulated, was often vague and inconsistent – but his extremely shrewd awareness of how to exploit a great variety of acting styles in order to drum up support for his Presidency. Roosevelt was a star of both radio and film who knew his audience and could intuit its needs. He mastered the media where other American presidents have been mastered by it. In his radio shows he was informal, humorous and self-assured; in newsreel film coverage he always took care that the cameras portrayed him as often as possible as the relaxed individual talking to the public, his natural friends.

The appeal of Frank Capra's films throughout the 1930s – *Mr Deeds Goes to Town* (1936), *Mr Smith goes to Washington* (1939), *Meet John Doe* (1941) – suggested that the film-watching public were happy with a politics that went no further than to emphasise the virtues of provincial decency and sentimental good-neighbourliness. Whenever 1930s cinema offered even the mildest of instructions in New Deal politics, the power of liberalism seemed severely limited. Whatever relief the voting public felt on the occasion of Roosevelt's inauguration in 1933, the film-watching public, immediately afterwards, was none too eager for a cinema of social consciousness. Roosevelt may have received overwhelming support through the ballot box, but Warner Brothers 'topicals' were never really integral to popular affections. Bottom-dog films of the 1930s which reminded the audience of the grimness of the times were never as popular as bottom-dog films in which the audience might participate with a character who fought against the bleakness of routine. The appeal of Paul Muni, in *I am a Fugitive* (1932), was thus not dissimilar from the appeal of Henry Fonda in *The Grapes of Wrath* (1940), since both Muni and Fonda played characters who, in spite of their experience of degrading conditions, impassively refused to accept their lot. Grim reminders of social conditions were not capable, on their own, of persuading the public to return to the cinema after 1933. Nor did the presence of New Deal agencies in 'topical' films provide the right answer to the call from Jesse Lasky in 1931 for those 'new ideas' which might reawaken interest in the movie industry.[6] It was not the appearance of the great Blue Eagle (symbol of the Administration's programme for national recovery) in the New Deal cinema of William Wellman (*Heroes For Sale*) and Alan Crosland (*Massacre*, 1934) which encouraged the public to return to the movies and witness the achievements of a benevolent federalism. The return to movie-going by the end of 1933 had much more to do with the gimmicks of salesmanship and the novelties of advertising. On certain nights Rialto chinaware was generously distributed in cinema foyers. On the cinema stage assistant managers came and spun a carnival wheel while the audience waited anxiously for the winning number. The lottery of the windfall, the lure of the miracle beyond grim endurance – not reminders of politics but distractions from it – these Banko, Keeno and Screeno games were popular fashions with cinema fans. It is hard to accept that a cinema public which responded so immediately to the lure of the novel and the promise of easy riches received its films in a mood that was shaped by sensitive responses to changes that occurred in the political culture.

It would be wrong to assume that the significance of popular culture in the 1930s may be simply explained by assessing the function of an entertaining style. Conventional politicians were successful when their style of performance was a derivative of that style which prevailed in entertainment industries. The same can be said of those neo-fascist leaders of the 1930s who relied for their appeal on providing their members with lavish costumes and presented themselves as theatrical superstars. But acting ability alone and the adoption of a theatrical style does little to explain the underlying significance of the appeal of popular culture in the 1930s or the range of needs it sought to satisfy. Successful politicians explain, at best, only the surface appeal of popular culture. They provide only limited satisfaction to consumer needs, the existence of which, in many cases, preceeded the arrival of the American Depression.

In the 1920s the appeal of politics had begun to split apart from the needs of a mass-consumption culture. In *Middletown* (1929), the Lynds quote a revealing *Saturday Evening Post* advertisement in which the very process of daydreaming is confidently offered as a replacement for positive action:

Go to a motion picture . . . and let yourself go. Before you know it, you are living the story – laughing, hating, struggling, winning! All the adventure, all the romance, all the excitement you lack in your daily life are in Pictures. They

take you completely out of yourself into a wonderful new world . . . Out of the
cage of everyday existence! If only for an afternoon or an evening – escape.[7]

The popularity of film-going in the 1920s suggests that the public
accepted the offer of 'escape'. Neither the nature of the offer nor the
public's acceptance of that offer changed significantly with the events of
1929. An evasion of political issues, personal needs and social
responsibilities was the key to the complicity which existed between the
public and the popular culture throughout the 1920s and 1930s. For the
most part the movies continued to reiterate in the talkies of the 1930s the
familiar, threadbare themes of the silent 1920s: that the rich, too, had
their troubles and were not to be envied; that a woman's life, however
useful, acquired meaning only in romance; that ladies of easy virtue, of
whom Mae West was the most prominent, could have hearts of gold;
that the ills of existence were mostly moral ills; that the cure for those ills
lay in preserving an unquenchable optimism and a sense of good-
neighbourliness. The *mores* of Hollywood remained more or less the
same in spite of the Depression.

The 1930s was not a self-enclosed decade. It is too easy to argue that
the collapse of the economy in 1929 evoked a similar collapse in the
nation's favourite cultural mythologies. One need only compare the
work of social and cultural historians of the 1920s and 1930s to see how
a dream of distraction and a need for heroes was common to the culture
of both decades.[8] One need only pick out one of the most pervasive
manifestations of culture-hero worship in the 1920s, the response to
Charles Lindbergh's flight from Long Island to Le Bourget in May
1927, and follow that hero-worship through into the 1930s, in order to
show how the appeal of individualism endured long beyond the point at
which it was supposed to have collapsed. The fact of the Crash did not
render irrelevant the appeal of an individual like Lindbergh. On the
contrary, the events of the Crash toughened up and tightened the need
for release from deterministic forces in the urban environment. The
need for heroes endured throughout the 1930s – heroes in space, heroes
in sports, products not of the city but of the farm, reminders of America's

uncomplicated beginnings. A dream of power and a dream of adventure retained its appeal in the American consciousness until Superman appeared in 1938 and presented to the imagination of the time all the yearnings of its dream of itself. In a sense both Lindbergh and Superman freed the fans from the constraints of politics and economic issues. They suggested the attractiveness of turning one's back on mean city streets and a humdrum technology. Lindbergh and Superman stimulated therefore a fantasy of urban escape but argued profoundly against self-limitation and social understanding. Both were presented and both were received by the American public as symbolic westerners, lone frontiersmen and space pioneers, creatures who made relevant the mythology of the West in defiance of gravity and urban restrictions. Their sale and acceptance was based entirely on escape considerations even though their success (and this was also true elsewhere of the gangster) was achieved through the benefit of sophisticated machinery and a modern network of urban communications. But the public in turn refused to discriminate between the lure of the symbol and the guarantee of status effected by machinery. The mass response to Lindbergh's flight vitalised a pseudo-frontier appetite for travel. It specifically introduced an aviation boom, 'but not an altogether healthy one, and it led many a flyer to hop off blindly for foreign shores in emulation of Lindbergh and be drowned'.[9] Superman, similarly, was thought so necessary as a power source that in the Second World War he was pressured by an insistent audience to proceed to Berlin, drop bombs on Hitler and bring hostilities to a quick end. In such a way the fans were committed to the miracle cures that liberated westerners might achieve; they believed in the relief that frontiersmen might bring to souls 'immured in city canyons and routine tasks'.[10] Personal power violently employed for social purposes and which did not necessitate a change in social structure, was extremely attractive. By the end of the 1930s Superman possessed a fundamental strength beyond the normal capabilities of American politicians. Where conventional politics in its highest form was becoming exposed by the personal limitations of the cripple in the wheelchair (the political meliorist chained to his desk and ever more deprived of his flamboyant gestures), the popular culture increasingly relied on a corpuscular detective who roamed the frontiers of space itself, who searched for adversaries and willingly defied the restrictions of the desk job.

In the 1920s and 1930s Hollywood cinema exposed and pandered to the need for escape routes. In the year following Lindbergh's crossing of the Atlantic, King Vidor's *The Crowd* (originally entitled *One Of The Mob*) defined the relationship between drudgery and fantasy as the inevitable outcome of living in the city. In 1936 *Modern Times* showed Charlie Chaplin walking away from the modern city and choosing instead the picaresque life-style of the open road adventurer. In *Modern Times* Chaplin displayed the needs of a man who must extricate himself from the clutches of society and who must turn his back on the life he has led as the helpless product of a mad technology. Chaplin was the link between Lindbergh and Superman, the cinematic hero as common man, the everyman committed to frontier escape routes. The idea of discovering a simple escape route, a way of evading the problems of living in a static community, was a favourite preoccupation with Americans in the 1930s. Not surprisingly the point is lost on critics who evaluate the decade in terms of a growth in political consciousness. Liberal court historians of New Deal politics like Arthur Schlesinger, Jr., see the 1930s as a period in which America moved from defeat to victory; a period of breakthrough for organised labour and in laws and regulations in favour of social welfare; a period in which America laid down the basis of future prosperity and prepared itself for an eventual triumph over fascist tyrannies. Radical progressives on the other hand, like Leslie Fiedler, consider the 1930s as a period of betrayal for the young radical – a period which began not with Lindbergh but with the notorious Sacco and Vanzetti anarchist trial – a period in which the radical energies of writers and intellectuals were tragically undermined by a dabbler in revolution like Roosevelt.

Popular culture offers a different perspective in exposing the needs of urban Americans in their leisure activities. In the 1930s the popular film and the best-selling book received their support from a persistent undercurrent of wish-fulfillment and fabulism which led an independent existence beyond ideology. W. H. Auden describes it as a 'disease of consciousness . . . incapable of converting wishes into desires. A lie is false; what it asserts is not the case. A wish is fantastic; it knows what is the case but refuses to accept it. All wishes, whatever their content, have the same and unvarying meaning – "I refuse to be what I am".' The rejection of self, situation and position, erodes desire and consumes belief, for whatever the individual wishes, Auden concludes, 'he cannot help knowing that he could have wished something else'.[11]

The ascendancy of wish-fulfillment thinking in the 1920s – the speculative desires for wealth fed by bond salesmen, Old Counsellors, newspaper hucksters – exploded in the 1930s on all levels; for now there lay a greater distance than ever before between the ideals of society and the democratic possibilities of fulfilling them. Literature seemed designed in the popular sector to provide a major avenue of escape. Popular literature in the 1930s was written on the basis of a shrewd recognition that those who had lost their money or their job would crave escapist fiction. On news-stands, with circulations ranging up to four million copies a month, pocket-digest magazines or newspapers like Bernard MacFaden's *Evening Graphic* contained not only an 'Advice to the Lovelorn' but a 'Lonely Hearts' column, in which lonesome girls were able to meet lonesome boys.[12] Best-selling novelists such as Hervey Allen (*Anthony Adverse*), James Hilton (*Lost Horizon*) and Margaret Mitchell (*Gone With The Wind*) exploited with nostrums and anodynes the public passion for surface maturation, conventional romance and local colour. As James Rorty confirmed, in the preface of *Where Life is Better*, some Americans remained resistant not just to politics but to any serious consideration of the problems facing them: 'I encountered in 15,000 miles of travel nothing that disgusted and appalled me so much as this American addiction to make-believe. Apparently, not even empty bellies can cure it.'[13]

Nowhere was Rorty's 'where-life-is-better daydream' more vigorously pursued than in Hollywood. During the depression in what almost seemed to be a grotesque travesty of the frontier movement, southern California became the goal of the dispossessed and unemployed, the idealists who believed in the rags-to-riches myth.[14] Once again it became the symbol of a second chance in the New World, the symbol of a dream of salvation and opportunity lived on in the beauty of Arcadian surroundings. Hollywood offered what Lewis Mumford terms a 'Utopia of Escape', an elementary-wish-fulfilment in the form of a perfect society — a desert island rather than a reconstructed social system.[15] With its sunshine and oranges, youth, fertility, optimism and progress, Hollywood seemed to offer a refreshing contrast to the industrial blight and freezing climate of the East and North. 'ALL ROADS LEAD TO HOLLYWOOD' flashes the neon sign in Horace McCoy's *I Should Have Stayed Home*. For McCoy's Mid-western emigré hero, Ralph Carston, Los Angeles is 'the most terrifying town in the world'. It is also a place of 'miracles' where 'today you are broke and unknown and tomorrow you are rich and famous'. Reality is displaced by a neon image; illusions have become so vivid and persuasive that people are committed to living within them. 'Hollywood . . . is where I belong, this is my destiny' murmurs Carston, a personal conviction which has its roots in the belief that America was fated to realise its 'manifest destiny' and extend across the continent from the Atlantic to the Pacific.[16] The faith is misplaced. Unwilling to acknowledge that the democracy of the frontier has been replaced by an oligarchy of big business, that the fluidity of the West has been succeeded by the standardisation of Main Street, the peripatetic hero in the California novel of the 1930s makes a solitary hegira to nowhere. On a landscape of decaying scenery, writers like Horace McCoy, Nathanael West and James Cain show the way the high hopes of a westward movement collapse on the Pacific shore in the vacant glare of a sunlight that gilds the cheapest artifacts of a transient American technology. The decline of the West is a decline in land, liberty and in human values. 'The great American dream', suggests Archibald MacLeish, is 'the singing of locusts out of the grass to the West and the West is behind us now'.[17] In Nathanael West's last novel, *The Day of The Locust*, the westerner is seen as a landlocked emigré symbolically re-enacting the West's destruction in the ceremonial dance riot of 'The Burning of Lost Angeles'.

Out in Hollywood West's locusts are an amalgam of bored
hinterlanders: retired midwest farmers, 'senior citizens' tired of ice and
snow, housewives, clerks and small merchants dissatisfied with the
tedium of small eastern towns. They have come to California to be fed
on a diet of sunshine, orange juice and exhilarating spectacles. But the
daily 'diet' which makes 'sophisticates' of them is too far removed from
their personal experience. The romantic dreams of passion and adventure
lived out in the darkness of the Bijou theatre only make more
unsatisfactory the ordinary lives which inevitably begin again on the
sidewalk outside. The boredom of the fans 'becomes more and more
terrible. They realise they have been tricked and they burn with
resentment.'[18] Unlike the production processes of Hollywood 'the lines
of human plasticity to continued frustration are finite'.[19] The cheated –
empty of talent, beauty, vitality and intelligence – revenge themselves by
turning on their idols. Neurotic, restive and excitable, the locusts emerge
from their catatonic state lean and miserable. They display a 'power'
which is 'awful' and 'anarchic'.[20]

It is not politics directly, suggests West, that makes the film-watching
public into witch-hunting fascists. It is a daily diet of meaningless
promises contemptuously delivered and impossible of fulfilment. The
search for a scapegoat derives from a desire to fix the blame for the sin of
contempt. Violent punishment is a necessary outlet for the tensions
which build up between consumer art and consumer desires – although
consumer desires are as much the product of escapist needs as they are the
consequence of an organised deceit. Riding through the slums of New
York City Miss Lonelyhearts recognises the explicitness of the joke: 'He
saw a man who appeared to be on the verge of death stagger into a movie
theater that was showing a picture called Blonde Beauty. He saw a
ragged woman with an enormous goiter pick a love story magazine out
of a garbage can and seem very excited by her find.'[21] Dreams and
aspirations are cheapened and commercialised by movies and
newspapers. 'So much does life promise, so little does it give. Mass man
senses this deception, rages against it and commits violence because of
it.'[22] West's people are rendered grotesque in a society that stimulates

and thwarts their desires; his novels are ironic and angry and trace a
pattern from expectation to despair to violence.

The authenticity of West's analysis of the relationship between
consumer art and consumer expectations was immediately affirmed by
Edmund Wilson in an early review of *The Day of The Locust*. Wilson
suggested that West, more than any other writer, had captured the
'emptiness' of Hollywood with an eye for detail that made his work into
'accurate reporting'. Budd Schulberg, planning his own Hollywood
novel, found West's book 'extremely authentic' not finding in it 'a single
wrong detail'. The novel, as Allan Seager put it 'was not fantasy
imagined, but fantasy seen'. West wrote about the novel to Jack Conroy
and talked about the quest for a 'superior truth' beyond ideology and
about Balzac who 'wrote with great truth and no wish-fulfilment'.[23]
Certainly West's portrait of the fan on the streets and in the cinemas of
Hollywood in the 1930s may give some indication of the dreams and
expectations of the film public generally and the 'tensions' they felt in a
world outside politics. The theory is a tempting one although it is
unsupported by conventional histories of the 1930s and the films
themselves. Hollywood rarely acknowledged the inadequacy of the act
of passive dreaming and the violence which, in serious literature, was
seen as being its natural outcome. On the contrary, it seemed to be
possessed of a belief that the American public was both unwilling and
unable to rely on its own imaginative resources; that it lived in a state of
imaginative impoverishment needing consolation with a style of cinema
which would relieve it of the necessity for coping directly with its
environment. As a Paramount advertisement put it: There's a
Paramount Picture probably around the corner. See it and you'll be out
of yourself, living someone else's life . . . You'll find a new viewpoint.[24]
All the major film studios gave the public a greater chance to live
someone else's life in preference to confronting the problems within one's
own life. Only when the process of 'living someone else's life' became
unsatisfactory, or the needs of the fan became impossible to fulfil, did
Hollywood resort to the providing of scapegoats and allow the public an
outlet for its rage. A dream of escape came to co-exist with a dream of

retribution. Hollywood contributed to a wish-fulfilment process but rarely admitted to the dangers involved; it gave outlets to anger but did not resort to rigorous self-analysis. Hollywood in the 1930s stimulated and thwarted the needs of a mass public but did not assess the function of mass culture.

In the early 1930s gangster film, the joys and frustrations of extravagant self-escape were exposed and satisfied at one sitting. The gangster figure became both a route to escape and an object of punishment; and eventually he was one because he was the other. The initial appeal of the gangster figure was contained in the pose he adopted – that of the modern-day agrarian who lived off his wits in an urban environment. The gangster insisted on sharing the untutored individualism of the cowboy in a society where conformity to rules and traditions was the price for security. In the petrified forests of big-city America the gangster of the 1930s possessed little of that soft-centred earthiness of the old-style heroes of Western films in the 1920s. As an outgrowth from a tough environment he exerted a forceful effect on a voyeurish audience which did not know at first hand the world of organised crime and gangland politics. As Robert Warshow put it: 'The real city, one might say, produces only criminals; the imaginary city produces the gangster: he is what we want to be and what we are afraid we may become.'[25] The gangster also expressed an unconscious protest against the sham optimism of a society in collapse. A psychopathic caricature of the Horatio Alger stereotype, he rose to success through diligence and self-reliance, hurting people and accepting, in turn, that he must be hurt by others. He attained temporary eminence and power, but his ultimate reward was punishment for rejecting the passivity of others and was a consequence of his presumption in setting himself apart from the masses. The individual could no longer rise on his own and he who chose to try without the assent of the audience – Scarface, Tommy Powers, Little Rico – was doomed. In traditional picaresque style the gangster became the Depression's favourite cultural scapegoat. For, as Warshow explains, 'The whole meaning' of the gangster's 'career is a drive for success' and 'he always dies because he is an individual; the final bullet thrusts him back, makes him after all, a failure'. It was the audience that found the gangster's individualism offensive. His death was a source of reassurance to an audience whose final response to the gangster was 'a response to sadism'. The audience gained 'the double satisfaction of participating vicariously in the gangster's sadism and then seeing it turned against the gangster himself'.[26] Urban passivity was justified; the twin myths of cowboy and vigorous urban Darwinist proved incompatible.

The popularity of the gangster did not derive simply from the public's awareness that legitimate institutions had failed them. Nor did the manner in which the outlaws operated entirely reinforce 'some of the country's most cherished myths about individual success'.[27] The public enjoyed what happened to the gangster. In his rise and fall he provided a vicarious symbol of social success and a necessary rationalization for eventual failure. The obligatory defeat of the gangster emphasised the danger and futility of trying to rise above one's station and class, of seeking wealth and power in an increasingly closed society, of attempting to deviate too extravagantly from the existing laws and customs of the community. It also emphasised the public's willingness to allow the gangster only momentary escape from the tedium of the times. Precisely because he lived so severely on a level beyond the reach of the masses his style occasioned an antagonistic response. Somewhere in a film the gangster switched from being a symbol of escape to being a symbol of contempt for those who had supported his initial efforts. The gangster's performance expressed a rejection not merely of those against whom he competed but of those very people from whom he had risen whose life lacked zest and a necessary agenda.

In the final analysis the gangster was contemptuous not merely of his rivals and inferiors but of life itself. In choosing to accept death more willingly than accept the life of a drone in a cinema seat he outraged the fans and removed himself too drastically from the common experience. In this respect he was different from Superman. Superman functioned as society's agent but assumed the disguise of Clark Kent. The presumption of Superman in setting himself apart from and above the masses was tempered by the ordinariness of his role as a crime reporter, as a bespectacled drone doing a nine-to-five job. Where the style of the early gangster rejected all passivities Superman was a hero who possessed the common touch. In a relatively short time after 1931 public outrage at the gangster's arrogance led to demands for increased censorship and government control over the film-making industry. The kidnap and murder in 1932 of Lindbergh's son stimulated those demands but ensured the continuation of Lindbergh's appeal. Only in the late 1930s did Lindbergh's sense of public relations fail him. When Lindbergh opposed America's entry into the Second World War and spoke of 'Jewish financing' of the war – when he became too greatly an advocate of the fascist cause – his public deserted him and turned to Superman. Superman, in turn, destroyed the West Wall and in *Das Schwarz Korps* was branded as a Jew by the Third Reich.

What the early gangster films gave with one hand the musicals took away with the other. The Warner Brothers musicals, *42nd Street* (1933), *Gold Diggers of 1933* and *Footlight Parade* (1933), stimulated new appetites while gangsters were being forced off city streets. The point was not lost on Nathanael West. West's Faye Greener, the principal source of lust and frustration in *The Day Of The Locust*, is more of 'a dancer' than 'an affected actress' and is closely modelled on the Goldwyn Girls. Her beguiling dances create an illusion of sexual intimacy and her song and dance routines which she performs for her male admirers are as suggestively erotic as Busby Berkeley's choreographies. In Berkeley's 'Bend down Sister' (*Palmy Days*, 1931) a long tracking shot presents the voyeurish audience with the cleavage of each Goldwyn Girl in turn as she bends toward the inquisitive camera. The coquettish eroticism of the dancers in the chorus line is similar to that of Faye in the novel who enjoys 'being stared at'. West's Faye Greener promises paradise to her audience but then cheapens their passions and drives them to release their energies in violence. The promise of the dancer leads not to satisfaction but only toward torment and insufferable frustration. No sex queen of the 1930s fully undercut the lies and false promises of the chorus line. Whatever new hope was contained in Mae

West's attempts to democratise sex — to reduce its mystique; to render sex a common, enjoyable and humorous experience — her invitations to sex remained for the audience exactly what they were — mere invitations. For the cinema audience sex remained a promise, a promise no different because it seemed genuine, a promise as likely to be realised by the fan as the promise that was issued from within a musical, or from one of Ernst Lubitsch's well-mannered sex dramas.

The attraction of punishment was never far away from the operative centre of the nation's consciousness in the 1930s. Just as the energies of the fans in *The Day of The Locust* had their outlet in violence so, in the reissued gangster films of the middle to late 1930s, the audience sought retribution against descendants of previous villains. After 1934 the gangster was stripped of many of the symbols of his power and appeal. In *The Petrified Forest* (1936) the gangster's fate was that of the fossil in a forest of stone; in *Dead End* (1937) he wandered alone, lost without his gang. But in a great many films the gangster's loss of power was shown in the way his deceptions were anticipated by lawmen, priests and crusading vigilantes — by agents and deputies of the cinema audience. The justness of the process was always secondary to the nailing of the criminal. In Fritz Lang's *You Only Live Once* (1937) a cynical world forces the individual into criminal ways, but its views are shared by the cinema audience. The involvement of the audience in the death of the gangster and the gangster's girlfriend is bleakly exposed at the ending of the film. As Henry Fonda and Sylvia Sydney 'appear on the sheriff's sight, we see them as he does and kill them just as certainly. Form and content correspond exactly: the sheriff pulls his trigger with our silent assent. He is society's agent and society has defined Fonda and Sidney as enemies'.[28] Such was the public's need for a bogeyman that all but a handful of Hollywood directors refused to endorse the actions of those who reduced the power of the supposed criminal. In *Angels With Dirty Faces* (1938) the priest asks the gangster 'to give up the only thing' he has left, his personal pride, and to make a spectacle of himself before dying in the chair. Humiliation from the priest became a natural follow up to humiliation from the President. In *Gabriel Over The White House*

(1933) the President declared war on American gangsters when his life was threatened by organised crime. As has been noted elsewhere, where the 'bogeyman' and scapegoat of Europe in the 1930s was a member of a political or religious minority group, in the United States he was presented by Hollywood as a member of a group of moral subversives.[29] Once the anti-gangster crusade gained momentum Hollywood made the criminal the reason for the Depression and so neatly sidestepped fundamental considerations of politics and economics. In films like *G-Men* (1935) and *Bullets or Ballots* (1936) Jimmy Cagney and Edward G. Robinson renounced their loyalties to the mobs and had their fire power legitimised by the wearing of badges. In Westerns like *The Texas Rangers* (1936) gang-style violence by defenders of the law was deemed a valid tactic in the punishment of wrongdoers. Hollywood refused to make crucial distinctions between the styles of violence of punishing officials and the violence of those who sought revenge outside the law. In order for society to function most peacefully the virtue of violence was considered more important than any moral consideration of the need for violence. Films were successful when they played to the mob, and lynch-law politics, particularly in films distributed after the kidnapping of Lindbergh's son, were seen as having considerable relevance. In Cecil B. De Mille's *This Day and Age* (1933) blue-eyed students were presented as heroes for taking the law into their own hands and for seeking revenge on gangsters who eluded official punishment. The fantastic energy in a torch-carrying mob, the fascist ethos of crusading vigilantes – these were issues which reappeared in *The Day of The Locust* and which West associated with massive frustration. But only a very few directors shared Nathanael West's fear of night-riding violence and vigilante methods. Archie Mayo's *Black Legion* (1936) exposed the common man's potential for fascist practices when dreams of success turned sour. But it was left to Fritz Lang in *Fury* (1936) and *They Won't Forget* (1937) to deal most fully with the terrible volatility of ordinary people and the psychopathic tendencies of small-town crowds.

If West's assessment of the mind of the mob in the American depression has much in common with the work of Fritz Lang it also invites us to make an assessment of the work of the Marx Brothers. West shared with the Marx Brothers – whose scripts he received from his brother-in-law, S. J. Pereleman – a desire to expose the fraudulence of mass society. But the irony here is that where West's fiction was largely ignored by the book-buying public of the 1930s the Marx Brothers' films were box-office successes. And yet, there is good reason for believing that the Marx Brothers were largely misunderstood and that the public missed, as Antonin Artaud puts it, their 'hymn to anarchy and whole-hearted revolt'.[30] In many instances cinema audiences viewed the horseplay of the Marxes as mere 'humorous' distraction and responded to their films on a level which 'laughed the big bad wolf of depression' out of sight.[31] As one reviewer indicated at the time: 'It is all amusement, of course, but nobody cares . . . It is all silly but everybody laughs.'[32] And to prove how silly it was all the audience needed to do was to point to those scenes where the Marxes got serious and performed for their fans with love songs, piano tunes and melodies from the harp.[33] But if the public went one way with a song and a chuckle the Marxes went another like 'laughing morticians'.[34] The outcome was ironic. The very appeal of what was seen as merely 'silly' only served to emphasise the very pointlessness of mass society (which the Marxes burlesqued) and the appetites which supported it. The randomness of style in the Marx Brothers' humour was a deliberate parody of that lack of pattern within consumer entertainments and those mass consumption styles which a modern audience found so appealing. An audience bombarded with non-sequiturs responded not to what the bombardment signified but simply to a method which took away attention from those uncomfortable statements of West and Lang. An endless patter of throwaway gags, a disconnected medley of ideas and impressions, things done incongruously and lacking in sequence – this was the welcome reassurance which the 'silly' gave to crazy consumers caught up in the boom of mad manufacture.

It is ironic that in the year (1934) the Marx Brothers were accused of conceit and effrontery by the fans (with the making of *Duck Soup*), Frank Capra should blast his way into box-office history with the breezy nuttiness of *It Happened One Night*. Where the Marx Brothers films were fantastic collages outlining the comic delineations of a nation's mind that had collapsed under a mass bombardment of drugstore supports and supermarket clutter, Frank Capra's comedies reached out to their audiences and offered reassurance through a dream of social unity. Capra dominated film comedy after 1934. In Westian terms the secret of his success lay in the fact that he never made his audiences feel sufficiently uncomfortable to need to seek revenge on the heroes he gave them. A 'where-life-is-better' daydream was less prone to have its outlet in a dream of violence if the common people were involved in the dream's realisation. Capra's social myth, as Robert Sklar has pointed out, required the recognition and participation of the common people to make it come true. It was a myth in which audiences were assured they had a part to play.[35] But it was also a myth which sentimentalised the past and tied the common man to the world of the farm. In *Mr Deeds Goes To Town* (1936) Capra suggested that the instinctive morality of the small-town American – not social reorganisation – was sufficient to solve the problems of the Depression. When Deeds receives an inheritance of twenty million dollars he philanthropically chooses to give it away. The economic miracle that will save the 1930s involves, it is suggested, the simple sinking of twenty million dollars into the land: the creation of a yeoman republic of small farms. Capra points a way out of the problems of the Depression by stressing the importance of an agrarian lifestyle and by paying attention to the innate fair-mindedness of the village democrat. The old-American way will win in the end. The moral sensibility of the common American patriot will balance the threat which is posed elsewhere by an immoral minority of criminals and gangsters.

Capra's evasiveness lay in his refusal to acknowledge the actuality of politics beyond neighbourly ideals, to acknowledge 'the existence of real incompatibilities of interest and real social problems not susceptible of individual solution'.[36] Nevertheless the Jeffersonian sentiments of Mr Deeds were a favourite retreat for 1930s film-makers. The search for a vanished innocence lay at the root of the popular back-to-earth films at this time: *King Kong* (1933), *State Fair* (1934), *Our Daily Bread* (1934), *The Life of Jimmy Dolan* (1933), *Stranger's Return* (1933). In spite of the burlesques of W. C. Fields[37] the romance of the frontier and the moral significance of the small-town community were favourite themes in films and novels. Film-makers like Walt Disney provided an image of history that the audience could consciously accept as fact and into which it might unconsciously escape from daily routine. The essential conservatism of Disney, as Richard Schickel makes clear, lay in his tendency to relieve the complexities of urban industrialism through jokes, musical cues and by emphasising the cultural traditions of the past. Disney purged nature and society of mystery and substituted a fictitious cuteness for its inherent discord; he affirmed the pioneer values of self-reliance, wit and eternal persistence and indulged in nostalgic longing for small-town amenities.[38]

The 1930s ended on a high note for agrarianism. As a bestselling novel in 1939 and as a box office success in 1940 John Steinbeck's *The Grapes of Wrath* (the film directed by John Ford) brought the decade to a close with a lyric appeal to Jeffersonian beliefs. In both film and novel practical politics were discarded in favour of an emotional rapport between dispossessed farmers living on the road in close togetherness. In their sublime belief in the regenerative earth and the moral potential of those who worked it both Steinbeck and Ford retreated from the active moment of American history with a propagandist vision of American life that was at once both dangerous and sentimental. They celebrated the farmer as the productive healthy member of society and suggested a primitivistic concept of nature: that the agrarian draws spiritual strength as well as sustenance from the soil. Set against these notions of Emersonian and socialistic agrarianism was the aridity of the city, the dishonesty of business and the inhuman unproductive nature of the urban machine. But at the end of the 1930s Steinbeck's Jeffersonian agrarianism, like Margaret Mitchell's plantation romance, was a bankrupt solution to the problems of the Depression. The disappearance of the family farm from the American scene by the early 1930s offered sufficient proof that the yeoman ideal could no longer be championed realistically as a formal way of life. To have faith in land was as inappropriate as to have a faith in those who had worked that land, seemed to want more[39] and were prevented from having it. When the Second World War came, the 'Okies' and 'Arkies' willingly disappeared into California's burgeoning munitions industries. They relinquished that dream of agrarian independence through which Steinbeck had so passionately defined their needs and identities. The conditions *The Grapes of Wrath* depicted were 'gone with the wind' and migrant labour became so scarce that California growers had to resort to the illegal importation of Mexican 'wetbacks'. Pearl Harbor and its aftermath affirmed that man's aspirations lay not in the land but in the city.

In Westian terms California's betrayal of that agrarian dream possessed by the 'Okies' was symbolically resolved through the issue of violence. The disappearance of the Okies into America's war industries meant the ending of one dream and the appearance of another. A dream of land was renounced in favour of a dream of retribution and scapegoats were found in foreign aggressors. But if America's war effort was a natural outlet for thwarted energies what was possible for the Okie was possible for the fan. The outbreak of war symbolically allowed an audience and readership whose dreams were similarly impossible of fulfilment (through what Steinbeck celebrated) the release of thwarted energies through violence in foreign lands. The Second World War and the pursuit of Nazi scapegoats was the final confirmation of West's vision of history.

Notes

1   Andrew Bergman, *We're In The Money: Depression America and Its Films* (New York, 1971), p. xiv.
2   Bergman, *We're In The Money*, p. xii.
3   Siegfried Kracauer, *From Caligari to Hitler* (Princeton, N.J., 1966 ed.), p. 5.
4   Bergman, *We're In The Money*, p. xii.
5   Leslie Fiedler, 'The Two Memoires: Reflections on Writers and Writing in the Thirties', in *The Thirties*, eds. Morton J. Frisch and Martin

Diamond (De Kalb, Ill., 1968), p. 60.

6 *The 1932 Film Daily Year Book of Motion Pictures*, p. 39.

7 Robert S. Lynd and Helen M. Lynd, *Middletown* (New York, 1929), p. 264.

8 See George Mowry, *The Twenties: Fords, Flappers and Fanatics* (Englewood Cliffs, N.J., 1963); F. L. Allen, *Only Yesterday* (New York, 1931); F. L. Allen, *Since Yesterday*, (New York, 1940); James D. Horan, *The Desperate Years*, (New York, 1962); Henry Morton Robinson, *Fantastic Interim*, (New York, 1943.)

9 F. L. Allen, *Only Yesterday*, pp. 219–20.

10 John W. Ward, 'The Meaning of Lindbergh's Flight', in *Studies in American Culture: Dominant Ideas and Images*, eds. Joseph J. Kwiat and Mary C. Turpie (Minneapolis, Minn., 1960), pp. 34–5.

11 W. H. Auden, 'Interlude: West's Disease', in *The Dyer's Hand and Other Essays* (London, 1962), p. 241.

12 Simon M. Bessie, *Jazz Journalism* (New York, 1938), p. 134.

13 James Rorty, *Where Life is Better: an Unsentimental American Journey* (New York, 1936), p. 13.

14 The idea of California as a frontier and land-abundant society had considerable appeal for the 'habitual' and 'removal' migrant of the 1930s. See Dorothea Lange and Paul Schuster Taylor, *An American Exodus: a Record of Human Erosion in The Thirties* (New Haven, Conn., 1969), p. 14; and 'I Wonder Where We Can Go Now', editorial, *Fortune*, vol. XIX (April 1939), pp. 90–119.

15 Lewis Mumford, *The Story of Utopias* (London, 1923).

16 Horace McCoy, *I Should Have Stayed Home* (London, 1938), pp. 1, 2, 68.

17 Archibald Macleish, *Land of The Free* (New York, 1938), p. 88.

18 Nathanael West, *The Day of the Locust*, in *The Complete Works of Nathanael West* (London, 1937), pp. 411, 412.

19 Virgil L. Locke, 'A Side Glance at Medusa: Hollywood, the Literature Boys, and Nathanael West', *Southwest Review*, vol. XLVI (1961), p. 42.

20 West, *The Complete Works*, p. 366.

21 West, *The Complete Works*, p. 115.

22 James F. Light, *Nathanael West: an Interpretive Study* (Evanston, Ill., 1961), p. 191.

23 See Jay Martin, *Nathanael West: the Art of His Life* (New York, 1970), pp. 305, 336.

24   Advertisement reprinted in *Motion Picture Herald*, 14 November, 1932.
25   Robert Warshow, 'The Gangster as Tragic Hero', in *The Immediate Experience* (New York, 1962), p. 131.
26   Warshow, 'The Gangster as Tragic Hero', pp. 131–2.
27   Bergman, *We're In The Money*, pp. 6–7.
28   Bergman, *We're In The Money*, p. 164.
29   Milton Mayer, 'The Myth of the G-Man', *The Forum* (September 1935), p. 145.
30   Antonin Artaud, *The Theatre And Its Double* (New York, 1958), pp. 142–44.
31   Rose R. Terlin, *You and I and the Movies* (New York, 1935), p. 24.
32   *Motion Picture Herald*, 6 September 1930, pp. 38–9.
33   It is no coincidence that *Duck Soup* (1934), which lacked any musical interlude, was the most poorly received of the Marx Brothers films. One suspects this as an important reason behind the public's adverse reaction. Since the Marxes' popularity had never been based on any political awareness of the implications of their satire it is difficult to accept Bergman's argument that the film was unpopular for political reasons.
34   Editorial, *Americana* Magazine, November 1932.
35   Robert Sklar, *Movie-Made America: a Cultural History of American Movies* (New York, 1976), p. 210.
36   Warshow, 'The Gangster as Tragic Hero', p. 110.
37   See *The Pharmacist* (1933), *The Dentist* (1933), *The Barbershop* (1933), *The Fatal Glass of Beer* (1933).
38   Richard Schnickel, *The Disney Version* (New York, 1968), pp. 51–3, 154–5, 157, 194–5, 210–13, 361.
39   See *A Companion to The Grapes of Wrath*, ed. Warren French (New York, 1963), p. 29.

Richard Maltby

The political economy of Hollywood: the studio system

The intricacies of Hollywood's economics defy compression into an essay of this length. Rather than attempting a comprehensive analysis of the studio system, my more limited intentions are twofold: to examine the influence of some economic factors on the relations of production within Hollywood; and then to consider the extent to which film producers achieved a relative control over their activities. Media theory has advanced a number of models to describe the relation between the industry's economic base and the ideological superstructure of its products. But theoretical distinctions between, for example, allocative and operational controls[1] over media resources can only indicate the potential dominance of ownership, whilst recapitulating a belief in economic determination in the last instance. They cannot establish the manner in which such determination operates in the process of media production. Ultimately, only empirical enquiry can provide satisfactory descriptions of the interplay of forces in the practice of film-making; unfortunately, the current dearth of primary source-material prevents anything more ambitious than a reassessment of known facts. That reassessment is based on the argument that a model of economic determination is necessary but not sufficient to comprehend the operation of the American film industry: insufficient because it cannot take into account the extent to which there was a debate over the status of product among the different sectors of the industry. Although the acknowledgement that film was primarily a commercial product pervaded all three branches of activity, the definition of what constituted that product diverged significantly between production on the one hand and distribution and exhibition on the other. That divergence of attitude provided the opportunity for factors other than the economic to come into play in determining the nature of production, and created an ideological space in which production personnel could exert a degree of autonomy over their activities.

The film industry during the height of the studio period may be best described as an oligopoly. It was dominated by five large vertically-integrated companies: Paramount, Loew's Inc. (MGM), Twentieth Century–Fox, Warner Brothers and RKO. The 'Big Five' were the largest producers, but their predominance in the industry came from their ownership of substantial exhibition circuits, and most importantly from their control over more than seventy per cent of first-run film theatres in the major metropolitan areas.[2] Although comprising only fifteen per cent of the total number of theatres in the United States, the major companies' properties were by far the most profitable sector of the exhibition market, and could expect to garner up to half the box-office receipts of any given A-feature.[3] These theatre holdings provided them with an économic power-base from which they could dominate both production and exhibition. As exhibitors, they controlled access to first-run exhibition, without which no A-feature could hope to be profitable. By giving preference to their own and each other's products, they substantially closed off the market to independent producers. They also guaranteed their bargaining position as distributors when dealing with the rest of the exhibition sector, who were obliged to accept the major companies' terms if they wanted access to the most popular and profitable films.

Since none of them manufactured enough films to meet the demands of its own theatres, co-operation amongst the Big Five was to their mutual advantage. Production was an expensive process; overproduction was an extravagance that could not be afforded. The companies thus relied on each other for much of their exhibition programme. They also exhibited the films of a few smaller producers – most importantly the 'Little Three' (Columbia, Universal and United

Artists) – who were principally engaged in manufacturing B-features for the bottom half of double-bills in suburban and neighbourhood theatres. Such oligopolistic co-operation secured several advantages: above all it guaranteed the stability of relations between the major companies. It reduced the intensity of competition, since a successful film produced profits for all the major companies through their exhibition of it. Their combined strength allowed them to dictate exhibition terms to other exhibitors, imposing practices such as block booking, 'zoning', and 'clearance'[4] which effectively constituted a system of price discrimination designed to maximise distributors' profits. What most clearly characterised the economic functioning of the film industry during the period of the 'studio system', then, was not the existence of the studios as production centres but the dominance of the Big Five as distributor-exhibitors.

However, while the major companies, acting in official consort through their trade association, the MPPDA, or in indirect collusion through non-competitive pricing and distribution policies, constituted a controlling oligopoly, they did not comprise an unequivocal monolith. The history of the film industry, from the formation of the MPPC to the present, may usefully be examined through an explication of the central opposition – financial, ideological, and to some extent geographical – around which it was structured: an opposition between competition and cartelisation. The industry's history has frequently been described as oscillating between periods of each form of economic activity, but in fact both have been consistently present since the formation of the Patents Company in 1908. In the studio era cartel practices were predominantly the province of the major companies' New-York-based operations, where the economies of scale denied to the studios' 'small batch production'[5] could be brought to bear on film distribution and exhibition through mass marketing techniques.

Block booking and other price-fixing practices severely curtailed the possibilities for competition between the Big Five, a fact emphasised by the geographical distribution of their theatre holdings. Each company owned prestige theatres in New York, but elsewhere one major company dominated the first-run trade in a State or region. Fox's ownership was concentrated on the West Coast, Warners in Pennsylvania and New Jersey, Paramount in Canada, New England and the South. Their cartel behaviour was even clearer in foreign sales, which in the late 1930s provided approximately thirty-five per cent of total industry income.[6] Where overt domestic collusion was prohibited by the anti-trust laws, cartelisation of the export trade was actively encouraged by the Neely–Pettingill Act of 1918, under whose permissions the Foreign Department of the MPPDA (which in 1945 became the Motion Picture Export Association) acted as the sole negotiating body for the American industry in dealing with foreign governments over quotas, tariffs and exchange restrictions.

In general, the MPPDA functioned as an instrument of cartelisation under the guise of 'business self-regulation'. Its restricted membership was dominated by the major companies, who used it both to increase their effective power within the industry and to improve their status within the community of American finance capitalism. Its president, Will H. Hays, had been Chairman of the 1920 Republican National Committee and Harding's Postmaster General: as 'czar of all the rushes' he brought the industry a Republican respectability that eased its relations with the New York banks in the 1920s. The industrial regulations formulated by the government and the MPPDA as part of the New Deal National Recovery efforts were designed to further the major companies' interests against both their own production employees and independent producers and exhibitors.[7] The Hays Production Code also became an instrument of cartelisation: the Code's Seal of Approval was a prerequisite for exhibition in all MPPDA-owned theatres and in most others. Its values, to which the studios of the later 1930s were efficiently geared, were therefore imposed on all producers who hoped for access to the American market.

The impetus to cartelisation came from the formation of vertically-integrated companies which failed to observe the conventional division of interest between buyer and seller in any transaction. While the Patents

Company constituted the first attempt to establish an umbrella organisation involved in every sector of the industry, the real architect of vertical integration was one of the Trust's principal opponents, Adolph Zukor. In 1919, having gained control of the Paramount distribution network and merged it with his own Famous Players–Lasky production organisation, he began acquiring and building theatres. In the next three years, Paramount developed a 600-strong theatre chain, and Zukor was in a position to impose block-booking practices on independent exhibitors requiring his popular product. It was inevitable that the other large companies would emulate Zukor's integration. In the early 1920s First National, Fox, Loew's and Universal, among others, became vertically-integrated organisations, concentrating their resources on establishing large theatre circuits, particularly for first-run exhibition.

The development of vertically-integrated companies was crucial not only for its effect on industry practice but also for its consequences for company ownership. The industry's investment in theatres during the 1920s was vast: in 1927 Halsey, Stuart and Co., one of Fox's backers, estimated the total investment in exhibition real estate at $1,250 million.[8] This was money the companies did not have, nor had they needed it in the past. They were obliged to turn for finance to Wall Street, and because they were seeking money for solid investment in real estate, Wall Street obliged. Initially, it was a matter of individual bankers recognising the potential of a previously disreputable industry: Otto Kuhn of Kuhn, Loeb & Co., who floated Paramount on the stock market in 1919 and financed Zukor's expansion; A. P. Giannini of the Bank of Italy (later the Bank of America), who backed United Artists and Columbia; and, most impressively of all, Waddill Catchings of Goldman, Sachs, who masterminded Warner Brothers' expansion from a small production company in 1924 to their takeover of First National in 1928. But the potential profitability and, more importantly, the growing stability of the leading companies provided by their enormous purchase of real estate, made the film industry an attractive investment proposition in the booming market of the mid and late 1920s.

The emergence of the new technology of sound added to both the expansionist impulse and the pressure to cartel action. The cost of conversion to sound was $500 million in capital expenditure,[9] and a doubling of production expenses. Sound aided the expansion of Warner Brothers and was directly responsible for the construction of the last of the Big Five, RKO, a vertically integrated company assembled by Joseph Kennedy and David Sarnoff on behalf of the Radio Corporation of America (RCA), whose Photophone system had been rejected by the major companies in preference for Western Electric's Movietone.[10] RKO's almost overnight appearance indicated both the size of the industry boom and the extent of cartel power: only by launching a concern of comparable size to the majors (three hundred theatres and $50 million working capital) could RCA hope to challenge the Western Electric monopoly and the cartel decision which endorsed it. Wall Street's confidence in the potential profitability of sound provided the capital.

A related development revealed by the appearance of RKO was that sound had introduced new interests to the film industry. Some of the largest corporations in America now had a stake in the movies. Western Electric was a subsidiary of the American Telephone and Telegraph Company (AT&T), itself under the control of the J. P. Morgan group; while RCA, AT&T's rival during the 1920s for domination of the radio industry, was controlled by the Chase National Bank, a part of the Rockefeller empire.[11] The consequences of Morgan–Rockefeller involvement were not fully evident until the shock-waves of the Wall Street Crash had struck the industry in 1932. The majors had heavily overextended themselves in buying theatres and converting to sound, acquiring massive long-term debts to be repaid from profits. The talkies had carried the industry over the first years of the Depression, but in 1932 profits vanished. All the majors except Warners[12] relinquished financial control to their backers of the previous decade. Sound and the Crash had attached the film industry irretrievably to the bastions of American capitalism.

Yet it was not a particularly undesirable place for them to be. While there was much temporary instability in the early 1930s, accompanied by theatre closures, salary cuts and declarations of bankruptcy, the five companies that had emerged by 1928 as the most powerful in the industry remained in existence and little-altered. The dross acquired in their over-ambitious expansion of theatre holdings was jettisoned, particularly when it had been noted that Loew's, which had not indulged in extensive real estate purchase and had the smallest theatre chain, was the only film company to declare shareholders' dividends every year through the Depression.[13] By 1935, when the Fox theatre chain was merged with the small Twentieth Century production company, the Big Five had resumed their stations and the oligopoly was secure against intruders. Only the ultimate ownership of the companies had changed.

That change of ownership, however, could hardly be described as inconsequential, although its precise effects remain elusive. With one brief and unsuccessful exception at Paramount, the companies (and in particular the studios) remained under the same managerial control as they had been in the 1920s. Their boards of directors now contained representatives from most of New York's largest financial institutions, but there is little evidence to suggest that this led to any significant interference in the day-to-day running of the companies. The enduring effect of monopoly capital ownership was to increase the already existing pressure towards the cartelisation of a stable oligopoly, a pressure which stressed the industry's broad long-term interest in internal and external stability, rather than the short-term interest of individual companies in immediate maximum profits. The industry's acceptance of the Hays Code was one example of this preference for long-term interest: it signalled the victory of Hays' consistent policy of encouraging the companies to aim their product at the larger and more stable family audience rather than directing their efforts, as they had in the early 1930s, at the sensationalist trade.

Another index of this emphasis on stabilisation was the decision on the part of each of the Big Five not to expand their theatre holdings, a decision reinforced by the 1940 consent decree which temporarily halted the Justice Department's anti-trust suit. A stable system of theatre circuits endorsed the major companies' oligopoly action, concerning the relative distribution of profits between the three sectors of the industry. Given their cartel power, the Big Five were in a position to dictate the division of profitability, within the broad limits of what the market could bear. There was an irresistible financial logic in maximising the profitability of early-run exhibition. Not only was this the area of largest single investment, constituting nearly two-thirds of the major companies' total capital investment; it was also the most reliable source of return on income, since it was freer from the vagaries of competition and audience taste than was production. The major companies exercised control through the price of film rentals, which for A-features were levied as a percentage of the gross box-office take. The higher the percentage, the greater relative profit could be directed into distribution, and the lower would be the profits of exhibition.

In the late 1930s, the Big Five typically received around one-third of their gross volume of business from film rentals, the remainder coming predominantly from their theatre holdings, with smaller amounts from the sale of film accessories and dividends from affiliated companies.[14] Considering that film rentals were garnered from the entire exhibition system, while theatre income came only from those theatres owned by the individual company, the disproportion between the two is striking. With some variation, rentals were set at a level which would produce a reasonable profit on investment in production/distribution, would not excessively upset the independent exhibitors, and would ensure that the most stable income sector of the companies' holdings was also the most consistently profitable. Since nearly half of the Big Five's film rental income came from their own and the other major companies' theatres, there was a typically oligopolistic pressure on each company to keep its rental percentages in line with the others'.

These decisions had an influence on the kinds of production undertaken by the Big Five, which may be illustrated by examining the case of Loew's Inc. Loew's was in one respect the least typical of the Big Five, in that it derived a significantly larger share of its total volume of business (around forty per cent) and of its total profits (around seventy per cent) from film rentals.[15] This was because it charged a higher rental than the others — for an average A-feature, in the region of forty per cent of box-office takings as opposed to the other companies' thirty per cent.[16] The higher price was justified by the company on the grounds of their productions' greater lavishness, cost and consequent drawing power. But that argument inverted the economic logic of the industry. Loew's had the smallest number of theatre holdings of the Big Five: a mere 139, compared to Paramount's 1,239 and Warners' 507, for example.[17] Since it had a smaller secure exhibition base for its product, it was obliged to compensate by securing a greater profit from distribution, and the logical means to that end was a higher quality, more expensive product that would justify higher rental charges.

The economics of MGM's luxury product was only an extreme version of the logic that applied to all the major companies' production activities. Since the largest share of their income came from their own early-run exhibition outlets, and the largest share of their distribution income came from first-run exhibition, the principal preoccupation of their production departments was to supply products for that market: A-features aimed primarily at the metropolitan market. That market required, and had come to expect, an expensive product with extravagant 'production values'. Ultimately, the Big Five's theatre ownership dictated the nature of their studio subsidiaries' activities, and this was reflected in the broad outline of the annual allocation of production funds. The New York executives would establish the total amount to be spent on production, on the basis of their own theatres' need for films and their assessment of what could be sold. They would also determine how this money should be divided between the classes of production, and commonly indicate specific requirements for star vehicles or genre films. Although this and subsequent stages involved consultation with the studio management, the broad pattern of film production was dictated by the profitable sectors of the industry which the studios merely serviced.

The cartelisation of the industry was concentrated on its New York activities. Competition was emphasised in Hollywood. That is not to say that there was a clear and precise division between the two, but there was an underlying tendency in that direction. Competition remained an effective force between exhibitors, and distributors also vied with each other to sell block bookings to theatres and theatre chains. On the other hand, the convenient arrangements by which studios would rent each other their stars, normally for 175 per cent of their studio salary,[18] was a cartel practice. Indeed, the star system itself was used to reinforce the major companies' oligopoly power. The high salaries paid to stars, executives and others were commonly justified on the basis that they rewarded unique talent, and that they provided the means of passing profit on to those who might well be held to be most responsible for its existence. There was, however, another effect. High salaries inflated the cost of film production, constituting roughly fifty per cent of an A-feature's budget.[19] High production costs and the majors' cartel practices over distribution and exhibition served to keep independent producers out of A-feature production. They were relegated to supplying material predominantly for the lower half of double bills, a section of the market the Big Five had only limited interest in, since their first-run theatres used very little of it.

However, while oligopoly practices existed among the major producers to keep independents out, the production system was geared to a much greater degree of competition *among* the Big Five than was true of the distribution and exhibition structure. The mutual benefits that accrued to the major companies through their exhibition of each others' films did not apply to production: while a successful Warner Brothers film might be good business for Loew's Inc, it did nothing for MGM. The studios, then, were in much more direct competition with each other than was true of their parent companies as a whole. That fact, however, serves only to emphasise the subordinate position of production in the industry's economy. Production itself could not make money; it was only through the distribution system that film rentals were collected and the investment in product recouped. From Edison's time production had been regarded as an inconvenient necessity by the profit-making part of the industry; after the formation of the studio era's mature oligopoly, competition in production came to possess a convenient ideological function for its cartelised supervisors in New York. Studio rivalry served to divert attention away from their parent companies' co-operation, just as Hollywood's prodigality gave the industry as a whole an undeserved reputation for extravagance. But there was no question about the unilaterial direction of economic pressure. Within the industry, it was abundantly clear who worked for whom.

Production was also inherently the most unstable sector, both for individuals and corporations involved. A general decline in the profitability of the industry might be blamed on any number of factors, but the more common occurrence of a poor annual performance by an individual company would almost inevitably be laid at the door of its production staff. Such an analysis was corroborated by the cartel practices of distributors and exhibitors, which reduced the probability of their performance fluctuating. The cartel system thus placed the burden of success, as well as the responsibility for maintaining the illusion of competition, on the production companies, while relegating them to an economically subordinate position within the structure of the industry. It was hardly surprising, then, with public attention focused on Hollywood's activities, that there should be a disproportionately high stress on the industry's instability, since it was in Hollywood that that instability was overwhelmingly evident. While the overall level of industry profits was comparatively stable and predictable because people continued 'going to the movies', the box-office success of an individual picture was subject to a wide variety of erratic and unpredictable factors, of which only one was the fickle taste of the public. Careers could be irretrievably damaged by a single failure, or destroyed by a change in industry fashion. It was, perhaps, inevitable that as a result the Hollywood community developed its second most famous behavioural tendency: 'an orientation to crisis'.[20]

A further financial pressure was imposed on studio performance by the New York management. Originating with the conservative business practices of company heads like Zukor and Nicholas Schenk, and reinforced by Wall Street influence, the Big Five developed the accounting practice of writing eighty per cent of the value of films off company books after a year, and writing it off completely after two years.[21] Films were required to recoup their investment almost immediately, and this stipulation affected not only the nature of the product, but also the fundamental attitudes brought to production. While theatre purchases had been financed in the main through long-term investments, film production subsisted on short-term capital, either from the company's own resources or borrowed from outside. The need to provide immediate returns discouraged producers from experimentation, and intensified their inclinations to stabilise their inherently unpredictable activity. Distributors and exhibitors also found a standardised product easier to merchandise, and it may reasonably be argued that the majority of Hollywood's production formulae, particularly in budgeting, derived from this pressure. The star system, genres, conventional narrative structures and other formulaic elements aided the predictability of box office returns by standardising the audience's pleasurable experience. The stress on formula that is so apparent in the studio product of the 1930s had its origins in a conservative attempt to deal with the assumed vagaries of audience response and the economic requirements of an industrial activity based on short-term high-risk capital.

Production was thus marked off from distribution and exhibition by a number of significant factors: its geographical separation, its method of financing, its relatively high emphasis on competition, risk and instability, and its unsuitability for the economies of scale brought by mass marketing. While these factors militated against it in the division of profitability within the industry as a whole, they also provided the film producers, and in particular the heads of studio production, with the opportunity to develop a defensive professional ideology which sought to protect their sphere of activity from external interference.

There were several strands to this ideology, but at its core was an alternative definition of the nature of the industry's product to that provided by the dominant sectors. It emphasised the uniqueness of film-making as an economic activity and relished its financial separation from the industry's more conventional operations. While company accountancy might conform to the most conservative business practices, the way each company actually spent its money did the very opposite. Hollywood's extravagance served the industry as a whole, but in particular it served the ideological purposes of the studio heads. The 'moguls' were extroverts who had left their quieter relatives in New York to manage the more conventional business of marketing while emphasising that their activity – the manufacture of individual artefacts for mass entertainment – was not susceptible to normative modes of economic behaviour, but required the elusive skills of 'showmanship'. Hollywood was, they averred, in the extraordinary business of selling dreams, and a dream factory was necessarily a fantastic place. Its fabled extravagance became a requirement of the commodity they manufactured. The various images of Hollywood, as well as most of its industrial practices, were the creation of this small group of men who ran the major studios. They more or less deliberately set out to create in Hollywood a separate, enclosed world, whose image to the rest of America was as important an ingredient in the product they sold as were the stars or plots of individual films. More than anything else, it was this construction of 'Hollywood' that constituted the key to their autonomy from East Coast control.

The rest of the industry's acceptance of these propositions encouraged the belief that organising production required unique managerial skills. While everybody in the industry was concerned to 'give the public what it wants', only the moguls were seen to have the expertise to supply suitable products. Each success – and in the studio era there were necessarily many more successes than failures – strengthened their claim that their talents in selecting material and supervising its production supplied a vital element of stability to a business enterprise that had already been defined as inherently unstable. This in turn reinforced the security of their own positions, and provided the basis for the further claim that their managerial expertise gave them a capacity denied others to predict public taste – a claim which found its most articulate expression in the 'Thalberg myth' of producer infallibility. The economic efficacy of this myth can be seen by the extent to which heads of production were considered to be the central props of their companies' edifices: Loew's executive personnel were rewarded with twenty per cent of the company's annual net profits on top of their massive salaries;[22] while the Twentieth Century production company which merged with the remains of the Fox exhibition empire in 1935 had as its most prominent assets Joseph Schenk and Darryl F. Zanuck. The idea of the star as an economic property was in a sense no more than an extension of the moguls' own position.

The mythology of the moguls' unique abilities, and indeed of their autocratic behaviour within the production system itself, must be seen in the economic context of the industry as a whole, as a defensive ideological construction to guarantee their autonomy. The forces exerted on them by the other sectors were explicitly financial; their response was to change the terms of reference by transferring their claim to power from the specifically economic sphere to one constructed around their ability to manage the irrational and unpredictable. However, because their ideology was necessarily defensive, it operated only in one direction, in their dealings with their financial superiors. The pressures they themselves placed on their employees were also of an economic nature, and essentially consisted in the financial logic of the studio system. If the professional ideologies and myths of production personnel are examined, a similar pattern may be found: resistance to economic pressure through a change in terms of reference, away from the explicitly financial to non-economic areas of creativity, unique talent and specialised skills.

Clearly such myths diverged from the economic realities of film industry activity. But equally, the myths had a real existence, and a real economic value. If film production was not as insecure as Hollywood's mythology insisted, nevertheless the Hollywood community behaved as if it was, and themselves lived permanently within a melodramatic fiction that could, and sometimes did, provide the basis for a movie. Hollywood's behaviour was an ideological construct symbiotically linked to those of the films themselves: part of the 'escapist' nature of the product lay in offering audiences the opportunity to enter the separate world of the movies that 'Hollywood' represented. The industry saw itself as merchandising a product, which was emphatically defined by the studio heads as entertainment rather than as a succession of specific films. Such a strategy clearly had an economic basis, in ensuring audiences' frequent return to the theatres to consume the product again. But the particular forms that entertainment took, and the specific political ideologies to which it corresponded, were not exclusively determined by the industry's economic structure, and certainly not by the fact of its ultimate ownership. That latter fact was sufficiently demonstrated during the early years of the Depression when, at the very moment the major companies came under the control of monopoly capitalism, the studio's product was at its most socially and politically radical. While such outbursts were inevitably followed by cartel action to depoliticise the cinema once again (the imposition of the Hays Code, blacklisting), that action was also always a reluctant industry response to external pressure.

That the industry sought to make its entertainment safe, and therefore depoliticised, is clear. That it had economic motives for doing so is equally evident: profit maximisation came through the manufacture of a product with the widest appeal, which meant, as Hays invariably argued, appealing to the family audience, which in turn meant minimising controversial content. But economic motives were not the only ones which might encourage such activity: the personal beliefs of the studio heads had consistently encouraged them to seek respectability for themselves and their industry, and as exhibitors in the Patents Company period, men like Zukor and Mayer had been instigators in the campaign to persuade middle-class audiences of the cinema's social respectability.[23] The moguls' common political beliefs achieved their fullest expression in the sentimental Utopian populism purveyed by the films of the late 1930s, almost certainly the period of Hollywood's greatest ideological consistency. However much it may have suited the mood of its audiences, or however tangential it may have been as a response to the political and economic circumstances of its period, it can hardly be characterised as an ideological product overtly working in the interests of monopoly and capital or cartelisation.

Rather, the American cinema may be seen as comprising a series of pressure relationships, each of which modified and mediated the behaviour of sections of the industry. Economic factors played a predominant part in deciding the quantity and cost of films produced, and the kind of market at which they would be aimed. Cartel practices imposed limits on their permissible content. But determining the limits of production's activities is as much as economic analysis can be seen to do. It may explain why the studios did not make certain kinds of films, but it cannot provide any more than a broad general explanation of why they made the films they did. Its failure to do so may perhaps be explained by the internal contradictions of the industry's economics – the opposition between long- and short-term interests, the irrational economics of production – but those contradictions served to create space for other factors to come into play. Professional ideologies, formulated in resistance to economic pressure and therefore trading in non-economic considerations, created spaces in which economic determination could be mediated. The American cinema cannot be comprehended without an understanding of its commercial operation, but equally it cannot be comprehended by such an understanding alone.

Notes

1   R. E. Pahl and J. T. Winkler, 'The Economic Elite: Theory and Practice', in *Elites and Power in British Society*, eds. P. Stanworth and A. Giddens (Cambridge, 1974).

2   Tino Balio, 'A Mature Oligopoly', in *The American Film Industry*, ed. Tino Balio (Madison, Wis., 1976), p. 213.

3   'The Hays Office', *Fortune*, vol. 18 (December 1938). Reprinted in *The American Film Industry*, ed. Balio, p. 301.

4   See J. C. Strick, 'The Economics of the Motion Picture Industry: a Survey', in *Philosophy of the Social Sciences*, vol. 8, No. 4, for a discussion of price discrimination practices.

5   Jeremy Tunstall, *The Media Are American* (London, 1977), p. 73.

6   'The Hays office', p. 311.
7   Robert Sklar, *Movie-Made America* (New York, 1975), p. 168.
8   Halsey, Stuart & Co., 'The Motion Picture Industry as a Basis for Bond Financing', reprinted in *The American Film Industry*, ed. Balio, p. 184.
9   Tino Balio, 'Struggles for Control', in *The American Film Industry*, ed. Balio, p. 118.
10   Robert Stanley, *The Celluloid Empire* (New York, 1978), p. 66.
11   F. D. Klingender and Stuart Legg, *Money Behind the Screen* (London, 1937), p. 70.
12   Stanley, *The Celluloid Empire*, p. 58.
13   'Loews, Inc.', *Fortune*, vol. 20 (August 1939). Reprinted in *The American Film Industry*, ed. Balio, p. 280.
14   Mae D. Huettig, *Economic Control of the Motion Picture Industry* (Philadelphia, Pa., 1944), pp. 60–1.
15   'Loews, Inc.', p. 281.
16   'Loews, Inc., p. 291.
17   Huettig, *Economic Control of the Motion Picture Industry*, p. 70.
18   'Loews, Inc.', p. 293.
19   Leo Rosten, *Hollywood: The Movie Colony, the Movie People* (New York, 1941), p. 79.
20   Janet Woolacott, *Hollywood: a Case Study* (Milton Keynes, 1977), p. 27.
21   Halsey, Stuart & Co., 'The Motion Picture Industry as a Basis for Bond Financing', p. 189.
22   'Loews, Inc.', p. 283.
23   Sklar, *Movie-Made America*, pp. 175–88.

Ralph Willett

The nation in crisis:
Hollywood's response to the 1940s

'I'm backed up in a dark corner and I don't know who's hitting me' (Bradford Galt [Mark Stevens] in *The Dark Corner*, 1946)

1

It was not only during the actual war years that the American film glorified the war effort and shaped the nation's attitudes towards foreign tyranny. By 1939 *Confessions of a Nazi Spy* (which identified a spy ring within the German–American Bund) was already directing attention to the infiltration of fascist ideology. The following year saw Hollywood using a European setting for anti-Nazi propaganda in such films as *The Mortal Storm* and *Four Sons*. It was at this time that the American cinema began to stereotype German soldiers and agents as efficient, even ruthless men, who were also suave and decadently self-indulgent in their taste for luxury, good food and wine, and culture. Germany's military leaders, however, while being presented as dangerous gangsters, were also caricatured as absurd, ridiculous creatures, an approach for which Chaplin (with *The Great Dictator* in 1940) must bear some of the responsibility, and one which he later regretted. But since dictatorship was, to Americans, anachronistic, it was a natural impulse to laugh at its practitioners, and *The Great Dictator* was at least unambiguous in its anti-Nazi feeling.

Contemporary Europe, which had been relatively neglected during the Depression, was being re-created by American directors, a number of whom were exiles from Germany itself. They assisted in the internalization of the old European–American opposition; while the German fascists lived in sumptuous, over-decorated apartments, the 'democratic' resistance fighters lived in mean cottages and plotted in cellars. Nazi officers, though sometimes portrayed by European exiles, were frequently played by English actors (George Sanders, Cedric Hardwicke) with upper-class accents; on the other hand, it was not unusual to hear American intonations in a 'European' village.

By 1940 European events had created a need in America for didactic newsreels, which made defence preparations, in the diluted form of parades and meetings, acceptable, even enjoyable. The reality of armed conflict was avoided; instead of death and mutilation, military leaders and troops in transit were featured. Further techniques employed were the mixture of documentary, instructional and fictional material in the propaganda series *Why We Fight* made from 1942 to 1945, and the use of a hortatory speech in the last reel to promote American readiness to join the war and to hasten rearmament. Hitchcock's *Foreign Correspondent* (1940), for example, ends with an impassioned radio broadcast from London: 'The lights are going out in Europe. Ring yourself around with steel, America.' Less successful, though, was the revival of *All Quiet on the Western Front* (1930) in 1941; the futility and horror of war and the stark images of dying men emerged too strongly.

Although in 1941 a Senate committee objected to Hollywood's anti-Nazi pictures, the Selective Service Act had been passed in the previous year; and after Pearl Harbor, the alliance between the American film industry and the American government became complete, with the authorities even suggesting particular themes that Hollywood should exploit. The Bureau of Motion Pictures, part of OWI, increased its influence over scripts and films especially during and after 1943 when the censorial Ulric Bell took over the Hollywood office.[1] Hollywood, on the whole, responded compliantly, and it is hardly surprising that, under these circumstances, the movies produced were simplistic melodramas, glorifying war and democracy (the 'civilised' nations), while vilifying the enemy as the representatives of barbarism. Even in

1944 James Agee, writing regularly in the *Nation*, was obliged, repeatedly, to call attention to the different levels of reality attained in Hollywood war fictions and English documentaries. The latter, he remarked, avoided the American disease of 'masked contempt and propitiation', and throughout his essays he persistently notes the absurdities and distortions perpetrated by the standard Hollywood product. The tendency to portray the inhabitants of Occupied Europe patronisingly, as foreign versions of folksy Middle Americans, has already been mentioned; Agee singled out the pro-Russian *Mission to Moscow* (1943), a thoroughly inaccurate film made by Warners with Roosevelt's approval, as a particularly blatant example of despising the American audience: 'there is no essential difference, it turns out, between the Soviet Union and the good old USA, except that in Russia everybody affects an accent and women run locomotives'.[2] In that film, and others like it (*The North Star*, 1943), the Russians, who sing folksongs but use cosmetics, are friendly, hard-working and heroic, while communism is an Eastern version of the New Deal. Such pro-Soviet attitudes later produced accusations and bitterness during the Cold War.

Equally false, Agee pointed out, was the bromidic treatment of death. Dying was not only sanctioned by patriotism but it was usually presented without a sense of horror or revulsion. Heaven and Hell were frequently depicted in 1940s movies, though neither these 'locations' nor their inhabitants were in any way disturbing. The majority of ghosts were pleasant, even charming, while in such films as *All That Money Can Buy* (1941) and *Heaven Can Wait* (1943) even the Devil (played by Laird Cregar) was made inoffensive and rather attractive.

Films which gave a true picture of combat conditions or of the psychological effects of war received short shrift from the Pentagon, with John Huston becoming the chief victim of official suppression. *Let There Be Light* (1945), which set out to show that the emotional casualties of war were neither lunatics nor social misfits, was banned, while *The Battle of San Pietro* (1944), which graphically depicted Americans in the Italian campaign being shot or burnt to death, was not allowed to reach the public. The truthful rendering of the sufferings of American soldiers in war was of little or no value to the propagandist machine. Reality needed to be manipulated rather than shown objectively, in order to intensify hatred of the enemy. Japanese soldiers, played by Chinese–American actors, were typed as subhuman animals, pitiless and, above all, sadistic in a continuation of popular culture racism; and into this psychological climate, Hollywood could inject an atrocity picture, *The Purple Heart* (1944), based on what were then unverified facts, with impunity. The army's *Screen Magazine* referred to the Japanese as 'rats' and 'cockroaches', and even *Guadalcanal Diary* (1943) more acceptable for its realism, contains its share of racist references: 'Where's the rest of the seven dwarfs?' 'They live in the trees like apes.'

Guadalcanal Diary is typical of the best and the worst of the American war film. It does show men wounded and shell-shocked, 'old before their time', and it does admit the omnipresence of fear: 'Anyone who says he isn't scared', says the sergeant, 'is either a fool or a liar.' Moreover, the class distinctions that were to bedevil English war films well into the 1950s are conspicuously absent. However, the 'realistic' shots are always brief; the question of the morality of war, of 'killing *people*' is abruptly settled by the sergeant: 'Besides, they're not people', he says of the Japanese; and the Brooklyn taxi-driver's mild protest against war ('I don't like it') tails off in pious fatalism ('I guess it's up to God'). War is inevitable, so there is no examination of the forces and pressures that create wars.

The formula element in the film lies not only in its attitude towards the Japanese, but in the multi-racial composition of the marine company: a Jew, a Mexican, a black American and a variety of WASP American types. This was the 1940s variation of the 'Pro-assimilative' process observable in 1930s films, encouraged by the OWI's *Government Information Manual for the Motion Picture* (1942), which recommended, among other measures, the use of 'colored' soldiers and servicemen with foreign names as a way of stressing national unity. Pictures of racial integration might help to allay racial tensions at home. Moreover, the emphasis on ethnicity offered an occasion for racial pride, while at the same time reassuring ethnic minorities that by participating in this communal enterprise they were demonstrating their 'Americanness', their shared values of freedom, patriotism, home and the family.

The melting pot was *allegedly* a reality, and wartime experience was a challenge for all Americans, whether abroad or on the home front, where immigrant girls and Claudette Colbert, a 'typical' suburban housewife, worked side by side in a welding factory (*Since You Went Away*, 1944). Hitchcock's *Lifeboat* (also 1944) has usually been seen as a criticism of complacent Western democracies, failing to respond to the Nazi threat until the last minute. But it is also a melting pot film, with its black American steward, its rich, cynical journalist with a working-class background, and its anti-Nazi German immigrant, once Schmidt, now a proud American Smith. And it is a film concerned with sacrifice and survival: the sacrifice of the Nazi officer is both his atonement and the redemption of those left on the raft.

There were other films, especially after Pearl Harbor, which focused on survival, even defeat. These were the 'last stand' pictures, depicting glorious American defeats in the Pacific in the cause of freedom. Like *Lifeboat*, these films masochistically exposed complacency and counselled unity; an example is *Wake Island* (1942), in which a feud between a marine commandant and the foreman of local construction workers is dropped in the face of the Japanese threat. And other kinds of non-didactic war films were permitted, such as *The Story of GI Joe* (1945), which, based on the career of a war reporter, Ernie Pyle, reflected a national mood of war-weariness.

2

The struggle with Germany and Japan preoccupied Sherlock Holmes, Tarzan and Donald Duck among others, but, in a sense, all Hollywood products between 1942 and 1945 were war films reflecting and supporting the war effort. In particular, the roles women assume in 1940s films are heavily influenced by the changes the Second World

War brought about. After Pearl Harbor, women were reclassified almost overnight by American industrialists so that they provided the basic labour force for the munitions industry – over four million by 1943. Nearly four times as many worked in heavy industry, manoeuvring giant cranes, cleaning out blast furnaces, servicing planes and so on.

The mass media responded by glamourising war work and pleading with women to enlist; the new working woman was symbolised as Rosie the Riveter, featured on the cover of the *Saturday Evening Post* and soon as familiar to the public as the girl with the Palmolive smile. Hollywood, whose audience in the war was largely female, responded by putting its stars into boiler suits (and, of course, into nurses' and army uniforms). Ann Sothern played an aircraft worker in *Swing Shift Maisie* (1943), Lucille Ball a defence plant worker in *Meet the People* (1944).

Attention was also paid to the ability of women to cope without a husband who was fighting, perhaps dying, abroad. That ability was symbolised on screen by the authority and independence of female stars, particularly Joan Crawford and Bette Davis. Even those actresses who played waiting, patient wives were possessed of a forbidding determination. Since they maintained homes instead of breaking them up, they can be seen as inverse images of the 1940s *femmes fatales*, as demonic agents of salvation.

The quintessential film about the women left behind on the home front was *Since You Went Away* (1944). It opens with a written announcement: 'This is the story of an unconquerable fortress, the American home, 1943.' Already, the military reference suggests the source of the film's emotional pull, the placing of civilian life in a wartime context. Racial tension is denied by the actions of the black maid (Hattie McDaniel) who has to take another job when the archetypal suburban family can no longer afford her wages, but who returns in the evenings to provide *free* labour. This environment glows with hygenic cleanliness, and the film's patriotic feeling emanates from the high school graduation scene, complete with 'America the beautiful' and the iconography of Lincoln's statue and the American flag.

The ideological stress in *Since You Went Away* on the single family group as the repository of worthwhile values is an indication that traditional ideas about the domestic role of women remained strong – and became stronger in the late 1940s when the returning troops learnt that most women (about eighty per cent) wanted to keep their jobs. As early as June 1945 *Atlantic Monthly* ran an article entitled 'Getting rid of the women'. In any case the treatment given by Hollywood to the career woman was much less reverential than that accorded the working wife, regularly forcing her into marriage and home life. *Mildred Pierce*, as portrayed by Joan Crawford in 1945, is the best example.

Mildred Pierce, labelled as *film noir* by Higham and Greenberg, but at its core, a melodrama or 'women's picture', presents and comments on a quest for upward mobility. It 'ended the playful admiration of the independent woman . . . If Mildred had succeeded both personally and in the business world she would have created a new social type: a career wife-mother . . ., precisely at the time when American society wanted to return to normalcy, to the *status quo anti bellum*. Mildred Pierce had to be destroyed to eliminate any troublesome thoughts held by working mothers.'[3] The heroine is a working-class girl (her father ran a grocery store, her mother, like Crawford's own, took in washing) who graduates from waitress to restaurateur during the Depression, by adherence to a rigid American ethic of hard work and self-reliance. This has been her way of escaping from a life which is just cooking, washing, and having children. Warned early on of the dehumanising effect of chasing success and abdicating maternal responsibilities by the loss of her youngest child, she accedes to the demands for money made by her snobbish daughter, Veda, and by the feckless Monty, with whom she spent the weekend when her daughter caught pneumonia; exploited financially and emotionally, Mildred persists in her 'nobility' which becomes near-suicidal self-sacrifice. Once again money and happiness are seen as antithetical, but, with the business sold, Mildred has the chance of a future as, at the end of the film, she walks off into the night with her first husband. Crucial to the film's significance is the reason for Mildred Pierce's punishment. Initially, she is blamed for simply not being a successful wife and mother; in addition, she seeks to explore areas of money and sex beyond her allotted class status, that is, she refuses to stay a consumer-wife-mother within socially imposed limits. The film is full of socio-sexual propaganda functioning as social control: strong, non-passive women are unlikely to achieve domestic bliss; career girls are lonely and lacking in warmth, a point underlined by the presence of Mildred's drinking companion, the asexual (i.e. independent) Ida (Eve Arden).

3

Along with the 1940s war films appeared a major genre of similar importance, known as *film noir*. For the present purpose it is useful to subsume under this heading those melodramas (private eye films, the 'Bogart as exile' films) which, despite obvious differences, overlap the *film noir* in theme, characterisation and information. Together, these categories form a genre which, through a persistent visual style, projects a menacing milieu of shadows and ambiguities. It is a world in which nothing is stable or reliable and in which inexorable violence frequently threatens to obscure the hero completely. The tone ranges from bitter nihilism to cynical stoicism; the plots end in isolated survival or personal (sometimes mutual) annihilation. Above all, these films are pessimistic explorations of what opportunities exist for human actions not committed to the war effort and 'democratic' values, and for personal and sexual relationships outside the conventional family. Indeed, in *film noir*, the family and romance are noticeably absent or brought into question; in *Double Indemnity* (1944), and *The Lady From Shanghai* (1948) sexuality and marriage are seen as incompatible.

The roots of the *film noir* lie in nineteenth-century Romanticism, which with its Gothic settings, fated solipsistic heroes and destructive women, was a major influence on Fritz Lang, a leading exponent of *film noir*. The essential images of the genre, expertly assembled by Higham and Greenberg in *Hollywood in the Forties* (1968) include: streets at night, in fog or rain; flashing neon signs; flickering street lamps; faces lit by car headlights, standard lamps or by the spotlight of a police interrogator; remote railway stations, coast roads; beach houses; and mirrors, the last used most memorably by Orson Welles at the end of *The Lady From Shanghai* (1948).[4]

Usually, the *film noir* does not entertain the possibility of a different world: the consistency of its gloomy, threatening atmosphere suggests it is as unchanging as its concept of human nature. Redemptive change is out of the question; so too is the placing of responsibility: 'It's not anyone's fault', says Martha Ivers, in *The Strange Love of Martha Ivers* (1946), 'It's just the way things are.' Evil is metaphysical, which explains the inadequacies of social institutions such as the law. In three films of 1946, *The Postman Always Rings Twice, From This Day Forward*, and *Deadline at Dawn* (the last-named written by Clifford Odets), the law is presented 'as an invincibly corrupt and terrifying force before which mere victims, whether innocent or guilty can only stand helpless or aghast'.[5]

The pessimistic vision of the *film noir*, implying a universal corruptibility, does not lend itself readily to social criticism and protest. In some of the films written or directed by Robert Siodmak (for example, *Christmas Holiday*, 1944, *The Killers*, 1946), moral squalor and irresponsibility are revealed beneath the suburban surface, but in these works and in others like them, the social context is not insistent, and the relations between the main characters are kept at the private level. When set beside the conservative affirmations of a film such as *Since You Went Away*, the *film noir* reveals a fundamental social meaning: it shows what happens when the individual tries to be exceptional, tries daringly for experience beyond the timid, middle-class world of order, family and deferred gratification. Typically, in *Double Indemnity* and *The Postman Always Rings Twice* (both based on novels by James M. Cain), the hero's dual desire for money and a particular woman ends in destruction. Neff in *Double Indemnity* concludes, 'I didn't get the woman and I didn't get the money'. Murder is both the result of and an analogue of uncontrolled passion; only in his own death does he succeed in overcoming the tension and despair of his isolation. When the protagonist is female, the social content is more obvious. Only in the home can a woman be happy and invulnerable; outside it, in a man's world, female aggression is unnatural and fatal.

Films noirs of the 1940s are filled with women who are glamorous and dangerous, seductive and duplicitous, their exciting sexuality underlined by a very expressive style. In seeking to satisfy their greed for money and power, they are unnervingly ruthless and destructive. They seem derived from the hard-boiled detective novels of Hammett and Chandler which, although a decade apart as books, were contemporaneous as films: *The Maltese Falcon* (1941), *The Glass Key* (1942), *Murder, My Sweet* (based on *Farewell, My Lovely*) in 1944 and *The Big Sleep* in 1946. The female protagonists in such books bewilder and threaten the detective-hero by means of an ambiguous combination of attractiveness and duplicity. Indeed, seduction may be a strategy to conceal participation in, or execution of, murder. Orson Welles indicated the hard-boiled hero's dilemma when he once observed, 'I hate women but I also need them'. In *Farewell, My Lovely* (1940), Velma Valento – now the rich Mrs Grayle – seeks to seduce Philip Marlowe with 'a half-sarcastic expression on her face'. She also deceives the romantic giant Moose Malloy turning him in for a reward and murdering him on his release. Marlowe agrees with Lieutenant Randall that his analysis of her suicide and its motivation is sentimental, but her single-minded and moral determination to hang on to her position and wealth are properly acknowledged in the book's last lines: 'It was a cool day and very clear. You could see a long way – but not as far as Velma had gone'.

Assuming the function of the gangster films of the early 1930s, *films noirs* offer their seductive women both as fantasies of power and as moralistic warnings. Their power lies in their sexuality, emphasised by dress or by the camera focusing on parts of the body. But through the narrative, the status quo of male domination is restored. The sexual mobility of such characters possibly articulates the soldier's nightmare, the paranoid fear of infidelity and change while he is overseas. So female sexual awareness in 1940s films becomes either a metaphor for or an accompaniment to ambition and the desire for independence.

The way in which the strains and apprehensions develop within the culture can be seen in two Rita Hayworth films, *Gilda* (1946) and *The Lady From Shanghai* (1948). In *Cover Girl* (1944) (and *Gilda*) the image of Rita Hayworth, carefully prepared, had been presented for audience approval which, immediately granted, made her a star. Mysteriously omitted from Alexander Walker's pantheon of sex symbols (*Sex in the Movies*), Rita Hayworth was manufactured into every man's pin-up. Born Margarita Cansino, her Spanish characteristics were only partly retained by the studios. Her hair was tinted auburn, and her hairline painfully altered by electrolysis. In *Cover Girl*, she comes across as physically attractive, healthy, all-American, as uncomplicated as Betty Grable and Ginger Rogers. But in *Gilda*, she is a far more ambiguous figure, ironic in defiantly asking her audience to 'Put the blame on Mame, boys', and sardonic in the way she plays up to the role of an untrustworthy, sexually insatiable woman that is imposed on her.

To the public, Gilda became an uncomplicated glamorous myth: the Bikini atom bomb was named Gilda, and had Rita Hayworth's picture painted on it. It was this image (of a cover girl or advertising model) that Welles took up and inflected in *The Lady From Shanghai*, showing Elsa stretched out sinuously on the boat's deck and showing her *blonde* hair caught in the wind. The radio advertisement 'Glosso Lusto in your hair' is relevant, as are the careful visual references to seeing and to voyeurism. Elsa's appearance partakes of another fantasy too, the mysterious fairy-tale princess (whom the gallant Michael saves in the opening sequence), an ethereal creature in a white dress who floats towards the bright lights of Acapulco. Welles's male discourse tends here towards those myths in which women are related to the desires of men. The major stereotype, which draws upon the illusionistic nature of traditional film narrative for its effect, is woman as glamour and sexual display, usually destined to become the property of the male hero. The romantic settings of Acapulco and the Caribbean make their contribution, but the dismantling of the myth soon begins to take place, with Elsa hinting fatalistically at the corruption of the trio she, Bannister and Grisby comprise. 'Everything is bad, Michael. Everything. You can't escape it or fight it. You've got to get along with it, deal with it, make terms'. She is a siren like Circe (the name of their yacht) and in the aquarium scene her face is juxtaposed with that of the alien sea creature. At the climax of the film the shattering of glass in the hall of mirrors signals not only her death (and Bannister's) but also the smashing of Hollywood's idols. Jacques Siclier writes: 'Every time a mirror falls in fragments, it carries with it the face of Rita. It is not only the body of the woman that perishes, but the idea, the allegory of woman. He [Welles] smashes the perfect shell of the ideal woman and the femme fatale is revealed'.[6]

In order to destroy one stereotype then, Welles has to resort to another, the wicked ruthless woman of *film noir*. Whether Welles convinces is debatable – he certainly strives to underline his vision of Elsa with Michael's fable about sharks, the aquarium scene, the intercutting with birds and reptiles during the river picnic, and the fairground in San Francisco with its grotesque laughing dolls. The process of revelation is the opposite of that which takes place in *Gilda*, where the heroine is *less* guilty than she seems. We may not be satisfied with that revelation of murderous evil in *The Lady From Shanghai* since the character's motivations are far from explicit. Orson Welles may have sought to betray 'Rita Hayworth', and so the mythological glamour-girl image is subverted by her games-playing husband.

But in both *Gilda* and *The Lady From Shanghai* (and Wilder's *Double Indemnity*) it is not only the visual discourse that is male, but the verbal discourse as well, through the use of voice over. The narrational voice, strongly resisted in *Gilda* by Hayworth's charisma, seeks to locate the audience in relation to the text. Fictionally, Elsa is mediated through Michael's romantic vision, which is Welles's in every way. And so the unhappiness and distaste she sometimes registers is consistent with the limitation of available roles for such a woman in what is still a man's world.

4

One major feature of the postwar American scene, the return of ex-servicemen, was treated in *Crossfire* (1947) and *The Best Years of Our Lives* (1946), films which took their place with other piously optimistic films, *Pinky* (1949), *Boomerang* (1947), and *Gentleman's Agreement* (1947), as part of a general movement to expose social problems in a more realistic style approaching that of documentary. Unfortunately, they were inclined to turn social and ethnic issues into personal questions and dilemmas, and (as Jim Hillier has shown) their realist aesthetic undermined their pose of critical fearlessness: 'On the most basic level they try to reproduce the world in a naturalistic way, an aesthetic which carries with it an ideological charge of affirmation, an essential faith in the world reproduced and in America's ability to solve its problems'.[7] The most relevant criticism to be made was expressed by Siegfried Kracauer. In his discussion of the 'vaguely liberal' films, he drew attention to the fact that 'they manage to suggest that liberal thought is receding rather than advancing', because 'they reveal the profound weakness of the very cause for which they try to enlist sympathy'.[8] Kracauer bases his conclusions on the weariness and disinclination to struggle he finds in the liberal-minded Police Captain of *Crossfire*, and the socially responsible bank officer of *The Best Years of Our Lives*; he might also have included the harassed DA in *Boomerang*, who discovers that his legal authority is ineffectual when in conflict with political power. Such men are talkers rather than doers, in a world where good nature is respected more than reason and ideas. Kracauer also refers to the spiritual atmosphere generated in these films by returning GIs: 'Visionless, at the mercy of any wind, benumbed even in their love-making, they drift about in a daze bordering on stupor'.[9]

Part of the problem for the returning male troops was the discovery that the pliable, passive wife or lover was yet another casualty of the war, and the divorce rate in 1945 was unusually high. In March 1946 the *New York Times* magazine published an article headed 'The American woman, not for this GI'. The ex-soldiers, however, some of them maimed, most of them uncertain and disoriented, needed images which translated that new female confidence into domestic competence, comfort and love. Two 1946 films, *Pride of the Marines* and the classic

The Best Years of Our Lives are equally dreams of male passivity – also present in *film noir*.

The latter, directed by William Wyler, derives from the cosy middle-class visual novelettes that MGM produced during the war. What separates this film from its predecessors is its specious aura of seriousness, as it tells the story of three ex-servicemen attempting to adjust to civilian life in a mid-Western town. In fact, the issues raised are resolutely shirked: there is no mention of the work of veterans' organisations; economic insecurity is mentioned several times, but real economic hardship is not shown; and there is no suggestion that ex-GIs might be at all resentful towards those who sent them to war. ('The Germans and the Japs pushed us in' is how the sailor, Homer, justifies America's part in the war and, by implication, the loss of his hands.) Nor is there a hint of class antagonism. It is conveniently precluded by army comradeship, which is maintained by regular meetings at a local bar. In place of rigorous social and economic analysis, the audience is offered the emotional resonance of the environment: the ball park, the high school football field, the fire station, the diner and the shoe-shine parlour which the men see, when they arrive home, are images of a traditional stability and security that is never really denied later in the film.

The essential dishonesty of the film, as Robert Warshow demonstrates in *The Immediate Experience*, is its refusal to acknowledge the actuality of politics, that is, 'the existence of real incompatibilities of interest and real *social* problems not susceptible of individual solution'. Warshow continues: 'the chief means of concealing the reality of politics is to present every problem as a problem of personal morality'.[10] This approach is exemplified in the film's attitude to economic problems, specifically the problem of returning GIs wishing to start a business without sufficient capital. Al Stephenson, the bank's new vice-president, makes the Mr-Deeds-like suggestion of small loans without collateral to *respectable* veterans who look hard-working, and so he manages to appear progressive in the perspective of conservative opposition. But there is nothing radical about this appeal to liberal benevolence; it in no way constitutes a challenge to the system, and Stephenson endangers his position more through his drinking than through his ideas. Despite its occasional gestures towards intelligence and realism, the film belongs fundamentally to the same category as *Since You Went Away*; both celebrate the family and the American way of life. In contrast to their nervous, ill-at-ease husbands and boyfriends, most of the women in this film are strong and wise: each of the leading men is at some stage put to bed by a woman. The roles acted by Myrna Loy, Teresa Wright and Cathy O'Donnell are maternal and domestic; the first two mentioned play the parts of mother and daughter. The exception is the role of Marie, the wife of a returning bombardier, the independent woman who cannot be domesticated. Unlike the other characters in the film, she appears to have no family (apart from her husband). Her sin, within the film's ethics, is *not* 'having worked during the war', but having enjoyed it to such an extent that she gives it up regretfully and, as the plot develops, only temporarily. Moreover, instead of building planes or, like the Teresa Wright figure, working in a hospital, she has been a nightclub dancer, a pin-up to her husband, who pastes her photo on the back of bombing patterns, but something more substantial, it is implied, to the men of Boone City. The sexual behaviour of soldiers overseas on the other hand, is practically ignored.

The film which most cogently portrays the mid-1940s state of limbo, 'that new troubling No Man's Land between war and postwar',[11] and its ambience of purposeless apathy and emotional misery, is *Crossfire*, in which bemused ex-servicemen spend their time playing cards, drinking, going to late movies, or engaging in pointless quarrels. In the film, a civilian warns: 'You can *feel* the tension in the air. A whole lot of fight and hate that doesn't know where to go'. But the world of *Crossfire* is the world of the *film noir*, as the elements of violence, intrigue and enervation determine. Elliot E. Cohen has criticised the compromises which the film's liberalism undergoes: Montgomery, the anti-semitic 'villain', is a psychopath, so only the most extreme form of prejudice is displayed. 'Anti-semitism', writes Cohen, 'is a pure irrational hate floating in space embodied whimsically against certain targets . . . This is the film's sociological wisdom . . .'[12] But the film is a dramatic narrative,

not a sociological tract, and it is because of the persistent amorality
Crossfire observes (Montgomery is betrayed and summarily shot),
because of its debt to the *film noir*, that the film transcends mere
melodrama.

Other attempts to make bold, liberal statements about social and
personal problems failed miserably through their timidity. *Gentleman's
Agreement* purported to deal with anti-semitism, but concluded that the
problem would disappear if people's behaviour improved. And like the
war film, it proposed that racial differences among Americans did not
really exist. *Pinky* limited itself to the problem of 'passing', its
black/white heroine being played by Jeanne Crain, while another stab at
the problem, *Home of the Brave*, explains its black hero's traumas (his
response to racism) through 'sensitivity' – a psychological (and curable)
condition. Racism is reduced to jokes and 'that chip on your shoulder'.

If such films seem naive and hesitant today, the constraints imposed
by an industry seeking profitability should not be forgotten. And
although *Gentleman's Agreement* and *Home of the Brave* were both
successful, in the insecure social climate of the postwar period, audiences
were prepared to accept liberal films about race only if they provided the
reassuring confidence which was difficult to find either in business or in
domesticity.

Notes

1   'From mid-1943 until the end of the war, OWI exerted an influence over
    an American mass medium never equalled before or since by a
    government agency.' Clayton R. Koppes and Gregory D. Black,
    'What to Show the World: the Office of War Information and
    Hollywood, 1942–1945', *Journal of American History*, vol. LXIV
    (1977–8), p. 103. See also Black and Koppes, 'OWI Goes to the
    Movies: the Bureau of Intelligence's Criticism of Hollywood',
    Prologue: the Journal of the National Archives, vol. VI (spring 1974),
    pp. 44–59.

2   James Agee, *Agee on Film*, vol. II (London, 1963), p. 39.

3   June Sochen, 'Mildred Pierce and Women in Film', *American Quarterly*,

vol. XXX, No. 1 (spring 1978), p. 13.

4 Charles Higham and Joel Greenberg, *Hollywood in the Forties* (London and New York, 1968), pp. 19–36.

5 Agee, *Agee on Film*, p. 199.

6 Jacques Siclier, 'Rita Assassinated or how myths are destroyed', *Cahiers Du Cinema*, 59 (May 1956), p. 24.

7 Jim Hillier, 'Out of the 40's, *Movie*, No. 19, p. 16.

8 Siegfried Kracauer, 'Those Movies with a Message', *Harper's Magazine*, vol. CXCVI (June 1948), p. 586.

9 Kracauer, 'Those Movies with a Message', p. 570.

10 Robert Warshow, 'The Anatomy of Falsehood', in *The Immediate Experience* (New York, 1964), p. 110.

11 Elliott E. Cohen, 'Letter to the Movie-Makers: the Film Drama as a Social Force', *Commentary*, vol. IV, No. 2 (August 1947), p. 112.

12 Cohen, 'Letter to the Movie-Makers', p. 113.

Richard Maltby

Made for each other: the melodrama of Hollywood and the House Committee on Un-American Activities, 1947

No discussion of the relationship between American film and politics can regard itself as complete without devoting some space to the encounters between Hollywood and the House Committee on Un-American Activities. No adequate history of the Cold War in America can be written without reference to the blacklist and other agencies of cultural repression that were generated by those encounters. But those events are now well documented, and their history has been written more than once. What remains to be said?

The Committee was a focus for hysteria, and in some respects that hysteria has provided its historians with a perspective too narrow to encompass the implications of the Committee's significance. The history of the Committee's encounter with Hollywood is not contained within the history of its victims, nor is it sufficiently described by an account which discusses only the conventionally political. Hollywood pursues its own politics, and they are different in kind from those practised in Washington. Rarely specifically issue-related, they concern themselves primarily with questions of status and constitute a dialectic between a concept of the movies as 'mere entertainment' and the several ideologies of Americanism.

The legal status of film was defined by a 1915 Supreme Court ruling, denying it the right to guarantees of free speech and legitimising censorship. Justice McKenna's opinion for the Court held that: 'The exhibition of motion pictures is a business pure and simple, originated and conducted for profit . . . not to be regarded . . . as part of the press of the country or as organs of public opinion'.[1] The cinema's social function was circumscribed within a framework that not only held it to be 'mere' entertainment, but potentially dangerous in its effects unless held in check by responsible social forces. As a result, the industry's Production Code Administration encouraged a conservative film content which sought to avoid controversy by keeping politics out of the movies and instead expressing a nostalgic melting-pot ideology that upheld the status quo.

The logic, ultimately, was financial: conventional Hollywood wisdom regarded films about politics as box-office poison, since anything controversial was liable to move the cinema out of its safe and profitable territory as entertainment into more dangerous areas. If the movies began to express their opinions about politics, politicians might want to express, and enforce, their opinions about the movies. 'Controversial' was a word useful only for advertising purposes; any other application was to be avoided. Not surprisingly, then, at all three of its encounters with the Committee, the industry wanted nothing so much as to play down the whole affair. That they were unable to do so suggests more than the greater effectiveness of the Committee's publicity. It implies that Hollywood, despite itself, had something in common with the Committee. That something was a mode of fictional construction.

In the early years of the Cold War, the Hollywood hearings comprised an interaction between two paranoid,[2] melodramatic definitions of political activity that set the terms of reference for the subsequent formulation of questions of loyalty and internal security. Those terms of reference cannot be understood merely in relation to the conventionally-labelled 'political' sphere in which the Committee normally operated. Hollywood did not only supply victims; it also perversely supplied a public rationale for the Committee's activities, and that rationale was by no means limited to the Committee's supporters in the film industry. The interaction between the Committee and Hollywood is above all an interaction on the level of rhetorical style and political aesthetics, and it is within that framework that I wish to explore the mutually supportive melodramas Hollywood and the Committee wove around their encounter in 1947.

The Committee enjoyed a tenuous relationship with Washington politics. Only two men of any repute ever sat on it: one, Nixon of California, made his reputation on it; the other, Walter of Pennsylvania, lost his through it. In more than thirty years of existence, the Committee was responsible for only one piece of legislation. And yet, despite a consistent lack of Presidential enthusiasm for the Committee's activities and its appalling legislative track-record, it was granted remarkably high appropriations by the House of Representatives with little apparent demur. It may be argued, indeed, that the Committee endured in Washington precisely because it did so little of conventional political consequence. It provided an outlet for a particularly militant vein of anti-liberal sentiment that, through its title, asserted itself as peculiarly American. Few Congressmen were prepared to face accusations from their own constituency backwoodsmen that they had voted against investigating un-Americanism. The Committee survived, by default, on its name. Its failure to occupy any substantial political ground meant that there was little reason for moderates to campaign for its abolition, however distasteful they found its activities. On the other hand, its power within Washington lay in the vagueness of its terms of reference. The Committee worked by power of suggestion, and it worked with constant aggression to demonstrate the need for its existence. With so nebulous a title, it could never run out of material to investigate. So long as it kept its fantasies outside the mainstream of Washington politics, it was no more than an occasional nuisance.

To Hollywood, however, the Committee appeared quite differently. On some level the Committee represented Washington and the entire weight of the American political institution. Insecurity was an article of faith in the film industry, which invariably responded defensively to external pressure. The Committee was both official and representative; Hollywood thus felt obliged to observe it warily and with respect. In that conjunction lay the effectiveness of the Committee's choice of

Hollywood as a target for investigation: if for Hollywood the Committee was associated with the official politics of Washington, for Washington the Committee and Hollywood shared a political importance that was based not on the realities of political practice but on the power of suggestion, and on a melodramatic oversimplification of political debate. By selecting Hollywood the Committee established itself as an agency for interaction between the political and the cultural, between the civic and the sensual. The Committee's aggressive attitude to the exercise of power by both institutions ensured that the encounter between them, of which it was the focus, was a violent one.

It may well be that the New Deal itself sponsored the growth of melodramatic fictions in American politics. Certainly Roosevelt's Hundred Days, his forging of the Imperial Presidency and his programme of governmental intervention all encouraged public belief in the simple, personal solution to the complex problems of the Depression. It was a political style that adjusted without difficulty to the need for national solidarity and ideological unity provoked by the Second World War. Regardless of the practical effectiveness of his policies, the manner in which Roosevelt conducted his political discourse arguably precipitated the paranoid attitude of the extreme right wing. His emphasis on the personal in his political presentation encouraged a reaction from his most virulent opponents which placed equal stress on the personal culpability of those responsible for their loss of power. When they themselves gained political influence, it was inevitable that they would convert that stress on the personal into a pursuit of victims. The House Committee on Un-American Activities was born, in 1938, of the increasingly cohesive alliance of Republican and Southern opposition to the New Deal. Throughout its active life it served as a barometer of anti-Roosevelt sentiment, growing increasingly obsolete as it grew more pointlessly vindictive. The Committee's historical importance lies not in what it did but in what it measured; with the passive ratification of Roosevelt's federal welfare state in the latter half of the Eisenhower administration, it became redundant. The

Committee's intentions and methods were locked into a political perspective that showed the other side of the melting pot's all-embracing populist vision; a perspective that found itself increasingly outmanoeuvred by the postwar liberalism of the Eastern establishment. American political fundamentalism has ever required its bogeymen; those unregenerate villains who refused the Jeffersonian promise could be explained away only by insisting that they gave allegiance not to an American democracy but to a conspiratorial and objectively evil alien power whose sole purpose was the overthrow of the government of the United States. In this perennial struggle to root out totemic victims to explain the failure of particular American Dreams, no lamb has ever led its populist executioners more willingly to the slaughter than the Communist Party of the USA. If it was not a conspiracy, too often it behaved as if it were. Even more than its transparent attachment to the foreign policy of the Soviet Union, what made it so ideal a target for the Committee was its insistence on secrecy, which lent it the same furtive air as the Masons or, for that matter, the Ku Klux Klan. The paranoid vision of the Committee's supporters was reflected and endorsed by the paranoia of those they persecuted.

Intriguing as the convolutions of paranoid politics are, by themselves they comprise no more than a subject of curiosity tangential to the mainstream of American political history. What gives them their significance is the extent to which, for the seven or more years of the early Cold War, their conspiratorial fantasies were adopted, sustained and practised by figures who in less melodramatic times would see themselves as the arbiters of political rationality. For those few years in the late 1940s and early 1950s, the Committee established the terms of debate for the major public issue in domestic affairs: loyalty, subversion, and the scope of the Red Plot. While, in the atmosphere of the Cold War, investigations into subversive activity might well have been considered a proper activity for the Government, the Committee's lines of inquiry were almost always peripheral to the more 'realistic' pursuits of official anti-Communism. Only occasionally (most notably in the Hiss case) did it manage to occupy the centre stage of Washington's strictly political theatre. More commonly it operated as the vanguard of those 'cultural vigilantes'[3] who sought to safeguard their diminishing political and social status by attacks on those New-Deal-sponsored groups they felt most threatened by. Operating as it did on the margins of the political stage, it sought a different limelight: the headlines of the nation's newspapers. Consistently it sought that limelight through the previous reputations of those victims it brought before its inquisition. Public personalities were a prime target of the Committee and its kind; that was undoubtedly one of the attractions of Hollywood. What ultimately made possible the Committee's success during its 'Great Decade'[4] between 1946 and 1956 was the decline of a 'realist' political dramaturgy in Washington, and its substitution by the melodramas of atom spies, microfilms hidden in pumpkins and the ever-growing Communist Threat.

The Committee's activities also established the manner in which the melodramatic debate would be conducted: around the public indictment of individuals whose past allegiances to causes now proscribed could be paraded as evidence of the moral unfitness of any organisations by which they were or had been employed. In that respect, the motion picture industry was the largest target they ever aimed directly at. The reasons for its selection do much to indicate the real intentions of the Committee in seeking to generate publicity for their conspiratorial vision. If it could be established that Hollywood, like the Federal Theater Project, was not merely a hotbed of radicals but had also regularly perpetrated acts of subversive propaganda, and moreover had done so with government support, then the Committee might achieve a breakthrough in convincing public opinion of the enormity of the Red Menace. The discovery that a filing clerk in the State Department was a card-carrying member of the Communist Party would have little effect on the public imagination; at best it might achieve a call to tighten up security procedures. But establishing that the writer or star of a popular movie perhaps half the citizenry of America had seen was a Communist was altogether a different kind of ball-game. The testimony of witnesses like Jack Warner that it was the 'intellectual' writers who were the most avid supporters of the Soviet and that 'Some of these lines have innuendos and double meanings, and things like that, and you have to take eight or ten Harvard law courses to find out what they mean'[5] were exactly suited to the Committee's attempts to induce paranoia. The Communists had done and were doing things to the movies, and they were so smart that Joe Public didn't even know he was being brainwashed. Naturally the Committee attacked the movies; they could not miss the opportunity to turn the dream factory into a paranoid fantasy. The concentration of their attack on writers and directors fitted equally well into the working of the Committee's paranoid style. They were the faceless ones, the backroom boys, the demonic brains behind the master-plan to destroy America's soul.

Such bizarre notions, as well as more concrete evidence, kept the film industry high on the Committee's priorities. As early as the year of its inception, chairman Martin Dies had expressed an interest in a number of Hollywood organisations he suspected of being Communist fronts. In July 1940 Dies carried out a brief one-man investigation of Hollywood, rapidly abandoned for lack of evidence. By 1947, however, the political atmosphere had changed to such an extent that a further attack on Hollywood could provide itself with both a more substantial basis and a broader target. The Popular Front had long since collapsed, to be followed by the partial disintegration of the Democratic coalition in the 1946 mid-term elections. Domestic political sentiment had swung sharply to the right with the onset of the Cold War. Moreover, the war had embedded in the public imagination a new villainous archetype: the espionage agent. Both the Committee and Hollywood had played significant roles in establishing the centrality of this new mythic figure in the political and cultural arena; while the Committee had doggedly investigated possible sabotage plots in war production and begun its forays into the murky world of atomic spies, the movies fed the public fantasies whose villains were 'agents' and heroes 'investigators'. While the spy cycle of the early war years claimed some allegiance to fact (*Confessions of a Nazi Spy*, 1939), and identified its villains as German (*Saboteur*, 1942, *Action in the North Atlantic*, 1943), the pressures of generic evolution developed new villains as well as new locales, and by 1943 the spy thriller had become more isolationist in underlying sentiment, with its 'agents' amorphously located as part of some vague European conspiracy (*Background to Danger*). In this European arena Americans were conventionally innocents abroad (*Journey Into Fear*, 1942), but the paranoia of such a narrative landscape was brought home more frequently in the stylistically related private eye genre, where the investigator hero strove to make sense of a world of deep shadows run by corrupt Machiavellian sophisticates (*The Big Sleep*, 1946). By the end of the war, the Bogartian individualist investigator had partially mutated into a government operative, and the European conspirators had brought their explicitly political fantasies home to the semi-documentary reality of wartime New York (*The House on 92nd Street*, 1945).

The war had also accustomed audiences to accept more readily an element of propaganda in film content. The military film units employed many Hollywood personnel, and documentary as a genre and set of stylistic idioms was reciprocally imported into Hollywood in the final years of the war, most notably in those same semi-documentary *policier* films. Hollywood's wartime fictions gave credence to the role of investigator at the same time that the tone of the emerging *film noir* reflected and produced a paranoid environment, into which the Committee's more extreme visions of an America overrun with conspirators seeking its destruction could be projected. The investigative narrative reflected and exemplified the self-defensive insecurity Hollywood felt in contemplating its newly-endorsed social function. No longer confident of his own heroic status, the equilibrium of social forms, or even the identity of objects, the *film noir* protagonist sought the end of the movie as a release from his quest for meaning and stability. As a form the genre still rigorously practised the melodramatic, but it now did so hoping for, rather than expecting, the happy ending. The investigator asked questions precisely to secure the retrospective structural guarantees earlier narratives had innocently assumed before Hollywood went to work for the government. One tactical approach to the recovery of narrative security (in both the *policier* and semi-documentaries and the liberal melodramas) involved a more overt commitment to the exaggerated fictional practices of one or other extreme American ideology. In such a context, the Committee's vision had become a valid option.

In June 1946 Congressman John L. Rankin of Mississippi announced the Committee's intention of investigating 'one of the most dangerous plots ever instigated for the overthrow of the Government'[6] emanating from Hollywood. Though the investigation failed to materialise, its announcement amounted to a declaration that the industry was likely to find itself once again on the Committee's agenda, a declaration renewed before Congress in January 1947 by the new Chairman, J. Parnell Thomas of New Jersey, in his eight-point plan for the Committee's activities in the coming year. There was an immediate connection between another of the Committee's investigatory targets of 1947 and Hollywood that ironically emphasised the relationship between their melodramatic paranoia. In November 1946 the Committee had unearthed an alleged Communist master spy of East German origin, Gerhart Eisler, who was brought before the Committee in February 1947, refused to take the stand, and was cited for contempt. Eisler's brother Hanns was a composer who had worked with Brecht on *Kuhle Wampe* and *Die Massnahme* and had since 1940 been resident in the United States, writing Hollywood scores (including those for *Hangmen Also Die* (1943) and *Woman on the Beach* (1947)). Hanns became a subject for investigation not only because of his brother but also because, when he was seeking an entry visa in 1939, he had obtained support from among others, Eleanor Roosevelt.[7] He, called by Committee Chief Investigator Robert Stripling 'the Karl Marx of Communism in the musical field', provided the incidental connection that led the Committee to Hollywood in May 1947. A closed session heard testimony from fourteen 'friendly' witnesses, including Jack Warner and Louis B. Mayer. On the basis of that testimony, the Committee scheduled public hearings in Washington for October, and issued an indictment which indicated their areas of concern. Its two principal charges concerned the injection of Communist propaganda into films, partly as a result of direct White House intervention with the studios, and the extent to which the National Labor Relations Board had assisted Communist-inspired attempts to take over Hollywood unions and thus seize control of the industry.

The anti-New-Deal thrust of these accusations was clear. The Committee might have adduced other, concrete reasons for their investigation of Hollywood; there was plentiful evidence of Communist Party fund-raising in Hollywood, and the Committee could easily have demonstrated a noticeable Communist presence on the periphery of the film industry. That it chose not to do so indicates either its incompetence or that its concern with Hollywood did not lie wholly within this area. Nearer to the Committee's heart should have been the matter of Hollywood's unions. The unionisation of the studios had been a protracted, bitter process, marked by wholesale corruption on the part of some labour leaders, consistent hostility from the studios, and a number of prolonged and violent strikes that were superficially inter-union jurisdictional disputes but ultimately reflected political antagonisms between Hollywood's left and right. The most recent of these strikes, in the autumn of 1946, had resulted in the effective defeat of the left-led Conference of Studio Unions and the firm establishment of the International Alliance of Theatrical and Stage Employees as the sole effective negotiating body for the industry's manual workers. The IATSE in Hollywood was dominated by Roy Brewer, a hard-line anti-Communist who was later to be a key figure in 'clearance' procedures for blacklistees, and was identified by one blacklisted writer as 'the strawboss of the purge'.[8] But despite its proud record of union persecution and its expressed interest in this area, the Committee made little attempt to plough this fertile soil, and concentrated its aggression against the numerically less significant Screen Writers' Guild (SWG). In this it again revealed both its melodramatic intent and its dependence on the particular prejudices of its informers. Several of the 'friendly' witnesses at both hearings were screenwriter members of the Motion Picture Alliance for the Preservation of American Ideals (MPAPAI), an ultra-right organisation founded in 1944; among them Rupert Hughes and James K. McGuiness, the founders in 1933 of a rival writers' organisation to the SWG.

In its early years the Guild had been dominated by Communists (its first president being John Howard Lawson), but since its reorganisation in the late 1930s, Communist influence had diminished sharply. Such factual considerations were, however, of little concern to the Committee: the Guild was a legitimate target because it was that most heinous of institutions, a trade union for intellectuals. Moreover, it could be clearly associated with identified long-term members of the Communist Party, who had also participated in dubious Rooseveltian schemes such as the War Activities Committee and Hollywood Writers Mobilisation, and who as screenwriters were ideally placed to insert undetectable Red propaganda into the movies. Since this line of attack coincided conveniently with the desires of the Committee's MPAPAI witnesses, the diverse influences which drew the Committee and Hollywood together found themselves most firmly focused around those members of the Guild later identified as the Hollywood Ten.

Potentially underlying all these opinions was an awareness that the American cinema had been a significant beneficiary of Rooseveltian liberalism. In 1941 Roosevelt had declared that films should not be subject to war censorship, and in a price control bill of 1942 movies were exempted, along with the press, from licensing as a condition of sale or distribution. The right of the screen to protection under the First Amendment had been tacitly granted by the Roosevelt administration's equation of motion pictures with newspapers so far as federal controls were concerned. Equally important, governmental acknowledgement of the morale and propaganda value of film during the war had legitimised the cinema's social consciousness. By providing the industry with an explicit set of tasks related to the war effort and affording it the same freedoms of information as the press, Roosevelt's wartime administration had provided the cinema with a social and political status. The use of Hollywood expertise in government propaganda films and wartime documentary units (and the industry's numerous feature productions intended to make specific, government-approved, propaganda points) had given purpose and technical experience to the employment of Hollywood's newly-defined social responsibility. In 1946 the industry assumed that its responsible contribution to the war effort would be converted to a responsible contribution to post-war political debate.

This new political freedom found its most obvious expression in a series of melodramas which took overtly political topics as their thematic content while remaining loyal to the formal structures of Hollywood's unselfconscious linear narrative tradition. The films thus operated within a framework established by wartime propaganda, in terms of both their narrative construction and their general political sentiment, which was liberal and integrationist. It was not surprising that many of the personnel involved in the production of *Pride of the Marines* (1945), *Mission to Moscow* (1943) and *Hitler's Children* (1943) also worked on *Crossfire* (1947), *Cornered* (1945) and *Body and Soul* (1947). Thus it was inevitable that several of the principal contributors to the postwar social realist movement should have found themselves brought before the Committee as members of the 'unfriendly Nineteen'. But the assumption they made that their most recent movies were the cause of their indictment, and that the Committee was launching an attack against Hollywood's emergent liberalism, was something of an oversimplification, for there were a number of significant industrial correspondences among the Nineteen as well as the obvious political ones. Eleven of them had worked for Warner Brothers, the studio responsible for the greatest output of wartime propaganda features. The progression from the studio's 'social conscience' films of the 1930s to the wartime films was a natural one, in that the inclusion of a more or less explicitly stated theme into a conventionally structured plot was a formula already well understood by studio writers and directors like Rossen, Koch, Pichel and Milestone. Success in a particular genre led to assignments in films of the same type, and to offers from other studios of similar work.

At the end of the war, many of these individuals found homes in other studios, where they established themselves in regular producer-director-writer teams: Adrian Scott, Edward Dmytryk and John Paxton at RKO; Louis de Rochmont, Henry Hathaway and John Monks Jr at Fox; Mark Hellinger, Jules Dassin and Albert Maltz at Universal. Collaborations such as these, along with a few independent production companies like Enterprise Studios, formed the core of the social realist movement, and the style of their films reflected their origins as clearly as their content reflected their political sympathies. But the direction they had taken since the war had been the result of a particular industrial trajectory and while they were now producing films for which the Committee had no affection, it was not their current work but their previous associations which made them vulnerable.

However, that 'Communist Infiltration of the Motion Picture Industry' should become a subject for investigation at exactly the time that the American cinema was expanding its wartime prerogatives of expression into areas of social controversy was not entirely coincidence. While, as in other areas of artistic or intellectual activity, the Committee and others dedicated to rooting out 'subversion' selected specific films and individuals for indictment, the right-wing backlash was intended to affect the expression of opinion by a much larger group. Since the cinema's postwar social conscience was in part the result of the industry's co-operation with the Roosevelt administration, it was not surprising that it should be a peripheral target for the attack on that administration's achievements. The very claim that the cinema was a socially responsible form of expression was an offshoot of the kind of liberalism which had brought forth the New Deal, and its partial legitimisation through government co-operation ensured that the Committee would find an opportunity to challenge it.

Such a notion may well have been behind the Thomas Committee's decision to raise the unprofitable issue of Communist propaganda in films, although it also served a more particular function that was as close to its heart. In selecting its subjects for investigation, the Committee clearly sought to establish a direct connection between individual film workers whom they could demonstrate to be card-carrying members of the Communist Party, and the Roosevelt administration. Their thin case on this point was constructed around a short list of films they and friendly witnesses declared to be 'communistic'; all made in 1943, most of them depicting Russia. On the basis of evidence taken in closed session in Los Angeles in May 1947, the Committee concentrated its investigations on *Mission to Moscow* (Warner Bros., 1943, directed by Michael Curtiz, script by Howard Koch) and *Song of Russia* (MGM, 1943, directed by Gregory Ratoff, script by Paul Jarrico and Richard Collins). The Committee's contention was that both films were communist propaganda, and that both had been made with direct encouragement from the Roosevelt government, in particular from Lowell Mellett, whom Roosevelt had personally appointed as head of the War Activities Committee, charged with assisting motion pictures to 'usefully serve the National Defence effort'.

Under public examination at the Washington hearings in October 1947, the case against Mellett collapsed ignominiously. Jack Warner, having apparently had time since May to check his files, retracted the statements he had made at the preliminary hearings that Ambassador Davies[9] had approached him about making the film and that allegations that it had been made at the request of the Roosevelt government were 'not without foundation'.[10] Robert Taylor, who in May had suggested that he had been 'coerced' into making *Song of Russia*, and that his commission into the Navy was specifically delayed in order that he might appear in the film, also withdrew his complaint, and stated: 'I think the script was written and prepared long before any representative of the government became involved in it in any way.'[11]

Despite their utter failure, the Committee's intentions were evident from their proceedings. Their eagerness to pursue the question of government involvement in what would, in the atmosphere of 1947, undoubtedly pass for a propaganda film, was shown by their choice of Warner as their first witness. That Warner and Louis B. Mayer both denied the existence of communist propaganda in their films was perhaps hardly surprising, and it may well be that Thomas and the rest of the Committee had little faith in their ability to make the specific case against Mellett stick. However, he remained a target. In questioning the 'expert' anti-Communist witness Ayn Rand, Chief Investigator Robert Stripling drew attention to a letter from Mellett stating that *Song of Russia* had no political overtones. Miss Rand then expounded imaginatively and at some length about the propaganda in the film, providing the Committee with the only detailed evidence they took to support their repeated assertions of communist-inspired content in the film.[12] Having established to their own satisfaction their case that communist propaganda had indeed been produced in Hollywood, the Committee and its witnesses seemed happy to revert to vague and generalised criticisms, which reached their nadir in Lela Rogers' assertion that 'It has been a long time since you could get a good American story bought in the motion picture industry'.[13]

The testimony of the friendly witnesses had in most respects been inconclusive: it amounted to allegations that there was communist propaganda in films, but it had been short on convincing evidence to establish the charge; witnesses had made accusations of communist affiliations among a number of Hollywood figures, and had repeatedly offered the opinion that the Hollywood communist conspiracy was strongest among scriptwriters, and in the Writers Guild. Other than that, much time had been consumed with their personal disapprobations of Communism, and with the Committee's attempts to persuade them to concur in its opinion that the Communist Party should be outlawed. Their most frequent charge related to the incessant characterisation of bankers, capitalists or Senators as the villain of the plot. Scriptwriter Rupert Hughes suggested: 'Where you see a little drop of cyanide in the picture, a small grain of arsenic, something that makes every Senator, every businessman, every employer a crook and which destroys our beliefs in American free enterprise and free institutions, that is communistic.'[14] Leo McCarey made a similar statement, but omitted to mention that his *Going My Way* (1942) had featured a businessman as the villain. But in an atmosphere where nobody, not even members of the MPAPAI, could guarantee their innocence, the vagueness of the charges was their essence and populist stereotypes were as good a target as any. If the Committee could establish an atmosphere of mass guilt by accusations which embraced almost everybody, then innocence could only be established by a willingness to co-operate with the Committee. Thomas's intention, expressed when he brought the hearings to an abrupt end after ten days, that it would resume its investigations of film content, may well have been an expression of his preparedness to continue this approach. In the event it was not necessary; the industry's institution of a blacklist was to provide an even more compelling reason for individuals to co-operate fully with the Committee.

In part the Committee was able in 1951 to avoid a return to the inevitably contentious area of film content by the alteration in the prevailing conditions in foreign and domestic affairs and in the affairs of the industry. But partly it was a result of the Committee's one palpable hit in the 1947 hearings: the co-operative refusal of the ten 'unfriendly' witnesses to co-operate. In one sense crucial to both the film industry and the Committee, the Committee had achieved its goal when the 'Hollywood Ten' were so christened. The press produced a phrase that could lodge itself in the public consciousness, and in the process indict 'Hollywood', the film industry's synonym for itself, along with the ten men actually cited in contempt of Congress. Hollywood had long been a fantastic place; the Committee redirected that fantasy for its consumers, and the extreme left, as was their historical heritage in America, offered a practical sustenance to their accusers.

Thomas contrived to eliminate Hollywood's liberal opposition in one simple manoeuvre. Eric Johnston, President of the Motion Picture Association of America, was scheduled to testify on 28 October. That day, the Committee for the First Amendment[15] sent a delegation of its most famous members to Washington to attend the hearings. Their publicly-stated intention was 'to see whether they [the hearings] would be fair', but they were also out to steal some of Thomas's publicity thunder. Instead of Johnston, Thomas chose to call John Howard Lawson, the first of the nineteen unfriendly witnesses, probably the most publicly avowed Communist Party member among them and almost certainly the one most likely to take a belligerently hostile attitude towards the Committee. Lawson fulfilled expectations perfectly. He engaged in a shouting match with Thomas, vigorously protested the Committee's refusal to allow him to read a statement, and repeatedly rose to Thomas's bait:

*The Chairman:*Mr Lawson, you will please be responsive to these questions and not continue to try to disrupt these hearings.

*Mr Lawson:*I am not on trial here, Mr Chairman. This Committee is on trial here before the American people. Let us get that straight.[16]

He was finally removed from the stand, and later charged with contempt. His performance had done more than simply establish the precedent by which the other ten hostile witnesses would be treated. The Committee's decision to examine Lawson as the opening witness on the day when a gathering of Hollywood stars was drawing even more public attention to the hearings than usual routed its liberal opponents. The Committee for the First Amendment had declared themselves anti-Communists, and their representatives in Washington had intended to keep away from the nineteen witnesses, in order, they hoped, not to confuse the issue of the witnesses' right to refuse to answer questions. Thomas had forcibly associated them with a public display of intransigence which demolished the basis of sympathy they had hoped to use as a weapon against the Committee. Bogart, Garland, Huston and the rest returned demoralised to Hollywood the next day.

Lawson's unintended co-operation with the Committee had extended beyond his performance. At one point in his testimony he had said: 'The pictures that I have written are very well known. They are ... such pictures as *Blockade*, of which I am very proud, and in which I introduced the danger that this democracy faced from the attempt to destroy democracy in Spain in 1937.'[17]That was the kind of remark the Committee would have been happy to hear from Lawson as a friendly witness. His posture before the Committee, his name-calling and refusal to co-operate with procedure did more damage, at least to his advocates, if not to himself, than his refusal to answer the $64 question. It was, at

the most charitable, a tactical error which in the main the other
unfriendly witnesses did little to correct. Albert Maltz was permitted to
read his prepared statement, Alvah Bessie was allowed to read the first
two paragraphs of his, but these were the only exceptions to an otherwise
regular pattern. The witness was identified, his request to read a
statement was rejected on the Committee's perusal of its contents, he was
asked and refused to answer the $32 question, 'Are you a member of the
Screen Writers or Directors Guild?' and then the $64 question, 'Are you
now or have you ever been a member of the Communist Party?' He then
stood down, a member of the Committee's staff recited his communist
affiliations, and his refusal to answer the two questions was offered as
grounds for his being cited in contempt of Congress. By the time the
ninth witness, Lester Cole, was called, the procedure was so refined that
he was on the stand for only six and a half minutes.

The rhetoric of both parties echoed each other. Where Thomas
sought to conjure up visions of Moscow-directed intellectuals
surreptitiously corrupting American minds in ways so subtle they could
hardly be detected, Dalton Trumbo, perhaps the most eloquent of the
Ten, suggested in his statement:

Already the gentlemen of the Committee and others of like disposition have
produced in this capital city a political atmosphere which is acrid with fear and
repression; a community in which anti-Semitism finds safe refuge behind secret
tests of loyalty; a city in which no union leader can trust his telephone; a city in
which old friends hesitate to recognise one another in public places; a city in
which men and women who dissent even slightly from the orthodoxy you seek
to impose, speak with confidence only in moving cars and in the open air. You
have produced a capital city on the eve of its Reichstag fire. For those who
remember German history in the autumn of 1932 there is the smell of smoke in
this very room.[18]

By the nature of their performance, the Hollywood Ten succeeded in
establishing the Committee's melodramatic persuasion. They acted as
unwitting foils in the creation of a public fiction that their employers
were then incapable of resisting. Prior to the hearings, the Association of
Motion Picture Producers had declared: 'Hollywood is weary of being

the national whipping boy for Congressional Committees. We are tired of having irresponsible charges made again and again and not sustained. If we have committed a crime we want to know it. If not, we should not be badgered by Congressional Committees.'[19] Throughout their testimony, Jack Warner, Louis Mayer and the other producers called rejected the Committee's explicit proposals for a blacklist:

> *Mr Warner:*Of course, I don't believe it would be legal – speaking only personally – to have the Association or any other men band together to obstruct the employment of any other man. I would not be a party to it and neither would any of the other men, from my knowledge of them.[20]

But the Ten's behaviour in front of the Committee undermined the basis on which this position was being held. The industry could no longer identify itself with them and maintain its appearance of conservative respectability. As in the Arbuckle and Taylor scandals of the early 1920s it was forced to make a public spectacle of its responsibility in punishing those who transgressed its boundaries of permissible behaviour. The public declaration of this responsibility was embodied in the Waldorf Statement, but the mood of the action was caught more precisely by the letters severing RKO's contract with Adrian Scott and Edward Dmytryk:

> By your conduct [in refusing to answer questions] and by your actions, attitude, public statements, and general conduct before, at and since that time, you have brought yourself into disrepute with large sections of the public, have offended the community, have prejudiced this corporation as your employer and the motion picture industry in general, have lessened your capacity fully to comply with your employer Agreement, and have otherwise violated your employment contract with us.[21]

The producers imposed a blacklist reluctantly, and they did so because they could see no alternative if they wished to resume their position of political neutrality in the new frame of reference the Committee had successfully created. Beset at the same time by a Supreme Court anti-trust decision that demolished the foundations of the industry's economic structure, and by competition from television that might swing the industry into permanent recession, they had little incentive to make a stand on political principle; something they were not, in any case, prone to do. As in 1934, when their claims to respectability had been challenged by a body who backed their demands with threats of economic sanction, the industry placed its mouth where its money was, and let its conscience take care of itself. The industry conceded to the American Legion rather than to the Committee, as it had conceded to the Legion of Decency rather than to Senator Brookhart. In both cases, it was seeking the same goal, and that goal was fervently noncontroversial, and desperately apolitical. It sought a return to that respectability which guaranteed it financial security, and thus it sought the simplest way out of a political controversy not of its making, so long as that way out left it free to carry on its own activities unimpeded by external organisations. It sought, in other words, to return to a position from which it could continue to construct its own melodramatic fictions, without the intervention of other scriptwriters like the Committee. What it never acknowledged was the extent to which its own melodramatic mode of representation had been a cause of the crisis it had experienced, and a contributor to the way issues were to be presented to the American public for much of the next decade.

Notes

1   236 US 230, 244 (1915). Quoted in Richard Randall, *Censorship of the Movies: the Social and Political Control of a Mass Medium* (Madison, Wis., 1968), p. 19.

2   'Paranoid' is here being used within the frame of reference articulated by Richard Hofstadter in *The Paranoid Style in American Politics* (London, 1966), to refer to the periodic re-location of the domain of politics in emotive rather than rational territory. 'The melodramatic' delineates one of a number of distinct attitudes which may be brought to the construction of a fiction.

3   Sidney Hook, *Heresy Yes, Conspiracy No!* (New York, 1950), p. 16.

4   Eric Bentley, *Thirty Years of Treason: Excerpts from Hearings before the House Committee on Un-American Activities, 1938–1968* (New York, 1971), p. xxvii.

5 Testimony quoted in Gordon Kahn, *Hollywood on Trial: the Story of the Ten Who were Indicted* (New York, 1949), p. 16.

6 Walter Goodman, *The Committee: the Extraordinary Career of the House Committee on Un-American Activities* (London, 1969), p. 172.

7 Goodman suggests that Eleanor Roosevelt was one of the Committee's prime targets for discrediting during this period. See Goodman, *The Committee*, pp. 204ff.

8 Quoted anonymously in John Cogley, *Report on Blacklisting: 1: the Movies* (New York, 1956), p. 47.

9 Joseph E. Davies, the US Ambassador to Moscow, 1936–8, on whose book the film was based.

10 Interestingly enough, in Eric Sherman's unpublished American Film Institute Oral History with Howard Koch, Koch claims that Roosevelt himself asked Warner to make the film, and that together they selected Koch as the screenwriter.

11 Bentley, *Thirty Years of Treason*, p. 138.

12 Bentley, *Thirty Years of Treason*, p. 112.

13 Cogley, *Report on Blacklisting*, p. 12.

14 Cogley, *Report on Blacklisting*, p. 12.

15 Formed by John Huston, William Wyler, and Philip Dunne shortly before the hearings began.

16 Bentley, *Thirty Years of Treason*, p. 154.

17 Bentley, *Thirty Years of Treason*, p. 156.

18 Kahn, *Hollywood on Trial*, p. 84.

19 Cogley, *Report on Blacklisting*, p. 13.

20 Kahn, *Hollywood on Trial*, p. 22.

21 Kahn, *Hollywood on Trial*, p. 191.

Brian Neve

The 1950s: the case of Elia Kazan and *On the Waterfront*

This paper represents a preliminary attempt to explore relationships between American film and American society. In concentrating on the work of one director, Elia Kazan, and in particular on one film, *On the Waterfront*, the paper seeks to explore ways of using feature films as source material for examining aspects of the wider culture and society of the United States.

Several models and/or influences could be mentioned, including Pauline Kael's piece on *Citizen Kane* and the essays in a recently published book on *American History/American Film*.[1] A number of factors that make *On the Waterfront* of interest relate directly to the film but others relate to the political pressures of the time and to the film's place in the career of its director. The influence of Kazan's 'friendly' testimony to the House Committee on Un-American Activities (HUAC) has been frequently referred to; the place of *Waterfront* in Kazan's constant but evolving concern with American society, and the impact of his involvement in the political/cultural 'movement' of the 1930s, have been less thoroughly explored. If the film partly reflects the 1930s, and partly the 1950s — with its box-office success strengthening interpretations that see it as reflecting contemporary society — in other senses it is possible to trace links with the society and 'movements' of the 1960s. Writing of *Viva Zapata* Leo Braudy has written as follows: 'Zapata may have been killed, Kazan may have named names. But the horse, the image, Brando as a star, live beyond the film — perhaps to infuse the more personal politics of the 1960s.'[2] While it is hoped that the detailed account of the genesis of *On the Waterfront* contributes something to an understanding of the development of the American film industry during the critical times of the early 1950s, this paper largely bypasses two other relevant concerns: firstly, the important and still rumbling debate about the behaviour of both 'friendly' and 'unfriendly' witnesses, and secondly, the wider analysis and debate concerning Kazan's work as a whole.[3]

1 Elia Kazan: the background

An Anatolian Greek, Elia Kazan was brought to America at the age of four, in 1913. Educated at the WASPish Williams College and at Yale Drama School, Kazan moved to New York in 1932, at the age of 23.[4] It was through the radical theatres that ethnic minorities in particular asserted themselves in the 1930s, with Jews and Armenians being particularly prominent in the new off-Broadway theatre groups that emerged.[5] It was in this 'movement' that Kazan 'started out' in the 1930s; Alfred Kazin writes of this period: 'There was a proud and conscious sense of personal 'vitality' and a flourish of dangerous experiences, that I saw in the sharp faces of James T. Farrell and Robert Cantell, of Clifford Odets and Elia Kazan.'[6] Kazan worked his way up in the Group Theatre, but also participated, in the early 1930s, in the more radical theatres; his agit-prop drama *Dimitroff*, written with Art Smith, was produced by the League of Workers' Theatre in 1934.[7] In playing the leading role in Clifford Odets's *Waiting for Lefty*, in 1935, Kazan described himself as 'full of anger, silent, unexpressed anger': 'The whole premise was that we were outcast, against the current of US life, and we thought that the revolutionary and the gangster had qualities that an artist needs in a hostile society.'[8] Kazan's performance as the racketeer Eddie Fuselli in the Group's *Golden Boy* (1937) led to his role as Googi in Warner Brothers' *City for Conquest* (1940) in which his lightning rise from rags to tuxedoed riches and his sudden demise seem to echo and parody the themes of the same studio's early 1930s gangster cycle. In terms of actors and acting styles there is a direct line from

Kazan's experience in the Group Theatre (with its concern with the work of Stanislavsky and the Moscow Art Theatre) to his co-founding of the Actors Studio in 1947, and his 1950s film work.

If fellow-travellers in the 1930s were generally attracted by the model of social progress that the Soviet Union seemed to represent, in the world of cinema and theatre the Soviet Union seemed even more obviously to be the source of all that was most admirable and progressive. Commenting on his membership of the Communist Party from 1934 to 1936, Kazan has said: 'There is no way for a man of your age to understand what it meant for us: we idealised the people in the USSR and what they did.'[9] Kazan left the Party in 1936; formally called to account for his failure to pursue its policies towards the Group, he regarded himself as being 'booted out' of the Party and remained bitter at their treatment of him.

While Kazan resisted the lure of Hollywood in the mid-1930s, failing, according to Harold Clurman, to 'adjust his turbulence to the vacuous serenity of Southern California',[10] in 1944 Darryl F. Zanuck signed him to make a picture a year for Twentieth Century–Fox. (Apart from two films for Warners as an actor Kazan's previous film experience comprised collaboration with Ralph Steiner on two 1934 agit-prop shorts, and his share of the direction of *People of the Cumberland*, for Frontier Films, in 1937.)[11] Thus while Kazan's Broadway career took off on one coast, on the other he learned film-making within the supportive studio system, quickly becoming associated with semi-documentary thrillers, and with a continuation of Zanuck's 1930s interest in big-budget 'social consciousness'.[12] (In terms of ideas, in *Gentleman's Agreement* (1947) it is the speeches of John Garfield, Celeste Holm and Anne Revere that are most striking – a mixture of genuine anger and political feeling and a naively optimistic and utopian Americanism.) According to his own account Kazan in 1945 was still 'very sectarian'. He supported the Hollywood Ten financially in October 1947, and his name appeared in support of a petition declaring that 'Any investigation into the political beliefs of the individual is contrary to the basic principles of our democracy'.[13] In his testimony to the House Committee on Un-American Activities in that year, Jack L. Warner described how *All My Sons* had disgusted him, adding that Kazan was 'one of the mob' − 'I pass him by and won't talk to him'.[14]

2 The making of 'On the Waterfront'

While working at Fox and on Broadway, Kazan began to think of producing his own films and/or choosing his own subject and working closely with a writer. When MGM sold its rights to a project on Emiliano Zapata and the Mexican Revolution to Fox in February 1949, Kazan as director and John Steinbeck began a long and increasingly tortuous collaboration on the film finally called *Viva Zapata*.[15]

The origins of Kazan's next step towards a greater independence are found in the events on the New York waterfront in the postwar period. Concern with hiring practices and with the infiltration of criminal and mob elements had increased in the late 1940s, and there was widespread rank and file discontent with the leadership of the International Longshoremens Association (and with its President Joe Ryan). It became clear that West Coast longshoremen worked in better conditions, for more pay and for more regular work, than did members of the ILA on the East Coast. It was similarly clear to observers that the ILA leadership had a collusive relationship with the shipping companies and with Tammany Hall politicians and that it controlled the hiring procedures (i.e. the 'shape up') in such a way as to control its members. Enforced kickbacks and loansharking were common, and those who had previously stepped out of line had often been dealt with by thugs brought in by the union (and condoned by the shipping companies) as hiring bosses. Writing at the time a journalist wrote: 'Let's face it. Neither the shipowners nor the majority of longshoremen want a change in anything. Both have been brought up in the tradition of the waterfront jungle which glorifies the law of the survival of the fittest.'[16] Malcolm Johnson made a similar point: 'Under the terror of the shape up, the longshoremen have learned from bitter experience to bow to the system, to keep their mouths shut.'[17] There is evidence of rank and file action against the ILA as early as 1939, when longshoremen led by Peter Panto opposed mob control of the union's six Brooklyn locals; Panto was found dead in a New Jersey lime pit in January 1941. In 1946 a Catholic priest, Father John Corridan, moved to the Xavier Labor School in New York and began to campaign for reform on the docks; he was convinced of the existence of a 'triple alliance of business, politics and union racketeering', and he began actively supporting a number of rebel longshoremen.[18]

In November 1948 Malcolm Johnson began a series of articles in the *New York Sun* on the waterfront situation, and the issue began to attract major public attention. Corridan provided information to Johnson, and also later to Daniel Bell, for his article in *Fortune* on the 'last of the business rackets'.[19] Corridan, Johnson and Bell all stressed the close relationship between Joe Ryan, the Irish leadership of Tammany Hall and a key business executive, William J. McCormack – a suggested model for the 'Mr Upstairs' character in the film. In January 1949 the rebels of Local 791 consulted Father Corridan on future strategy.[20] Their leader, John Dwyer – whom one source inaccurately identifies as the 'prototype' for Terry Malloy – was said by Corridan to have the overwhelming support of his local.[21] The wildcat strike of 1951, like those before, was prompted by an agreement between the ILA and the shipping companies that the rebels considered a sell-out.

As early as 1949 Arthur Miller, who lived in Brooklyn, had written a film script based on the waterfront situation, and in particular on the case of Peter Panto.[22] Elia Kazan had directed both of Miller's successful Broadway productions of the 1940s, *All My Sons* and *Death of a Salesman*, and they were natural allies in the quest to film the story once the script, 'The Hook', was finished early in 1950. At first there were ideas about a co-production with Kermit Bloomgarden (formerly business manager of the Group Theatre), and there were also talks in August 1950 with Jerry Wald and Norman Krasna, who were collecting material for their new RKO independent unit. But in January 1951 Kazan and Miller visited Hollywood with the intention of setting up a deal for the production of 'The Hook'.[23] Miller recounts as follows:

'suffice to say now that as the fifties dawned, Kazan and I presented it for financing to Harry Cohn, owner and head of Columbia Pictures'.[24] Miller's story is that Cohn was prepared to go ahead in order to sign up Kazan for a series of films, but that objections were raised by Roy M. Brewer, then a key figure in the film industry's defence against (or complicity with) the Congressional investigations. (Brewer's role is discussed in Richard Maltby's paper on HUAC in this volume.) Brewer knew Joe Ryan and apparently put forward Ryan's traditional line on waterfront opposition to his leadership – that it was communist in origin. While there is no evidence for this interpretation, Miller reports that Brewer and Cohn, after consulting the FBI, suggested to him that they would approve the project if Communists, and not racketeers, were seen to be the villains. The proposed deal with Columbia fell through in February 1951 and in August of that year *Variety* announced that Miller and Kazan had 'pushed off' for a year their plan to produce 'The Hook'.[25] Kazan remembers only that Miller withdrew rather suddenly from the project, and that his script, 'The Hook', was different in feeling and less individualistic than the later Schulberg script.[26]

Budd Schulberg first visited the New York waterfront in 1950 after reading Malcolm Johnson's articles. He had attended the first Soviet Writers' Congress in 1934 and joined the Communist Party in 1937, leaving three years later following a dispute in which Party leaders had criticised drafts of his Hollywood novel, *What Makes Sammy Run*.[27] In 1951 Schulberg completed a 'waterfront' script, but attempts to arrange financing for an East Coast independent production to be directed by Robert Siodmak were unsuccessful. Some time in 1952 Schulberg met Kazan at the latter's request – in order to discuss some ideas Kazan had for a project on corruption in an Eastern city – and their collaboration on a 'waterfront' story began.[28] Schulberg later recalled his research in New York: 'I talked to the 'insoigents' – as they call themselves – who think the time is finally at hand when honest unionism can remove the killers, grafters and seller outers, and institute regular and honest employment on the docks.'[29] The script went through eight drafts, and was turned down by a number of studios, including Fox: Zanuck's comment was

'Who gives a shit about labour unions'.[30] Quite apart from a possible reluctance to deal with Kazan following his HUAC testimony in April 1952, the studios had steadily reduced the proportion of their output dealing with social and political issues, and in 1953 few subjects involving controversy were being considered.[31]

Following the strike of 1951, which spread until most of the port was inactive, Governor Dewey ordered (in November 1951) an investigation by the New York Crime Commission. The Commission investigations, involving the appearance of witnesses at public hearings beginning in December 1952, brought much of the corruption of the waterfront into the open, and the hearings were headline news until the Commission issued its report in May 1953. Numerous witnesses gave testimony to the Commission and this, together with the reform literature of the period, was reflected in re-writes of Schulberg's script. The model for the Terry Malloy character was Anthony 'Tony Mike' de Vincenzo, who was given police protection when he testified to the Crime Commission.[32] Later he and John Dwyer campaigned and organised for the proposed new American Federation of Labor (AFL) union, Dwyer in Manhatten and de Vincenzo in Hoboken.[33] (The Commission's report led to the creation of a bi-State waterfront commission to regulate dock employment and abolish the 'shape up'; it also led the AFL to expel the ILA and to the holding of an election in which the independent ILA and a new AFL union competed for representation of longshoremen.) Charles Larrowe describes Dwyer and de Vincenzo as men who emerged from the rank and file. De Vincenzo testified against Ed Florio, the highest ranking ILA officer in New Jersey, although he had known him since childhood (they were second cousins). De Vincenzo, who later argued that he was 'proud to be a rat', testified of assault, murder, loansharking and of payments from businessmen to Florio and other ILA officials for their efforts in strikebreaking and controlling jobs. He talked of meetings at the Oxford Democratic Club and Skelly's Restaurant with key figures in politics and on the waterfront.[34]

In May 1953 Kazan met with Schulberg in Los Angeles and there, after failing to interest the major studios, they persuaded Sam Spiegel to back the *Waterfront* project.[35] An independent producer, Spiegel had founded Horizon Productions with John Huston in 1948; while their *The African Queen* had been a success in 1951, Spiegel's most recent production, *Melba* (directed by Lewis Milestone) was to be a box-office disaster when it was released later in 1953.[36] Kazan and Schulberg continued to work on the script, which was finally finished in November of that year. In December 1953 the vote of longshoremen in New York narrowly failed to dispossess the ILA from its representative role; the ILA gained 9,060 votes to the 7,568 votes for the AFL union led by John Dwyer. Location filming took place in November and December 1953 and January 1954; a distribution agreement was reached with Columbia Pictures (despite Harry Cohn's reluctance), and the film was released in October 1954.[37]

3 Kazan and HUAC, 1952

When the House Committee on Un-American Activities resumed its hearings on Hollywood in 1951, Budd Schulberg was an early 'friendly witness'. While immunity from any prison sentence could be gained by pleading the Fifth Amendment, witnesses who could neither disprove allegations of Communist connections, nor would recant their past and name names, faced the blacklist. In December of that year *American Legion Magazine* published an article – entitled 'Did the movies really clear house?' – which led Hollywood executives to renewed efforts to demonstrate their anti-Communism.[38] The Legion later wrote to the studios naming some three hundred persons whose names had been linked with communist or 'front' organisations or petitions. Whether or not Kazan was specifically cited in this list, Spyros Skouras, the president of Twentieth Century–Fox was quick to respond, telling representatives of the American Legion that he was collecting all allegations against his employees and inviting them to arm him with 'written, signed explanations or denials' to prove their innocence. In this context Lillian Hellman's account of a meeting with Kazan in March

1952 has been widely quoted. She writes that Kazan told her that Skouras had told him that unless he became a 'friendly witness' for HUAC, he, Kazan, would never make another movie in Hollywood.[39] In a contemporary letter John Steinbeck remarked of Kazan that 'this Congress thing tore him to pieces'.[40] Kazan had first appeared before HUAC in January 1952, but the testimony had not been made public. On 10 April 1952 he appeared voluntarily before the Committee and named eight members of his party cell within the Group Theatre. (He also named three well-known Party officials, and four officials involved in the League of Workers' Theatres.) The named members of the Group Theatre included Clifford Odets (who named Kazan in his own friendly testimony on 19 May 1952) and Art Smith, who, although his name, like others, was already known to the Committee, was – according to one source – blacklisted following Kazan's testimony. Kazan publicly recanted his communist past in a quarter-page advertisement in the *New York Times* of 12 April 1952. In this he argued that he believed that 'any American who is in possession of such facts has an obligation to make them known, either to the public or to the appropriate government agency'. In addition he provided the Committee with a list of all his credits in film and theatre, giving a short summary of the intention of each; the list strains to present attitudes that will appeal to the Committee: the 1938 play *Casey Jones* is described as 'thoroughly and wonderfully American in tone, characters and outlook', while *Viva Zapata*, released in February 1952, is described as an 'anti-communist picture'.[41]

The long gestation period of *Zapata* has been chronicled elsewhere.[42] Despite Kazan's greater cinematic self-confidence, the political pressures of the time led to a shift in interest from Zapatismo to Stalinism, and to substantial cuts made by Darryl F. Zanuck. The film was poorly promoted and was not a commercial success. Immediately after the second HUAC appearance Kazan started on a contract film for Fox, a mildly 'Cold War' thriller, *Man on a Tightrope*.[43] Released in March 1953, the film was a critical and commercial failure, while at that time the major companies refused to touch the waterfront project. Kazan also had to face the fury of former friends and Party colleagues. John Howard Lawson wrote of Kazan's behaviour as follows:

> We are accustomed by this time to the dreary spectacle of frightened men and women, who lie and supplicate and repent, denying all that is decent in their professional and personal lives in order to secure absolution from the ignorant politicians who have become the arbiters of culture in the United States. But Kazan seemed determined to outdo other informers, in treachery to his friends and in personal abasement.[44]

More important was Arthur Miller's comment on the ethics of the witch hunt in *The Crucible*, first performed in January 1953 and not, as were Miller's previous two Broadway plays, directed by Kazan.[45] The experience clearly had an effect on the *Waterfront* script: asked if the film was a defence of his (and Schulberg's) testimony before HUAC, Kazan answered that 'Well, I think it's partly affected by that, naturally'.[46]

4 'On the Waterfront': some interpretations

How accurate is Kazan's claim that 'it happened like that'?[47] While the actual politics of the waterfront are not central to their arguments, several critics make reference to them.[48] Contemporary accounts indicate that there was much more rank-and-file activity than appears in the film, but they also provide evidence of widespread alienation, fear and cynicism, and this the film does reflect. The waterfront of the time, with its labour surplus and the semi-corporatist collusion between city hall, employers and the union, provided little basis for vigorous union democracy; the Tammany and Ryan machines may have been doomed, but at the time they had the clout (in all senses) to block most possibilities of reform.

Father Barry reflects a good deal, in terms of ideas and passion, of the character of Father Corridan, a figure well represented in Malcolm Johnson's articles and Budd Schulberg's script. (Schulberg's subsequent book, *Waterfront*, gives far more prominence to the priest – relative to Terry Malloy – than does the film.)[49] Father Barry's role can be compared to 1930s forerunners, notably Father Jerry Connelly (Pat

O'Brien), who in *Angels with Dirty Faces* (1938) finally gets James Cagney to do the 'right' thing. While Father Barry's role is manipulative, it is worth pointing out that Father Corridan's actual role, in advising and encouraging the rebel longshoremen, was not — in broad principle — dissimilar. Arguably Peter Biskind exaggerates the role of Father Barry as the agent of Terry Malloy's 'awakening'.[50] As will be argued later, Terry is the greater focus for emotional identification in the film, and Terry's character and consciousness are too thoroughly and strongly drawn (and portrayed) for him to be seen as merely being manipulated by official and unofficial 'social engineers'.

There are elements of the experience of Tony de Vincenzo in Terry's character, as is indicated by de Vincenzo's testimony to the New York State Crime Commission. But de Vincenzo seems to have been a more conventional rank and file 'leader' than Terry, and he subsequently campaigned for the AFL union in the representation election. The result of that election — narrowly favouring the ILA — suggests a popular cynicism among longshoremen about the reform pretentions of the proposed new union and its leaders. 'Pop' Doyle, nursing his wounds and unwilling to 'stick his neck out', appears as an authentic figure, and the *film noir* scenes — especially those involving cars and trucks — convey something of the menace that undoubtedly existed at the time.

The documentary element of *On the Waterfront* is significant even if, particularly in the character of Terry, the film has wider dramatic and social implications. While its interest in the complexities of waterfront life is selective, the film was seen at the time as a return by Hollywood to the real world.[51] The exact nature of the power structure was not of primary interest to the film-makers, just as the governmental investigations of the 1950s, most prominently the 1957 McClellan Committee inquiry into Jimmy Hoffa, the Teamsters and the underworld, neglected some of the wider issues implied by corrupt business unionism.[52] The role of the stevedore companies and businessmen is treated obliquely, and there is no discussion of the role of politicians in the power structure of the waterfront. There are several references, however, to 'Mr Upstairs', and to his close liason with

Johnny Friendly. When Terry is testifying to the Crime Commission the 'boss' figure is seen from behind his chair, watching the hearings on television. His role is suggested by the rich surroundings, large cigar and deferential waiter: 'If Mr Friendly calls,' he says, 'I'm out.' The shot recalls the caricatures of mid-1930s agit-prop – of the boss in Steiner and Kazan's *Cafe Universal*, or the labour racketeer Harry Fatt in Odets's *Waiting for Lefty*.[53]

The case for testifying is put by Father Barry and the Crime Commission investigator: Father Barry talks of 'getting the facts to the public'; the investigator, complaining about the effort of climbing flights of stairs, remarks that it will be 'worth it if we can tell the waterfront story the way the public have a right to hear it'. Terry's motives are more complex, however, and it is only *after* his testimony that we see Kazan's passionate feelings in Brando's performance: 'Terry Malloy felt as I did. He felt ashamed and proud of himself at the same time. He wavered between the two, and he also felt hurt by the fact that people – and his own friends – were rejecting him. He also felt that it was a necessary act.'[54] It is difficult not to see Terry's final verbal challenge to Friendly – 'I'm glad what I done to you' – as deriving some of its power from Kazan's own feelings about the party, and his treatment by it (albeit some sixteen years before). 'Kayo' Dugan's argument at the church meeting, that 'No matter how much we hate the torpedoes, we don't rat', is matched by Kazan's own reference, in his *New York Times* 'Statement', to the 'specious reasoning which has silenced many liberals': 'It goes like this: "You may hate the Communists, but you must not attack them or expose them, because if you do you are attacking the right to hold unpopular opinions and you are joining the people who attack civil liberties".'[55] Rather like Arthur Miller in *The Crucible* Kazan has expressed a view on the HUAC experience while changing the context and the situation in which it arises.[56] Whereas Terry Malloy testified about murder, Elia Kazan talked about the political preferences of former Party colleagues. Kazan has no doubt that 'Tony Mike' was right to do what he did; his attitude to his own behaviour has been more ambivalent.

To Terry the old loyalties finally make too many demands on his ease of mind: he is required to set up Joey Doyle, to ignore Edie Doyle and to take a sinecure job in return for keeping quiet. There is an indication of the decline of the old ethnic loyalties, and the decline in the need of working men to rely on the compromised services of the 'machine'.[57] Edie Doyle was educated in the suburbs (and disagrees with her father), while Terry is detached from his old machine loyalties, becoming something akin to David Riesman's 'autonomous individual'.[58] Under pressure from Father Barry, Terry redirects his obligations from one form of social organisation, the local machine, towards another, the State.[59]

Brando's public image was already partly established by *Streetcar Named Desire*, *The Wild One* and *Viva Zapata*, but it was not until 1954 that Brando entered the 'top ten stars' list – he was included in 1954, 1955 and 1958, but was not to appear again until 1972–3 and *The Godfather* and *Last Tango in Paris*.[60] Despite the drama and passion of the film Terry Malloy – a self-confessed 'bum' and loser, a boxer turned longshoreman – seems an unlikely hero for his times. Yet secretly (under the safety of dark), it was perhaps the anti-conformity of Terry Malloy that was attractive. Like Prewitt (Montgomery Clift) in *From Here to Eternity* or even Miles Bennell (Kevin McCarthy) in *Invasion of the Body Snatchers*, the 1950s saw the emergence of heroes who were anti-conformists, advance-men for the 1960s counter-culture. In addition the box-office success of *East of Eden* and *Rebel Without a Cause* signalled Hollywood recognition of the emerging 'youth culture', and the growing importance of the young cinema audience. Arguably the 'generation gap' in *On the Waterfront*, between Terry and his older brother Charlie (and Johnny Friendly) is as central to the film as are the more conventional family conflicts in the two films of 1955. Discussing the Method actors and actresses in the 1950s, Leo Braudy has commented as follows:

They brought into films experiences and feelings that official culture either ignored or actively attacked. By representing and articulating the feelings of insecurity and impotent rage felt by many in what was being billed as a secure and settled society, Brando and Dean allowed their audience a sense of release.[61]

Peter Biskind argues that Terry Malloy is manipulated by Father Barry, and while this is true in relation to Terry's testimony to the Crime Commission, it is *his* doubt, and *his* final decision to 'take it out on their skulls' that have most emotional effect. In creating the role of Terry, Kazan, with the 'Method', and Brando provided a focus for identification and/or release in the 1950s and an image of personal authenticity in the 1960s. Kazan, simply because he did play a role in the 'movement' of the 1930s, was able to provide a bridge to the 'movement' of the 1960s.

The mix of racketeering and boxing in *On the Waterfront* points back to the Group Theatre production of *Golden Boy* in 1937 (in which Kazan, Lee J. Cobb and Karl Malden appeared), and to Robert Rossen's and Abraham Polonsky's *Body and Soul* (1947).[62] A more general comparison could be made with Warner Brothers' gangster films of the 1930s, and 'topicals' such as *Marked Woman* (co-written by Robert Rossen), in 1937. (Although there are similarities of theme between the two films, *Marked Woman* has a far greater emphasis on class conflict than does the later film.) Thematic links have also been traced with *I Am a Fugitive from a Chain Gang* (1932) and *The Grapes of Wrath* (1940); Paul Muni, Henry Fonda and Marlon Brando have been seen as similar 'little men' who slowly see that they are victims of the system.[63] Returning to *Golden Boy*, there is something of the Joe Bonaparte of that play in Terry Malloy. Johnny Friendly has bought 'a piece' of Terry just as Eddie Fuselli controls and exploits Joe. Both men are given a more sensitive, more authentic self; the mob (and the 'love of an easy buck') have robbed them of their individuality. The differences between play and film reflect something of the movement toward 'other-directedness' in the postwar years. Joe, like the early 1930s gangsters, rides his ambition and shoots for the stars; Terry reckons that he'll live a bit longer without ambition.

The softer, more authentic self of Terry is seen in his private roof-top world, and in the pained honesty of his final conversation with his brother. It is the truth of this private testimony – of failure, of an unfulfilled American dream – that is the prevailing truth of *On the Waterfront*, not the public testimony to the Crime Commission. (Impressionistically, the cab scene seems to reflect something of John Garfield's feeling with Ida Lupino in *The Sea Wolf*, in 1941; there are differences, but in both cases there is a kind of doomed resignation, a fleeting, mutual awareness that the world is closing in on them.) Arguably the 'feminised' aspects of the male persona revealed for the first time in 1950s cinema were also genuinely subversive.[64] The film certainly has much in common with early New Left thought, and the question of personal integrity, and authenticity. Terry's 'philosophy of life' reflects the ideas of the alienated young in the late 1950s – distrust of commitment, rejection of parental values, pessimism about human nature, and lack of interest in social and political activity.[65] Such dissent from existing norms led directly to the concern of the Port Huron Statement with 'finding a meaning of life that is personally authentic'.[66] Elsewhere the 1962 statement (from Students for a Democratic Society) echoes themes in the film: it argues that 'the object is not to have one's way so much as it is to have a way that is one's own'.[67]

Also arguably it was in part the ideas and techniques that came to be known as 'the method' that gave actors their own authenticity and aided the crumbling of the established star system.[68] In a sense other than that of the subject matter, *On the Waterfront* saw a renewed concern of American cinema with real people.[69]

Some particular comment on the ending seems necessary. While many critics were disturbed by the parallels with Kazan's own behaviour, or by Father Barry's human sacrifices to his conscience, Lindsay Anderson draws attention to what he sees as the élitist and fascist implications of the last scene.[70] Anderson argues that the men are shown as craven, first ignoring Terry when he is refused work (following his testimony) and then following the 'new master' like 'leaderless sheep'. Firstly, nothing in Terry's character seems to support the view that either consciously or unconsciously he wishes to be a leader of men. That the men are apparently docile (as well as not being completely true) is – to the extent that it is true – not greatly surprising. While Friendly may have lost the support of Mr Upstairs, it is far too early to suggest that he or his successor have lost their position of power. They still control the jobs, just as in reality the ILA (despite expulsion from the AFL following the State Crime Commission's report) continued to be the bargaining agent and union for the longshoremen. Even given conceptions of union solidarity more traditionally associated with Britain, the 'sense of liberation' and the collective action that Anderson wants seem too much to expect given what has gone before. Evidence from the automobile industry of the time suggests that workers tended to blame themselves for their misfortunes, rather than blame the system collectively.[71]

When the shipper orders Friendly to get 'his' men back to work, and Friendly says he will have them working in two minutes, the first comment from the rank and file is an inquiry about Terry and the second a statement that if 'he don't work, *we* don't work' (emphasis added). Johnny Friendly responds as follows: 'Work. He can't even walk. You want to know who works – the men I pick to work.' Friendly makes efforts to herd the men towards the holds, and his success with one group of men (in a sequence that resembles one in *A Face in the Crowd*) does bring Anderson's sheep imagery to mind. Friendly picks on that most acquiescent and defeated character (for his own good reasons), Pop Doyle, but Doyle replies that Friendly had pushed him around all his life and nudges the union boss into the dock. A longshoreman makes the comment that if 'Terry walks in, *we* will walk in with him'; 'They *are* waiting for him to walk in' (emphasis added). Another longshoreman suggests that perhaps they can run the union on the 'up and up'. It is true that Father Barry is also there pushing Terry into his final walk. But it does seem that the rank and file do play a role in the last scene of the film, and that this role is not that of a 'passive herd'.[72]

Cynical and suspicious they are surely likely to be, of Terry only slightly less than Johnny Friendly. (When Terry is beaten up a worker suggests that he is 'one of theirs anyway'.) Is it so unnatural that the men respond to personal courage? 'He fights just like he used to', says one.

What kind of collective action – to take over the leaderless (in Anderson's view) union – does he expect? Collectivism and solidarity are not to be assumed; they do not emerge overnight and should not be dragged on as the *deus ex machina* of the drama of socialist realism. They have to be worked for. And given the individualistic bias of American culture they have to be worked hard for. Working for them in the 'divide and rule' conditions of the New York waterfront of the film – with excess labour and mob controlled shape ups – is harder than elsewhere. To suggest that collective action is easily achieved in adverse conditions is not to make a socialist film. Friendly pledges that he will be back: despite the emotional triumph of Terry – his own personal redemption through action – the ending is ambivalent. The last shot of the film is not of Father Barry and Edie – plainly satisfied with the resolution, Edie incomprehensibly so – but of the shutters coming down, adding to doubts about how much has changed.[73]

Notes

I would like to thank Elaine Burrowes, of the National Film Archive, British Film Institute, for arranging film viewings; and the British Academy, for a grant which enabled me to make several additions to the paper in New York, in September 1980.

1   Pauline Kael, 'Raising Kane', in *The Citizen Kane Book* (London, 1971); John E. O'Connor and Martin A. Jackson, *American History/American Film: Interpreting the Hollywood Image* (New York, 1979). See also Keith Kelly and Clay Steinman, ' "Crossfire": a Dialectical Attack', in *Film Reader 3* (February 1978).

2   Leo Braudy, *The World in a Frame: What We See in Films* (New York, 1977), p. 244.

3   See Michel Ciment, *Kazan on Kazan* (London, 1973); Roger Tailleur, *Elia Kazan* (Paris, 2nd ed., 1971); *Movie*, No. 19 (winter 1971–2); Jim Kitses, 'Elia Kazan: a Structural Analysis', *Cinema* (USA), vol. 7, No. 3 (winter 1972–3); Gary Collins, 'Kazan in the '50s', *The Velvet Light Trap*, No. 11 (winter 1974); and Estelle Changas, 'Elia Kazan's America', *Film Comment* (summer 1972). On *On the Waterfront* see in particular Peter Biskind, 'The Politics of Power in

"On the Waterfront" ', *Film Quarterly*, vol. XXIX, No. 1 (fall 1975), and Kenneth Hey, 'Ambivalence as a Theme in "On the Waterfront": an Interdisciplinary Approach to Film Study', *American Quarterly*, vol. XXXI, No. 5 (winter 1979).

4   Ciment, *Kazan on Kazan*, pp. 9–15.

5   Judd L. Teller, *Strangers and Natives: the Evolution of the American Jew from 1921 to the Present* (New York, 1968), pp. 139–140 and pp. 143–4.

6   Alfred Kazin, *Starting Out in the Thirties* (London, 1966), p. 13.

7   On Kazan and the Group Theatre see Harold Clurman, *The Fervent Years* (London, 1946), and Morgan Y. Himelstein, *Drama Was a Weapon: the Left Wing Theatre in New York, 1929–1941* (Westport, Conn., 1976; reprint of 1963 ed.). On *Dimitroff*, Himelstein comments that 'While some of the scenes still consist of the old Communist slogans, other episodes contain realistic human drama' (p. 27).

8   Ciment, *Kazan on Kazan*, p. 19.

9   Ciment, *Kazan on Kazan*, p. 16.

10   Clurman, *The Fervent Years*, p. 205.

11   See Joel Stewart Zuker, *Ralph Steiner, Filmmaker and Still Photographer* (New York, 1978). Frontier Films condemned the initial footage that Kazan and Steiner brought back from Tennessee (for *People of the Cumberland*), as 'too artistic and too apolitical' (p. 32).

12   Colin McArthur, *Underworld USA* (London, 1972), ch. 9; Russell Campbell, 'The Ideology of the Social Consciousness Movie: Three Films of Darryl F. Zanuck', *Quarterly Review of Film Studies*, vol. 3, No. 1 (winter 1978).

13   'Who's Un-American', *Variety*, 29 October 1947, p. 14.

14   Stephan Kanfer, *A Journal of the Plague Years* (New York, 1973), pp. 44–5.

15   Paul J. Vanderwood, 'An American Cold Warrior: Viva Zapata!', in *American History/American Film*, eds. O'Connor and Jackson, p. 188.

16   Ed Reid, *The Shame of New York* (London, 1954), p. 146.

17   Malcolm Johnson, *Crime on the Labor Front* (New York, 1950), p. 135. Other sources for the account of the waterfront situation are Charles P. Larrowe, *Shape Up and Hiring Hall* (Berkeley, Calif., 1955); Allen Raymond, *Waterfront Priest* (New York, 1955); William Keating and Richard Carter, *The Man Who Rocked the Boat* (London, 1956),

and John Hutchinson, *The Imperfect Union* (New York, 1970). Also Aleine Austin, 'The Revolt Against Joe Ryan', *The Nation*, 1 December 1951, pp. 473–4; Richard Carter, 'Waterfront Revolt: Wanted: A Real Union', *The Nation*, 31 October 1953, pp. 346–8; and Gus Tyler, 'The Waterfront Loot, Blood and Politics', *New Republic*, 5 January 1953, pp. 6–7.

18 Raymond, *Waterfront Priest*, p. 94.

19 Daniel Bell, 'Last of the Business Rackets', *Fortune* (June 1951); and Daniel Bell, *The End of Ideology* (New York, 1960), ch. 9.

20 Raymond, *Waterfront Priest*, p. 81.

21 *Time*, 27 September 1954, quoted in Pauline Kael, *I Lost It At The Movies* (Boston, Mass., 1965), p. 53.

22 See Arthur Miller, 'The Year it Came Apart', *New York*, (30 December, 1974), pp. 30–44.

23 *Variety*, 30 August 1950, pp. 3, 14; 17 January 1951, p. 4.

24 Miller, 'The Year', p. 42.

25 *Variety*, 1 August 1951, p. 102.

26 Ciment, *Kazan on Kazan*, p. 102.

27 Danial Aaron, *Writers on the Left* (New York, 1965), p. 451.

28 Budd Schulberg, 'Why Write it When You Can't Sell it to the Pictures', *The Saturday Review*, (3 September 1955), and ' "Waterfront": From Docks to Film', *New York Times*, 11 July 1954, II, p. 5.

29 Budd Schulberg, 'Joe Docks, Forgotten Man of the Waterfront', *New York Times Magazine* (December 1952), p. 3.

30 Ciment, *Kazan on Kazan*, p. 109.

31 "H'Wood Nix on 'Message' Pix", *Variety*, 22 April 1953, pp. 5, 18. Social problem movies represented 28 per cent of the industry's output in 1947 but only 9.2 per cent in 1954. See Garth Jowett, *Film, the Democratic Art: a Social History of American Film* (Boston, Mass., 1976), p. 368.

32 Edward C. Burks, ' "On the Waterfront" Returns to Hoboken', *New York Times*, 24 May 1973, p. 53; on Anthony de Vincenzo see Dick Russell, 'The Original Brando', *The Village Voice*, 6 January 1975, p. 10.

33 Larrowe, *Shape Up and Hiring Hall*, p. 207.

34 Testimony of de Vincenzo to New York State Crime Commission, reported in *New York Times*, 16 December 1951, p. 40.

35 Press Release, Columbia Pictures, in British Film Institute microfiche on *On the Waterfront*, London.

36   Stuart Kaminsky, *John Huston, Maker of Magic* (London, 1978), p. 62;
     Kingsley Canham, 'Lewis Milestone', in *The Hollywood Professionals*,
     vol. 2 (New York, 1974). See Budd Schulberg, 'The Inside Story of
     "Waterfront" ', *The New York Times Magazine*, 6 January 1980, pp.
     28–36.
37   Bob Thomas, *King Cohn* (New York, 1967), pp. 346–7.
38   Cogley, *Report on Blacklisting*, pp. 123–6.
39   Lillian Hellman, *Scoundrel Time* (Boston, Mass., 1976), pp. 63–4.
40   Letter to Annie Laurie Williams, 17 June 1952, in Elaine Steinbeck and
     Robert Wallsten, *Steinbeck: a Life in Letters* (London, 1975), pp.
     450–1.
41   Eric Bentley, ed., *Thirty Years of Treason, Excerpts from Hearings Before
     the House Committee on Un-American Activities, 1938–1968* (New
     York, 1971), pp. 484–95. For Schulberg's testimony see pp.
     434–57. See in general on Kazan's testimony, Roger Tailleur, 'Elia
     Kazan and the House Un-American Activities Committee', *Film
     Comment*, vol. 4, No. 1 (1966). The reference to Art Smith is from
     Kanfer, *A Journal of the Plague Years*, p. 179. The most thorough
     examination of Kazan's stance before HUAC is in Victor S. Navasky,
     Naming Names (New York, 1980), esp. pp. 199–222.
42   Paul J. Vanderwood, 'An American Cold War Warrior: Viva Zapata!'
     Despite the emphasis on the corrupting influence of power, and the
     creation of the character of Fernando to point a lesson about Stalinism
     (and in this sense Kazan can view the film as anti-communist), the
     film's sympathetic portrait of a revolution remains powerful and
     remarkable for its time. See the exchange between Peter Biskind and
     Dan Georgakas in *Cineaste*, vol. VII, No. 2 (spring 1976), pp.
     10–17.
43   *Variety*, 28 May 1952, p. 3.
44   John Howard Lawson, *Film in the Battle of Ideas* (New York, 1953), p.
     40.
45   Eric Bentley, *The Dramatic Event: an American Chronicle*, (New York,
     1956), pp. 244–62.
46   Quoted in Stuart Byron, ' "Waterfront" Politics', *The Real Paper*, 30
     May 1973, p. 24.
47   'Kazan vieux comme la monde', an interview with Elia Kazan by
     Claudine Tavernier in *Cinema 70*, No. 143 (February 1970).
48   Biskind, 'The Politics of Power', p. 38; Kael, *I Lost It At The Movies*. p.
     53; Raymond Durgnat, *Durgnat on Film* (London, 1976), p. 72.

49 On Father Corridan see Allen Raymond, *Waterfront Priest*; Budd
    Schulberg's novel is *Waterfront* (New York, 1955). In *Waterfront*,
    reflecting the failure of the New York State Crime Commission to
    produce fundamental change, the ending is down-beat: Terry, like the
    real life Peter Panto, is murdered and found dead in a lime-pit (pp.
    308–9).

50 Biskind, 'The Politics of Power', p. 29.

51 Kael, 'The Glamour of Delinquency' (1955), in *I Lost It At The Movies*,
    pp. 44–62. Schulberg's commitment to his subject is undoubted: the
    'Original Screenplay' (Film Studies Center, Museum of Modern Art,
    New York City) is headed as follows:
    TO THE AMERICAN LONGSHOREMEN
    Whose muscles move food into our homes
    and steel to our defense lines –
    AND TO THE WATERFRONT PRIESTS
    Who serve God by serving men.

52 Grant McConnell, *Private Power and American Democracy* (New York,
    1966), p. 314.

53 *Cafe Universal* (1934) now exists only as a series of stills; see Shot 10,
    captioned 'The Capitalist Puffs his Cigar', in Zuker, *Ralph Steiner*. See
    also the stage directions for *Waiting for Lefty* in *Six Plays of Clifford
    Odets* (New York, 1939).

54 Ciment, *Kazan on Kazan*, p. 10.

55 Elia Kazan, 'Statement', *New York Times*, 12 April 1952, p. 7.

56 Arthur Miller, *Collected Plays* (London, 1967).

57 Gary Wills, *Nixon Agonistes: the Crisis of the Self-Made Man* (Boston,
    Mass., 1969), p. 464. See also Stanley Aronowitz, *False Promises: the
    Shaping of American Working Class Consciousness* (New York, 1973),
    pp. 105–8.

58 David Riesman, *The Lonely Crowd* (New Haven, Conn., 1950), p. 255.

59 In this context the prominent role played by the Supreme Court, in
    reform and social change in the 1950s seems relevant. Albeit
    supported by pressure groups, Black Americans gained more in the
    1950s by individualised appeal to the judiciary than through the
    legislative or executive arms of the State.

60 Cobbett Steinberg, *Reel Facts* (New York, 1978), pp. 406–8.

61 Braudy, *The World in a Frame*, p. 241.

62 The link is pointed out by Penelope Houston in her contemporary
    review; see Joy Gould Boyum and Adrienne Scott, *Film as Film:*

Critical Responses to Film Art (New York, 1971), pp. 301–4.

63   Frank McConnell, *Storytelling and Mythmaking: Images from Film and Literature* (New York and Oxford, 1979), p. 245.

64   Peter Biskind and Barbara Ehrenreich, 'Machismo and Hollywood's Working Class', *Socialist Review*, vol. 10, Nos. 2/3 (March-June 1980), pp. 109–30.

65   Kenneth Keniston, *The Uncommitted: Alienated Youth in American Society* (New York, 1965), for example pp. 56–7, and pp. 80–1.

66   Christopher Lasch, *The Agony of the American Left* (Harmondsworth, 1973), pp. 167–8.

67   Extracts from the Port Huron Statement, in Massimo Teodori, *The New Left: a Documentary History* (London, 1970), pp. 163–72; see especially pp. 167–8.

68   See in particular the case of Marilyn Monroe, and the change in her performance and image following study at the Actors Studio, in *Bus Stop* (Joshua Logan, 1956).

69   Thomas W. Bohn and Richard L. Stromgren, *Light and Shadow: the History of Motion Pictures* (Sherman Oaks, Calif., 1978), p. 338.

70   'The last sequence of "On the Waterfront" ', *Sight and Sound*, vol. 24, No. 3 (January/March 1955). For a defence see Robert Hughes, *Sight and Sound*, vol. XXIV No. 4 (spring 1955).

71   Ely Chinoy, 'The Tradition of Opportunity and the Aspiration of Automobile Workers', in Lawrence W. Levine and Robert Middlekauft, *The National Temper: Readings in American Culture and Society Since 1865* (New York, 1972), pp. 339–46.

72   Biskind, 'The Politics of Power', p. 30.

73   At the end of the 'Original Screenplay' there is a greater sense of popular victory – a police sergeant arrives to inform Mickey (Johnny Friendly) that he is wanted as a material witness to the Joey Doyle and Charlie Malloy murders; the men stand proudly behind Terry, and 'The blast of a ship's whistle seems to sound a note of triumph as we . . . FADE OUT'.

Philip Davies

A growing independence

In recent years Hollywood has seen the rise to predominance of independently produced films; the studio system has been in decline for some thirty years or more. A convenient starting place for discussing the process whereby this change has taken place is the year 1947 when not only was the House Committee on Un-American Activities posing a highly visible threat to the film industry,[1] but also various other developments damaging to the studio system and to film-making in general were coming to a head. The contemporary political investigations disrupted working relationships within the industry; a long-fought legal battle approached resolution in the Supreme Court, whose decision would outlaw certain practices fundamental to the studio system; and the American public began to desert its movie-going habits. None of these challenges to the motion picture industry was sudden – the political investigations and legal battles spread over two decades – but in the late 1940s they combined to alter substantially the environment of the film industry. Prescient observers of national life might have noticed a number of social and economic factors which were to influence the development of the industry, but few can have predicted that these outside pressures would lead to dramatic adaptations in the economic structure of film-making.

There began in 1947 a progressive decline in cinema-going which continued until the audience had more than halved. Box-office receipts fell dramatically and over four thousand cinemas closed in the next decade. This fall in the audience for movies is often attributed to the growth of television viewing. Certainly television use has had a considerable effect on the movie industry but, as Michael Pye and Lynda Myles point out, the fall in paying customers at the box office actually began just before the sales boom in television sets.[2] Cinema audience figures reached their peak in 1946 with 4,060 million admissions during the year, but the annual total fell by more than six hundred million in the next two years. Although television sales were brisk and accelerating, only about one million sets had even been produced by 1948, and fewer than one million households had a television by the following year. In 1947, the first year of declining cinema audiences, fewer than two hundred thousand television sets were sold, a number that can in no way account for a fall of over four hundred million cinema seat sales (see Table 1).

Table 1: Changing leisure patterns in the United States: cinema and television, 1946–49.

Date	Cinema attendances (millions)	Box-office receipts ($M)	Number of TV stations	Number of TV sets produced	Households with TV
1946	4,060	1,692	30	6,000	8,000
1947	3,653	1,594	66	179,000	14,000
1948	3,422	1,506	108	975,000	172,000
1949	n.a.	1,451	69	3,000,000	940,000

Sources: M. Pye and L. Myles, *The Movie Brats: How The Film Generation Took Over Hollywood* (London, 1979), pp. 19–21; and US Bureau of the Census, *Historical Statistics of the United States, Colonial Times to 1970* (Washington D.C., 1975), pp. 400, 796.

The change in cinema-going habits is closely related to more general changes in American family lifestyle in the postwar era. By 1965, takings at the nation's cinema box offices were down to just over one thousand million dollars, representing a fall of 37 per cent since the high point of 1946, whilst the 1950s and 1960s saw an increase in expenditure on every other form of recreation monitored by the US Bureau of the Census.[3] Spending on books, magazines and other reading matter doubled; money spent on recreational equipment such as sporting goods and boats tripled. The sales of flowers, seeds and potted plants increased threefold; in 1965 these garden products attracted $1,272 million. By the mid-1960s the American public were spending more on their gardens than on going to the movies, and by the early 1970s this choice was even more marked, annual expenditure on gardens being ahead of movie-going by over one billion dollars. While it would be an exaggeration to say that a movie-going nation had become a nation of gardeners, these figures suggest a growing concentration of leisure activities around the home and family. Each individual sector of growth – gardening, participatory sports, television viewing, books, magazines and records – is a symptom of an overall change in emphasis in family leisure patterns, which is itself partly consequential upon the movement of the population out of the cities and into the suburbs.

Postwar America faced a shortage of housing. It has been assessed that in the immediate postwar period more than six million families were either searching for better housing or planning to do so.[4] At this time the housebuilding industry was beginning to adopt mass production methods, thus cutting building costs and reducing profit margins. The large tracts of undeveloped land on the city's edge provided the perfect location for mass building projects. Hence the large builders made housing available to the population by building in the suburbs. The rate of new residential construction in the 1940s was approximately two-and-a-half times that in the 1930s, an expansion characterised by large-scale residential development in the suburbs, where almost seventy-five per cent of metropolitan growth took place.

Lifestyles in the suburbs were not dramatically different from those in the cities but some differences were evident. In the low-density, sprawling, decentralised suburbs accessible forms of institutional recreation were few. By moving away from the cities the population was also moving away from the major down-town cinemas. Following the population shift there was a development of drive-in theatres to attract the automobile-transported suburban population with low budget movies, but this was no answer to the swing away from cinemas.

While facing the economic squeeze of falling box-office proceeds the movie industry also came under political and legal pressure to put its house in order. Congressional concern over the influence of revolutionary groups in American institutions became focused on the film industry.[5] Investigations begun in 1940 produced little of note, but the attacks launched by the House Committee on Un-American Activities in 1947 and 1951 were very damaging to Hollywood. In a series of hearings going on until 1958 the Committee labelled some 325 members of the film industry as past or present members of the Communist Party. Never before or since has the film industry been subject to such a concerted and damaging campaign of political vilification.

The undermining of the studio system consequent upon changes in the law dates from the federal courts' decisions in the case of U.S. *v.* Paramount Pictures.[6] In 1938 the United States Department of Justice had filed suit against the major studios charging them with offences against anti-trust laws. A District Court decision handed down in 1946 agreed with the government's accusation that the studios had 'unreasonably restrained trade and commerce in the distribution and exhibition of motion pictures and attempted to monopolise such trade and commerce'[7] and declared a number of distribution practices illegal. An appeal to the Supreme Court elicited an even more drastic response. Certain booking practices which maintained the major studios' grip over the programme of films shown in cinemas were banned, and most significantly the decision insisted that the production/distribution side of the industry be completely divorced from the exhibition side. The studios had to divest themselves of all their motion picture theatre holdings in the United States. The decision blocked the major studios' direct access to one reliable source of income, box-office takings.

After its best-ever year in 1946 the industry faced falling attendance; in its weakened state it was little able to tackle the problem. Investment in films was damaged by the political 'exposés', since as well as the usual financial risk, investors now faced the problem that a surprise discovery of a red under their particular bed could wreck the film's commercial prospects. Divestiture of the theatre side cut the producers' reliable incomes markedly, and falling audiences contributed to a further fall in cash flow. The studios responded with investment in technical gadgetry such as 3-D, Cinemascope, Todd AO and expensive attempts to design surefire 'blockbuster' hits. However, the audiences continued to decline, and these substantial investments weakened the industry even more. The age of studio-dominated Hollywood seemed to be over; independent producers became the dominant force in making films, and commercial conglomerates gained control of studio assets.

The independent producers saw a great opportunity in the wake of the Paramount decisions. The mechanisms whereby the major studios kept cinemas full of their own product were prohibited by the Supreme Court's anti-trust decision, leaving the way open for exhibition of independently produced films. Studio-controlled movie output declined, leaving these film factories with empty backlots and underused equipment. Faced with an unpredictable market, and struggling with a lack of confidence from investors, the major studios began hiring out studio space. The result was that the independent production companies – formed to produce a single film or a portfolio of films – found the facilities to make films available for hire, and the exhibitors free to accept independent production.

An independent film producer has to assemble a script, director, and actors that will attract investment. Potential investors of the several million dollars needed to produce and advertise an average feature film have to be convinced that a particular package is likely to make a profit. The risk/profit ratio can be phenomenal – *Star Wars* (1977) has taken over $431 million at the box office world-wide. Other smaller budget successes can give a very high ratio of return – *American Graffiti* (1973) has given a fifty-dollar return for each dollar invested.[8] Certain tax benefits have encouraged money into the production of independent motion pictures. At a time when the top personal income tax rate was 81 per cent, actual tax paid could be reduced to 60 per cent or as low as 25 per cent by forming a production company and having investment income taxed in accordance with corporation or capital gains legislation. Manipulation of tax law has allowed investors to redistribute their income over several years, thus altering the margins at which tax was payable, possibly avoiding paying tax, or at least deferring tax payments for a few years to benefit from inflation.[9] At one time it seemed possible to base an independent production on 'a consortium of upstate dentists, Florida realtors, or Seventh Avenue garment kings who were looking for a little protection from a fifty per cent tax hike'.[10] In 1976 the revenue laws were revised to stop these tax shelter practices, although it was recognised that investment in films made in the United States should be liable for the same tax credit as any other investment, but by this time independent producers had managed very successfully to make their mark on the film industry.

A significant feature of independent production is the importance of individuals. Under the studio-controlled system of the 1930s and 1940s, actors, directors and other personnel were under contracts which bound them to the studios and closely controlled their careers. Studios maintained a consistent output of films with the ultimate aim of making an overall annual profit. A film which failed at the box office was a disappointment, but, being part of a programme of films, would not necessarily be a disaster for the studio. Independent production companies, basing their hopes on a single film or small portfolio of projects, can less easily withstand box-office failure. In order to attract finance the project must contain some quality which inspires substantial confidence in its potential to give a return to its investors. To do this, box-office receipts and other sales must cover all the costs of production (salaries, technical services and so on), the advertising and publicity costs, and the expenses and profit margins of the distributor and the exhibitors. Anything left after all these disbursements is profit for the investors, but automatic expenditures are so large that the returns from the film must be two-and-a-half to three times initial production costs for the film to go into profit. Given that the average production costs of a film in 1979 were $6 million, any package needs to be very persuasive to inspire the confidence of financiers. An extremely skilful film script may be enough to attract investment, but when each product is a marketing gamble a script alone gives little indication of the final size of the audience. There is no clear guide to the profitability of a film, but among the few tangible assets that one can put into a package are stars and the director.

Stars and directors became involved in independent film production at a very early stage; in 1919 United Artists was set up by Mary Pickford, Douglas Fairbanks, D. W. Griffith and Charles Chaplin to help finance and to distribute independent productions. In the 1950s the pressures on the studios led to a demand for independently produced films, and at the same time actors were being freed from their expensive studio contracts. Investment in film by actors provides them with the opportunity of making substantial profits, as well as continuing their careers in the film industry, and having greater personal control over the final product. Furthermore, the involvement of a well-known actor in a film gives confidence to other investors.[11] The power of a director to imbue a project with investor confidence is a relatively new factor. The pattern of success or failure established in the independents' Hollywood can no longer be attributed to a particular studio's formula of production. Therefore the major box-office movies of recent years have attracted particular notice to the individuals involved, including the directors. The development of the *auteur* theory, assigning authorial status to film directors, provided justification for this new recognition of the director's importance.[12] Films such as *The Godfather* (1972) (directed by Francis Coppola), *Obsession* (1976) (Brian De Palma), *American Graffiti* (1973) (George Lucas), *Jaws* (1975) (Steven Spielberg), *M*A*S*H* (1970) (Robert Altman), *Mean Streets* (1973) (Martin Scorsese) have played a major role in establishing the investment potential of particular directors. As individual blockbusters, or as part of a series of successful movies they have helped these directors develop financial muscle in Hollywood, either because the director becomes wealthy enough to invest heavily in his own production (such as Francis Coppola with *Apocalypse Now* (1979), or Robert Altman with the many films produced by his company Lion's Gate Film) or because his name on a project inspires confidence in its potential to make money.

If the commercial viability of a film is seen by potential investors as substantially reliant upon the involvement of actors and a director of some status, then these persons are able to demand substantial payment for their services. In an interview with James Caan the discussion turned to *A Bridge Too Far* (1977):

Caan: I really enjoyed that. It was eight or nine days of work.
Interviewer: Word is that they paid you a cool million for it.
Caan: Is that what the word is? They paid me close to it. Yeah.[13]

Caan asked for two million dollars and Steve McQueen for three million to act in *Apocalypse Now*. Francis Coppola commented, 'I began to see that if this kept up, the industry would someday be paying three million dollars for eight hours, plus overtime, and have to shoot at the actor's house'.[14] The opportunity to demand such high fees translates into further potential power if actors choose to use their wealth in the production of other movies.

The desire for personal control has often led actors and directors into production. For example, careful husbanding of financial power and a highly successful screen image have put Clint Eastwood into a position of almost total control over his film output. Through his own production company, Malpaso, he can assert final say over the director, screenplay, writer, co-stars and other personnel in any film he makes.[15] Kirk Douglas, whose production company, Bryna, was an early example of a star going into production, claims that:

The reason I formed my own company originally wasn't financial – no, really – it was so that I could express myself more. Because of it I was able to pick *Spartacus*, to help with the financing of *Paths of Glory*, to make *Lonely Are The Brave* which the studio would not otherwise have touched . . . My company has given me the muscle to get things done when I would otherwise have been helpless.[16]

If Douglas is expressing a general truth, then whereas the studio-controlled product might be characterised by artistic and ideological uniformity,[17] one might expect recent independently-produced films to cover a wide range of styles and approaches.

The growth of independent production may have allowed for the exposure of controversial political attitudes. Some members of the film industry have long recognised the political potential of the medium, but there has been a general reluctance to admit this potential, especially since HUAC showed such a devastating interest in the connection between film and politics. Kirk Douglas, while stressing the artistic freedoms allowed by independent production, rejects the idea of films carrying 'messages'; 'You don't go to the cinema to have messages rammed down your throat. If there is a message to be picked up, it must be as a by-product of the entertainment.'[18] The alleged dichotomy between 'entertainment' and 'message' depends on the perception of a message as something heavy-handed and probably partisan. A similar division is made by Charles Chaplin when talking of his film *Modern Times*.

Our only purpose was to amuse. It was just my old Charlie character in circumstances of 1936. I have no political aims whatever as an actor.

It started from an abstract idea, an impulse to say something about the way life is being standardised and channelised, and men turned into machines – and the way I felt about it. I knew that was what I wanted to do before I thought of any of the details.[19]

Here clearly the film contains a 'message'; Chaplin succinctly outlines the idea, but there is still the careful denial that the film is really anything other than an amusement. The message, however clear, was not part of a political aim. That films aim to amuse and entertain is a basic tenet of the industry, but films may nevertheless convey a particular political or social analysis, whether this is inserted intentionally, or is the accidental by-product of a film-maker's approach. A film which attempts in part to show a particular vision of society inevitably contains a 'message' in the manner in which it portrays events.

Clint Eastwood does not consider that his films contain a particular political emphasis. He has expressed a willingness to take on any kind of film project with the caveat that 'I'm very anti-war. I wouldn't do a film that was pro-war. I'll do most anything, but I won't do that.'[20] However, consistent images of individualism and toughness in the characters Eastwood plays provide an indirect comment on a society which is seen as needing vigilantes who answer to a higher morality than the law (for example Harry Callahan in *Dirty Harry* (1971)). This kind of rugged individualism is carefully distanced from the identifiable fascism of the execution squads in *Magnum Force* (1973) and the laughable and pathetic Black Widows in *Every Which Way But Loose* (1978), nevertheless the films as a body give a bleak and conservative view of human nature and contemporary society.

While the Eastwood style of conservatism may share something with the image of individualism portrayed earlier by John Wayne, and might not have been considered out of place under the studio system, some independent productions have taken a more liberal line. Political activists in a position to influence the form of a film have at times effected a particular bias within the film; indeed, once identified as politically committed, stars and directors tend to find that responses to their work emphasize the supposed political messages whether or not such were the intended aims of the film. For example, both Robert Redford and Jane Fonda, noted political activists with the power to wield significant influence over film projects, find that their films are treated in this fashion. Their collaborative effort, *The Electric Horseman* (1979), was reviewed in one publication as 'a thoroughgoing delight of a picture that gets extra resonance from the known political interests of its two stars'.[21] Both these film actors would agree with Kirk Douglas that, to be a success, a film must have entertainment value, but they have both been involved in explicitly political movies. Redford says of *All The President's Men* (1976), a film he produced and in which he starred, 'History made the statement, not us ... I don't think of it as a propagandist film'.[22] Fonda, on the other hand, is concerned to put progressive films in front of a mass audience by skillful and responsible use of film-making conventions. As she points out: 'People in my generation all grew up hating Indians, objectifying women, fearing 'mobs' and all that. Those movie makers really knew how to manipulate people's emotions. Well we have to do the same thing. We have to learn how to move people, but in other directions. We have to learn the tried and true techniques of movie making.'[23]

Directors also can have explicitly political motives. For example, Martin Ritt has directed films with 'socio-political' themes, for example, *The Molly Maguires* (1970), *Conrack* (1974), *Sounder* (1972), *The Front* (1976) and *Norma Rae* (1979). Whereas he has never directed a 'blockbuster' he has a reputation for quality and, as he puts it, 'I've had a lot of films that have paid off, from which people got their money back. I've a high batting average and I'm eminently hireable.'[24] Ritt does not evade the political role of film: 'With sex and psychology today, the cinema can go all the way. Lesbianism, homosexuality and drugs don't threaten the Establishment. But ideas do. You're into the area of propaganda, like it or not. The only ideas the cinema used to accept were the old ideas of patriotism, dissolving to an American flag at the end of a John Wayne movie . . .'[25] His films have shown a consistent awareness of politics and he himself expresses concern that public political awareness must be heightened in order to prevent the recurrence of McCarthyite tyranny (he was himself blacklisted). In spite of his financial success investors still find his consciously political topics difficult to accommodate. He related that when trying to find backing for *Norma Rae*, 'I was turned down by the first studio I went to. "Who needs it? A film about working people – it'd be depressing." '[26] Discussing another proposal, a film about America's migrant workers, Ritt says, 'The problem will be the money. It's a problem to get money to make anything, particularly serious work.'[27]

As the case of Martin Ritt indicates, the new independence of the film industry's production methods does not necessarily allow an ideological *carte blanche*. The costs of production are such that few individuals are in a position to risk financing a film completely alone and they therefore rely on money from elsewhere. Groups of like-minded people may form a film-making organisation, but for the most part independent producers use their own and their partners' cash to attract institutional investment. Most of this investment comes from the film distributors. The former

studios, shorn of their American theatre chains, have taken on the role
of bankers in the economic structure of movie-making. If stars and
directors can demand high payment because of their corner on saleable
talent, the distributors have strength through their control of access to
the market. In 1978 six major distributors (Columbia, Paramount,
Twentieth Century–Fox, United Artists, Universal and Warner
Brothers) accounted for 89.1 per cent of American distributors' film
rentals in the United States and Canada. American International and
Buena Vista (Disney) accounted for 6.2 per cent, leaving all other
distributors with only 4.7 per cent of the market.[28] This domination of
distribution means that the major companies receive a constant flow of
rental income, making them the natural providers of risk capital to invest
in films which will ensure the rents keep coming. They operate on such a
scale that they are able to develop a portfolio of films to produce overall
profits, and thus withstand the occasional flop. Independent producers
may have more detailed control over their films than was true of
producers under the studio system, but the major companies are still the
main source of finance for production, and the opinions of the financiers
cannot be ignored.

The major companies with which the independent producer has to
negotiate have much the same names as the studios of the 1930s, but
they are quite different economic structures. In this age of diversification
a single-product industry is at a disadvantage. During the 1960s several
of the film studios were acquired by conglomerates wishing to expand
into leisure-related industry. Columbia and Twentieth Century–Fox
have resisted takeover, but have diversified their own interests and
reduced their financial dependence on motion pictures.[29] Being the
prime guarantors of film-making funds, it is the major companies who
decide whether a package is 'bankable', based on the script and the line-
up of director and actors.[30] There has always been a tension between the
commercial prospects of a film and the freedom of the film maker to say
what he wishes. Martin Ritt believes that 'A successful film has *content*; it
can never be totally successful if it doesn't upset anyone';[31] his stance
contrasts with the wariness of investors who would prefer their film to

have a wide box-office appeal.

Independents wishing to make films have on occasion expressed their frustration about the restrictions imposed by the distributors. James Caan, talking about his directoral debut *Hidden In Plain Sight* (1979), said 'It's unfortunate that you have to deal with conglomerates. It's pretty tough for a creative person to go hat in hand to some fuckin' conglomerate and start talking creatively.'[32] Less stridently Glenda Jackson said of being 'a bankable actress', 'It's all right as long as they're offering something they want you to do. If it's something *you* want to see off the ground, you're suddenly a whole lot less bankable.'[33] Financiers generally avoid serious and potentially controversial topics, hence commercially-inspired censorship will often have an ideological character. A report of the making of *Missouri Breaks*, whilst it may be apocryphal, illustrates this tension: 'Marlon . . . saw his character . . . as an opportunity for "a serious study of the American Indian". "Gee, Marlon, not at these prices", said Arthur Penn (referring to Brando's $1.5 million slice of a sizeable budget), so Brando settled for having fun.'[34]

Haskell Wexler, whose work as a cinematographer and director has included *Medium Cool* (1969), *The Conversation* (1974), *One Flew Over the Cuckoo's Nest* (1975) and *Coming Home* (1978), is convinced that Hollywood is incapable of producing a truly left-wing film; the financiers say that such a film will not sell, and writers do not even bother to write or submit such scripts knowing that they will go nowhere.[35] Mike Gray who made *The Murder of Fred Hampton* (1971), and wrote the original script for *The China Syndrome* (1979) does not agree. He is convinced that socially relevant films can reach the screen as long as they contain some traditional Hollywood element – 'tits and ass, guns, and a chase'.[36] In attracting the attention of Mike Douglas and Jane Fonda to his project he managed to get *The China Syndrome* off the ground, although he did have to forfeit directoral control to a more 'bankable' person. Certainly there seems more scope for politically aware movies if Gray's assessment that 'the people in charge of this industry couldn't care less about the subject of the picture as long as it makes money'[37] is correct.

Film-making is still the prerogative of the few. While the mode of independent production allows stars, directors, scriptwriters and promoters to put together a film package, the bulk of investment in such packages comes from the major distributors. Even if a film is produced without any investment by one of the major companies, the distributors are not obliged to handle the film, and without distribution services an independent producer may be left with a very expensive print and no way of obtaining any box-office receipts. There is a reluctance to support films that deal with controversial subjects, owing to preconceived ideas about what kind of subject matter makes profits. Since investment now comes through the entertainments division of a large corporation, the film-maker cannot even appeal to the individual styles of the old Hollywood studios. The re-emerging economic strength of the motion picture industry has been based on two main factors: sales to television, and the 'event' movie. Pre-sales give movie makers some guarantee against their investment. 'Event' movies such as *Jaws* (1975), *Grease* (1978) and *Close Encounters of the Third Kind* (1977) attract crowds to the box office while also providing substantial spin-off profits to the conglomerate on the sales of 'tie-in' products such as records, paperbacks, posters and toys. Subjects unlikely to lend themselves to this kind of treatment, and which may prove difficult to show on television, will find it ever more difficult to attract investment from the major sources.

Distributors are still particularly uneasy about becoming involved in anything they perceive as a 'political movie'. This is so despite the success of such films as *The Candidate* (1972) and *All The President's Men* (1976), as Alan Alda found when setting up *The Seduction of Joe Tynan* (1979).[38] Financiers are worried that movies with a message might be jeopardised at the box office. As William F. Thompson, Senior Vice-President of The First National Bank of Boston, says in an interview,

Do you want to be an advocate of a cause on the screen, and with your stockholders' money? You can catch the public fancy with what I call problem movies, but I think you've got to be awful attuned to what the public is going to like two years from now. I think the public basically doesn't go to see cause-type things . . . They don't care about drugs or homosexuality, really. I think those kinds of causes, if you will, are better left either low-budget, if you really have a yen to make those things, or better yet, on Broadway.[39]

Notes

1 See Richard Maltby, 'Made for each other: the melodrama of Hollywood and the House Committee on Un-American Activities, 1947', elsewhere in this volume.

2 Michael Pye and Lynda Myles, *The Movie Brats: How the Film Generation Took Over Hollywood* (London, 1979), pp. 19–21.

3 US Bureau of the Census, *Statistical Abstract of the United States: 1977* (98th edition) (Washington, D.C., 1977), p. 235.

4 See Barry Checkoway, 'Large builders, federal housing programs, and postwar suburbanization', *International Journal of Urban and Regional Research* (March 1980) for an excellent discussion of suburban expansion.

5 For a wide-ranging discussion of political investigation in the 1940s and 1950s see David Caute, *The Great Fear: the anti-Communist Purge under Truman and Eisenhower* (London, 1978).

6 United States *v.* Paramount Pictures 334 US 131 (1948). See E. Borneman, 'United States versus Hollywood: the Case Study of an Antitrust Suit', in *The American Film Industry*, ed. Tino Balio (Madison, Wis., 1976), pp. 332–45; and M. Conant, 'The impact of the *Paramount* decrees', in *The American Film Industry*, pp. 346–70.

7 Quoted in Borneman, 'United States versus Hollywood', p. 339.

8 James Monaco, *American Film Now: the People, the Power, the Money, the Movies* (New York, 1979), p. 394.

9 See Conant, 'The impact of the *Paramount* decrees', pp. 349–51; and Pye and Myles, *The Movie Brats*, pp. 47–54.

10 Monaco, *American Film Now*, p. 4.

11 See Richard Dyer, *Stars* (London, 1979). Dyer points out that 'Stars are widely regarded as a vital element in the economics of Hollywood' (p. 11). He is referring primarily to stars under the studio system, but his discussion of the economic significance of stars could also be applied to independent production.

12 For this point I am indebted to Richard Dyer, who discussed it in his

lecture, 'The Redefinition of Hollywood', given at the Silver Jubilee Conference of the British Association for American Studies, 29 March 1980.

13 Ralph Applebaum, 'Conditioning' (interview with James Caan), *Films and Filming*, vol. XXV, No. 10 (July 1979), p. 19.

14 Tony Crawley, 'Coppalypse Now! Part 2', *Films Illustrated*, vol. IX, No. 99 (November 1979), p. 97.

15 See P. Agan, *Clint Eastwood: the Man Behind the Myth* (London, 1975).

16 David Castell, 'Kirk Douglas' (Interview), *Films Illustrated*, vol. I, No. 11 (May 1972), p. 11.

17 See, for example, T. Bennet *et al.*, *Hollywood: a Case Study* (Milton Keynes, 1977), pp. 43–8.

18 Castell, 'Kirk Douglas', p. 11.

19 David Robinson, '*Modern Times*', *The Movie*, part 9 (March 1980), p. 170.

20 Agan, *Clint Eastwood*, p. 127.

21 Review of *The Electric Horseman*, *Films Illustrated*, vol. IX, No. 104 (April 1980), p. 308. See also Richard Dyer's comments on Jane Fonda in *Stars*, pp. 89–98.

22 David Castell, 'Redford' (interview), *Films Illustrated*, vol. V, No. 59 (July 1976), p. 424.

23 David Talbot and Barbara Zheutlin, *Creative Differences: Profiles of Hollywood Dissenters* (Boston, Mass., 1978), p. 139.

24 David Castell, 'The cinema of Martin Ritt', *Films Illustrated*, vol. VI, No. 67 (March 1977), p. 255.

25 Castell, 'The cinema of Martin Ritt', p. 255.

26 Tony Crawley, 'Martin Ritt: the bison of the Hollywood veldt', *Films Illustrated*, vol. IX, No. 102 (February 1980), p. 231.

27 Crawley, 'Martin Ritt', p. 232.

28 David Gordon, 'The movie majors', *Sight and Sound* (summer 1979), pp. 151–3.

29 James Monaco, 'Who owns the media', *Take One*, vol. VI, No. 12 (2 October 1978), pp. 24–8, 58–9.

30 See P. McGilligan, 'Bank shots', *Film Comment* (September/October 1976), pp. 20–5 for a discussion of the role of banks.

31 Crawley, 'Martin Ritt', p. 232. Emphasis in the original.

32 Applebaum, 'Conditioning', p. 15.

33 David Castell, 'Act One, Scene One, Take One: Glenda Jackson on the different demands of stage and screen', *Films Illustrated*, vol. V, No.

51 (November 1975), p. 95.
34 Review of *The Missouri Breaks*, *Sight and Sound* (summer 1976), p. 190.
35 Talbot and Zheutlin, *Creative Differences*, pp. 121–2.
36 Talbot and Zheutlin, *Creative Differences*, p. 315.
37 Talbot and Zheutlin, *Creative Differences*, p. 318.
38 Tony Crawley, 'Alan Alda on How *M*A*S*H* Makes Smash Ratings', *Films Illustrated*, vol. IX, No. 100 (December 1979), p. 139.
39 McGilligan, 'Bank shots', p. 25.

Christopher Frayling

The American Western
and American society

Ever since the early 1950s, when the American Western was first established as a legitimate subject for serious academic study, the critics have been debating about whether the Western 'myth' is best interpreted as part of an entrepreneurial culture, or a folk culture. And on the whole, the 'folk culture' people have succeeded in dominating the debate. For the French neo-realist critics, such as André Bazin, J.-L. Rieupeyrout and Jean Wagner,[1] the most appropriate way into this American genre 'par excellence' was through the question of historical *authenticity*. The Western had to be 'historical at base', although this did not necessarily mean that Westerns could be expected to be historically accurate – rather that they had to be 'faithful to history' in the sense that specific events (and 'historical references') provided the particular context within which 'the great epic Manicheism which sets the forces of evil against the knights of the true cause' was presented. Pre-1950 Westerns, which kept the 'epic' simple, represented the purest form of the genre for this school of thought, and the arrival on the scene of 'super-Westerns' like *High Noon* (1952) and *Shane* (1953) (which tended, according to Bazin, to be self-reflective, to be Westerns about Westerns) was greeted in Paris with fear and trepidation. Jean Wagner, a later contributor to the debate, attempted to relate the origins of the movie Westerns to the same search for an American national identity as stimulated Frederick Jackson Turner's thesis about the political and cultural implications of the frontier process. 'Crises in America's national identity' – for example, in the 1910s, the mid 1930s, the early 1950s – were in consequence, directly 'reflected' in the changing shape of the genre during these crucial periods: 'the Western, by its very nature, is rooted in an objective thing which is the history of the United States'.

This neo-realist frame of reference – whether presented as a discussion of the historical bases of the genre, or of the relationship between the Western and American folk culture – became fashionable in the 1960s, and survives today only in the general surveys of the origin of the Hollywood Western, such as those by Fenin and Everson, or Kevin Brownlow, which stress the 'authenticity' of the genre (between 1903 and 1929) in terms of landscape, clothing, actors and general historical detail.[2] But Bazin's stress on the 'epic' qualities of the Western still survives in more mainstream criticisms of the genre which explore the interconnections between the Hollywood product and a series of American 'foundation myths' – rugged individualism (preferably of a Puritan type); the cleansing of the American paradise of sinful elements through the efforts of a Saviour-Hero; the 'last gentleman' who represents a strict, but dying code of honour; the conflicts between the contrasting images of 'desert' and 'garden'; and so on. This approach, much loved by American Studies departments, is epitomised by the work of Jim Kitses and John G. Cawelti.[3]

To Cawelti the function of the Western is to 'resolve' in its own way 'the conflict between key American values like progress and success and the lost virtues of individual honour and natural freedom'. The Western 'presents for our renewed contemplation that epic moment when the frontier passed from the old way of life into social and cultural forms directly connected with the present'. This feature of the Western ('its extension of basic plot patterns to express shifting contemporaneous tensions') explains why the genre has continued to flourish. Cawelti at least attempts to present a definition of the genre which incorporates a *dynamic* component: but the base-point remains the 'major American ideals' of progress, advancing civilisation, and 'the heroic virtues of individual honour and masculine independence'. Perhaps this explains why Cawelti (in common with most auteurist critics of the films of John Ford, Howard Hawks, Anthony Mann, or Sam Peckinpah) is fond of celebrating what is special about an individual director's 'vision of the West' – as if an unlimited number of such visions are available to the director at any one time. Only if the field of ideological battle in the Western is a fixed one, in which the values of 'individualism' or 'populism' fight it out with each other in a never-ending variety of combinations which always refer back to 'the major American ideals' can this concept of a 'vision of the West' make any real sense. Since Cawelti makes no attempt to relate a given 'vision of the West' to a socially-constructed consensus, but rather assumes that it is a vision of something that is fixed, or static, his analysis seems definitely to belong to the tradition of interpreting the Western in terms of immutable 'foundation myths'.

Up until very recently, these two schools of thought – the 'neo-realist' and the 'mythic', both based on the assumption that the Western is best interpreted as part of a folk culture, have dominated serious study of the Western. There have been attempts to challenge them from an auteurist position,[4] and the semiologists, with their emphasis on the grammar of the image as a mechanism for the production of meaning, have tried to make redundant more normative approaches to the problem. Much has been written about the syntax of the Western, in terms of Metz's 'grande syntagmatique', precisely in order to characterise some earlier critiques of the Western as woolly-minded, reductionist or, worst of all, uncinematic. Perhaps the most obvious example of such a Western 'syntagm' is the stock panning shot of a valley, showing a stagecoach (originally John Ford's *Stagecoach* (1939)) in the middle distance, and 'discovering' a group of waiting Apache warriors on a bluff overlooking the valley as the camera moves from right to left: the effect was one of John Ford's favourites, becoming something of a visual cliché in the heyday of the Cowboy and Indian film of the 1940s and 1950s; the Indians are associated with the highlands, the 'above', the settlers with the lowlands, the 'below'. In a film like *The Searchers* (1956), Ford was able to exploit audience expectations about this piece of visual grammar, by having John Wayne and the Rangers appear on a bluff *above* the Comanche encampment.

But despite the combined assault of 'scientific' semiologists and (some) auteurists, the two schools of thought – which one might categorise as 'traditional film theory' and 'American Studies' – have continued to predominate in the accessible literature on the Western. The purpose of this chapter is to look at a fresh development in critical analysis of the genre, and the various criticisms of this development, in order to suggest the directions which surveys of the American Western and American society might take in the future: in particular the argument will be that critics have still failed to resolve the question of whether or not the Western forms part of an 'entrepreneurial culture'. This fresh development is based on the realisation that, at root, the popular Western film is a *social* phenomenon. On the face of it, not an earth-shaking discovery – but arguments (presented by the neo-realists) about historical accuracy, and (presented by the semiologists) about classifications and taxonomies had tended to push considerations of the *social* dynamic which lies behind changes in the genre well into the background: and in a sense, the attempt to explore the sociology of the Western which I will be discussing represents a reaction against precisely those arguments which, since the 1950s, have dominated the field, even if it implicitly owes something to the 'foundation myths' school and thus to Jean Wagner's work.

There had, of course, been various attempts to explore the relationship between the Western and changes in American society (or politics) long before Will Wright published his *Sixguns and Society* in 1975.[5] Andrew Bergman, for example, had looked at the Westerns of the Depression era in terms of 'the values, fears, myths and assumptions' of the culture which produced them.[6] Bergman's main concern was to explain the resurgence of their popularity in 1935 and 1936. His conclusion was that the Westerns of the 1936–7 season, and especially those produced by Paramount Studios, had as their main theme the external threats to prosperity – in the form of Indians, or corrupt small-town politicians – and the ability of the Texas Rangers (or equivalent federal authority) to cope with these threats: evil was personified, scapegoats for social dislocation had been found, and the possibility of individual success was kept alive through the medium of a series of adapted Western plots. Bergman's general argument was that 'the audience is obviously limited by what it is offered, but what it is offered depends a good deal on what it has accepted previously' – an argument which in practice tends to blur the distinction between Hollywood as a culture industry ('a circus for the masses') and the sovereignty of the consumer ('some movies are popular and others are not'). The blurring of this distinction, together with the looseness of Bergman's criteria concerning the relationship of films to popular thought make some of the connections he develops seem rather arbitrary at times – and directly link his work to more recent attempts at establishing connections between Westerns and specific examples of 'popular thought' (Vietnam and Indians, the Third World and Revolutionary Mexico, post-Vietnam dislocation and post-Civil-War rootlessness, etc.). But at least Bergman had attempted to interpret the Western as *both* entrepreneurial culture and folk culture.

Michael Wood's genial look at America in the movies was also explicitly based on shifting criteria:

> the relation between the America of the movies, and the other America out there in reality is a relation of wish, echo, transposition, displacement, inversion, compensation, reinforcement, example, warning – there are virtually as many categories of the relation as you care to dream up, and I don't see why we should try to keep the number down; what remains constant is an oblique but unbroken connection to the historical world.[7]

This rejection of attempts to 'keep the number down' was allied to an attack on two of the most fashionable theories for pinning down 'the relation' in more concrete terms – the Frankfurt School model of a 'culture industry' (which was deemed 'too conspiratorial'), and the Lévi-Straussian concept of 'myth'. Having dismissed the most sustained attempts by sociologists and structuralists to relate culture and society in a coherent way, Michael Wood proceeded to look at a random selection of 1950s Westerns in terms of the distinctively American notion that the 'nice guys finish last' – a notion which is never historically located, needless to say. Not surprisingly, given Wood's retreat from anything that looks remotely like a rigorous analysis, he has subsequently reacted strongly against the thesis contained in Wright's *Sixguns and Society*.[8] Wood reckons that Wright 'might well have arrived at his conclusions without the application of all his critical apparatus . . . since the films themselves are clear enough about where their values lie'. The trouble with the Wood alternative, as Wilfred Sheed has pointed out, is that by 'using Wood's methods one could conceivably prove that almost anybody is typically American . . . as sociology this has limited value, since we can only trust the bits we already know, but as entertainment it's fine'.[9]

Philip French has reacted even more strongly against *Sixguns and Society*, seeing it as 'an ambitious, not to say arrogant, and by no means convincing academic thesis'.[10] Unlike Wood, however, Philip French *had* previously made some attempt to look at developments in the Western over the past twenty years through a series of simple categories: French's system 'depends upon making connections between the style, tone and content of movies and the rhetoric, beliefs and public personae of four prominent politicians'. In this analysis, the Westerns of the period parallel the career and political philisophies of Kennedy, Goldwater, Johnson and William F. Buckley: some generalisations about the symbolic significance of these politicians are put side by side with summary remarks about a given group of films – thus *The Magnificent Seven* (1960) derives from Kennedy's Green Berets, *Guns in the Afternoon* (1962) from Kennedy's Peace Corps, and *Butch Cassidy and the Sundance Kid* (1969) from Kennedy's chic image. As French admits, these categories are far from 'clear-cut'; the notion that a politician is in some *social* sense 'typical' either of his age or of a section of the community may be a 'relatively bold' one, but seems to allow for rather too much flexibility both in the treatment of the politicians' careers, and in the isolation of Western themes and motifs which may or may not 'connect'. Before Philip French gets tired of his 'schema', about a third of the way through *Westerns*, he does succeed in raising two important questions: how can a critic incorporate both the studios *and* society into his or her analysis of the Western, and how can we account for *variations* in the 'style, tone and content' of movies which were released at *much the same time*, without forgetting about the audiences at which they were aimed? In so far as these questions are not seriously discussed by Will Wright, Philip French's criticisms of *Sixguns and Society* are telling ones.

As will have become clear from the foregoing survey, Will Wright's *Sixguns and Society* aims to explore the relationship between the Western and American society with much more methodological rigour. This has put a lot of critics off. But the book remains the most serious attempt to treat Western movies as versions of social thought – not simply reflections of prejudice or fantasy, but narrative vehicles for the display, displacement and 'resolution' of what is on Americans' minds – and, as such, it deserves more attention than most critics have been prepared to give it up to now. Whatever one's reservations about Wright's extensive 'critical apparatus' – and whether these reservations stem from methodological timidity, pluralism, aesthetic sensitivity, or, more simply the feeling that Westerns should never be treated quite *that* seriously – the book's ambitious attempt to bring the 'scrambled messages' of Hollywood films into sociological focus both serves to resolve some of the problems we have encountered in previous offerings on the subject (arbitrariness, suggestion rather than analysis) and manages to incorporate the more interesting aspects of Jean Wagner's neo-realistic account into its explanation as well.

Wright begins by assuming that 'films are ideological productions – so that the popularity of the genre mainly depends on how well the ideology of the film fits the social experiences of its audience' (rather than on 'the whims of a few powerful men in the industry'). The audience is seen as 'an active participant in choosing, with regard to its own needs, which types of stories it will watch and enjoy'. Wright's analysis is thus limited to a study of only the most commercially successful Westerns (those which earned, or were expected to earn more than four million dollars in the United States and Canada – sixty-four films in total) and, specifically, to the narratives and plot structures of these films. His main thesis is that there has been a development in the Hollywood Western from a concern with solitary heroes fighting it out with villains (who usually go around in gangs) for the sake of the weak, but growing community (and in defence of the family), to a concern with 'élite groups' of heroes, who have rejected the (still weak) community, and who fight simply to affirm their sense of themselves as professionals. In the former case (which Wright calls 'the Classical Plot'), the gunfighter tends to get the girl; in the latter ('the Professional Plot'), he tends to be quite happy with his fellow gunfighters. 'The Classical Plot' begins with the hero outside society, and shows his progressive integration into society; 'the Vengeance Variation' begins with the hero inside society, shows his going outside society for a 'job', and then returning to society (abandoning his 'job') because in the end he believes in the same values as the 'Classical' hero; 'the Transition Theme' begins with the hero inside society, and shows his progressive disillusionment with society; 'the Professional Plot' begins with group of men outside society – where they stay throughout the film. In this way, slight alterations in individual features of the plot ultimately result in a 'leap' – to a whole new plot variant ('the Professional Plot'), where there is no individual hero, society is no longer seen as constructive ('the Classical Plot') or even destructive ('the Transition Theme'), but as irrelevant, and where group solidarity is all that is needed to provide the 'acceptance' that society once provided for the 'Classical' hero. According to Wright, this structural progression in the Western is a response to a change in America, specifically American institutions, from the ideology of a market economy (the gunfighter as *homo economicus*) to the ideology of a corporate economy (the gunfighter as the self-image of the technocrat). The old American small town ('society' for the Classical hero) gradually disintegrates as a credible narrative device, to be replaced by what Frederic Jameson calls 'that suburban Los Angeles-type decentralisation, dominated by multi-national corporations and transcontinental networks of various kinds, in which only professional castes and individual networks of acquaintances are able to feel any kind of group identity'. In this new context, the 'Classical Plot' – and the last bastion of the rhetoric of 'possessive individualism' – can no longer have any credibility: even in its heyday, the inapplicability of 'individualistic thinking' to contemporary social realities (say, in the 1950s) had been explained away by the presence, 'alongside the hero', of 'society' as a separate entity (represented by the homesteaders or the townsfolk) to which this way of thinking was not expected to be relevant. Jameson continues: 'the final acceptance of the hero seals the narrative trick: we have been shown the ideology of individualism as still very much alive, but that it need not apply to us – so that its apparent inapplicability to the present-day world cannot amount to a disproof or refutation'. By the time of 'the Professional Plot', even this *rhetoric* of individualism has been definitively outmoded by the full development of a corporate kind of socio-economic organisation.

As Wright's introduction points out, the traditional 'mythic' approach to the Western has tended to fall back on rhetoric, mystification, and above all ethical judgement, as a substitute for historical or structural analysis of the genre; those studies which attempt to explore the 'psychological needs' served by the Western (and especially the 'B' Western or TV series) have also tended to fuzzy conjectures about 'human nature', 'our unconscious inner needs', 'the drive to violence' and 'the adolescent fear about adulthood' as a substitute for an *historical* view of reading (or viewing) publics; analyses of the Western which derive from old-fashioned studies of the novel (the Eng. Lit. approach), by laying emphasis on the point of view of the author (or director) have also, according to Wright, tended to deflect their findings about individual texts (rather than about a 'textual corpus' – which would be well beneath their visual threshold) in an ethical direction – and this approach may also involve a few individual Westerns by assimilating them to 'high culture' and insisting on their literary (or filmic) value, in a defensive way. Let's give John Ford the good housekeeping seal of approval by comparing his work to the 'great poets' of the pastoral (even if he would, as Andrew Sarris maintains, have been 'the last to admit it himself'). What is needed, says Wright, is a study of the historical limits to a whole group of authors' 'choices' at a given time, and an analysis of the historical situation of the genre, as well as of the constraints operating upon the authors' 'visions' of that situation. Better still, why not make the whole notion of an 'author' (a hangover from Lit. Crit. days) redundant? – it only raises more problems than it can solve. Who is this theoretical construct called 'John Ford' anyway? We may be accustomed to the thesis that a particular artist's hidden 'vision' should be treated as the most important variable in a given range of films. But this piece of received wisdom raises a criterion that an analysis which calls itself structuralist cannot cope with – for if structural analysis is used to decipher a web of meanings or a set of relations in a film or films, then the role of a director must become problematic, even irrelevant. In the same way, the 'worth' of a film or its director should be of no concern, for *all* films are, in principle, open to a structuralist analysis that explores or 'uncovers' meanings. Even the attempt by critics such as Peter Wollen to elevate the *auteur* to the level of a code, or sub-code so that we may write about 'Ford' or 'the Fordian world-view' (though not the real Ford, who would be a problem for us), so that in turn the ideas (or 'intentions') of the 'director' become a set of objects (or coding) on a level with other codes which run through 'his' films, is equally problematic for the card-carrying structuralist – since it encourages the creation of hierarchies of films which tend to 'close' rather than 'open up' further readings of a given range of material.[11]

So Wright has tried all these 'literary' approaches and found them wanting. He also seems to be taking issue with the traditional 'sociological' approach: for example, his introduction implies a rejection of the Frankfurt School model of 'mass culture' as 'cultural history'. If 'mass culture' is simply an 'industry', related to advertising techniques, and invested in by big business, then it must be about consumer brainwashing and very little else – by definition: so there cannot possibly be any intrinsic interest in its formal analysis. Yet Wright is primarily concerned to develop a coherent method of formal analysis, and he also believes that audiences vote with their feet, so he cannot be expected to find much common ground with these critical theorists. Against the view that American tastes and preferences are not reflected but moulded in successful films by 'the powerful studio heads, directors and movie stars', Wright points to the 'many instances' where star-studded films with millions of publicity dollars have been box office disasters, and the similar number of cases where low budget films have 'become quite successful . . .'. Wright sees the plot structure and setting of these latter films as 'similar to the standard Western', and concludes that 'it is essential to look at the *genre itself* for a complete understanding of what makes for popularity'.

So much for the idea that the Western is part of an 'entrepreneurial culture'. For the same reasons, Wright's method implies a rejection of some more recent neo-Marxist criticisms of the Western – for example the *Cahiers* collective text on John Ford's *Young Mr Lincoln* (1939).[12] Any such attempts to 'read' a film scene exclusively in terms of the apparent interests of the studio which produced it (Twentieth Century–Fox), and the direct relationship of that studio to the power politics of the time (Big Business and the Republican Party, just before the election of 1940), will tend to limit the scope of questions we are permitted to ask about the 'choices' made by (and available to) film-makers, and can tell us very little about the ways in which these 'choices' might be built into the structure of a work: at most, Wright implies, such studies can elucidate one 'specific political meaning' which may have been intended by the makers (in so far as such intentions are recoverable from the available evidence). Will Wright's rejection of the 'culture industry' model also implies a rejection of the classical Marxist concept of ideology in general – for this concept seems to have underpinned the position of the critical theorists: the 'culture industry' idea works, if ideology is seen to be simply 'false consciousness', or 'collective error' (to be set against some scientific 'truth'); it does not work if one does not share this view of the nature of ideology, or of its function in the big business end of culture. Will Wright's mode of analysis seems to be closer to Althusser's more recent definition of ideology as 'the representation of the imagery relationship of individuals to their real conditions of existence' – a definition which, by stressing the 'quasi-narrative' function of ideology, perhaps re-opens the way to a formal analysis of the relationship between the narrative bases of a given cultural formula, and the 'contradictions' these narratives may be said to resolve.

Wright has been accused by critics of being a 'theoretical maverick'. But by using Lévi-Strauss to lay the foundations for an account of how Westerns might be received, and then using Propp to provide a method of categorising these Westerns, Wright is actually fighting on two fronts at once – he wants to get away from the accusation, often levelled at formalists, that he is detaching films from their historical context, and he also wants to analyse the films in a rigorous, structural way – and, rather than mix the two traditions up in a (very) uneasy synthesis, he does, in fact, hold to the position that one activity must always inform the other, or, in other words, that the social interpretation of a given text is integrally related to a structural reading of it, and *vice versa*. But you cannot do them both at the same time.

First, then, Wright's use of Lévi-Strauss. The structural anthropologist argues (and Wright quotes him) to the effect that 'the myths of totemistic societies serve to resolve conceptual contradictions inherent in those societies', or, in other words, they provide an imaginary resolution of ideological (and, perhaps, social) 'contradictions', and, in the process, reassure the audience (the members of that society) that the 'contradiction' need not exist; if for 'myths' we read 'narratives' (as Wright seems to do), then Strauss's focus on the various 'codes' or 'signs' (expressed as binary oppositions) out of which these 'myths' are constructed, can be adapted to suit the basic oppositions at work in the Western film narrative – for Wright, these are 'inside society/outside society', 'good/bad', 'strong/weak', 'wilderness/civilisation' (although not the famous Straussian opposition between 'nature' and 'culture', which literally becomes part of the landscape). These 'codes' or 'signs' may then be used to evaluate the behaviour of the main characters in Western narratives ('where does he stand *vis-á-vis* . . .?'), and can also help to decode the 'message' of a given sequence of episodes ('when are things getting dangerous . . .?'). Wright has neatly side-stepped the problem raised by Michael Wood – that films cannot be compared with fully-blown myths – by using Lévi-Strauss at a primary stage of his analysis: the points of intervention in specific narratives come much later.

In order to subdivide Western stories into a set of episodes, narrative units, or 'functions' (whose presence in a given order 'may be said to constitute the Western genre'), Wright then adopts criteria gleaned from Vladimir Propp's method of analysing the production of narratives.[13] The main focus of *Sixguns and Society* is on the permutations which have happened to these 'functions' since the arrival of the sound film: Wright's study of these permutations (or 'variations') is not restricted to a simple *categorisation* of narratives, however (as was Cawelti's analysis of changing Western 'formulas', and, perhaps, Propp's original study of the Russian folk-tale), for he is also concerned with looking at the relationship of his categories – once established – to the changing social context, or rather (in Frederic Jameson's words) to 'that external limiting situation or condition of possibility which accounts for the coming into being of a given variant and excludes the others'. Wright can now attempt to extend Propp's formal study of the changing role of narrative 'functions' to cover the social interpretation of texts as well. He calls this extension 'a liberalised version of . . . Vladimir Propp' (an extension which goes well beyond the role of equivalent organising devices in the studies by French and the Brauers).[14] We have already looked at both the more traditional modes of analysis against which Wright seems to be reacting, and the general conclusions about the Western society which emerge from his unusually rigorous theoretical framework. How have these conclusions been received?

Sixguns and Society has been criticised (as one might expect) from many different perspectives: from the point of view of film studies, Wright's emphasis on plot (and his method of analysing plot, which as we have seen derives from Propp's attempt to classify the *narrative* sequences in Russian folk-tales) and consequent neglect of performances, production structures, and technical developments seems inadequate. His aggressive rejection of the traditional normative approach to the study of film has made many enemies: Demetrius Kitses, to take one example, criticises Wright for 'tearing the Western from its own industrial context', for 'nowhere evidencing an interest in *films*', and for having 'an unnecessarily narrow and conservative base'. A big-budget Western has rather more to it, perhaps, than a fairy story which is often communicated from one person to another, which can accurately be retold by an anthropologist, and which obeys a rigid set of narrative conventions; Propp was studying a group of oral texts which had already been collected, and set down on paper: thus he saw no reason to incorporate the *act of communication* (tone of voice, 'style' of the narrator) into his model, in any systematic way. But, whether one believes that the audience is supine (Adorno, Godard), or active (Bergman, Wright), it is clear that narrative films are at some level an *act of communication*, so the adaptation of Propp – even the improvement on Propp – since the Soviet formalist made little attempt to systematise the relationship between social change and developments in the folk-tale – does raise at least one key problem that Wright does not address. If Wright had restricted himself to using Propp as the starting-point for a *classification* of individual films (as many critics, such as Peter Wollen, have done),[15] this might not have mattered. But he is concerned with relating his classification to the concepts and attitudes implicit in the structure of American institutions, so he finds himself in the position of having to *suppress* many of the ways in which meaning is produced and communicated, in his search for 'simple and recognisable' meaning and correspondences. To give two examples: he has nothing to say about the specific ways in which 'language and conventions of film' can be manipulated and, since he studies film at the level of narrative action only, he has to ignore those (many) characters in Westerns whose motives are not directly reflected in their behaviour (or in what Propp calls their 'spheres of action'). Time and time again, Wright reluctantly admits that individual characters in Westerns simply do not fit his 'simple and recognisable' categories: 'people like him may exist in real life, but they seldom do in the Western'; 'she is one of the few psychologically complex characters in Westerns'; 'he is the kind of complicated and ambiguous character who almost never appears in the Western myth'; etc., etc. So many exceptions, even in a genre which is alleged to be about people who 'gotta do what they gotta do', would suggest that a lot of suppression is going on to make actors behave in a recognisably formularised way. In some films, the more interesting ones in fact, narrative action may not even be dominant in the production of meaning. Yet Wright soldiers on, as if semiology had never happened, and as if Propp had not been adapted by literary critics to accommodate more complex characters into 'value-laden categories'.

From the point of view of sociology, as we have seen, the breadth of Wright's social and political perspective has been seen as one of the reasons why so much of what he says verges on the tautological: by placing the 'structure of feeling' of a given time (the kind of 'hidden history' which is contained within the films) alongside its undifferentiated 'social character' – to hi-jack Raymond Williams's terms – Wright has been accused of presenting a 'self-confirming circularity'. When dealing with both the films and the society, he seems obliged to distort his descriptions by ignoring the complexity he finds exceptional. Wright's straightforward version of the objective changes which have happened in American society (as well as of changes in *perceptions* of American society by audiences) is only as good as his sources – and in a book which is marked by a rare degree of self-consciousness (he tells us what he is going to do, what he is doing, what he has done, and invariably how he has done it), some reference to where his sources found their judgements would perhaps have helped. Wright gets around the thorny problem of 'how we are to undertake the difficult task of making connections between a model of the "real" world and a model of the world derived from films'[16] by bringing in *his* version of the 'quasi-narrative' function of ideology. But, by presenting an undifferentiated account of what 'society' is, he fails to explore the ways in which films communicate to specific groups and social classes. Frederic Jameson's recent analysis of the ways in which social classes are represented in popular films – with special reference to Lumet's *Dog Day Afternoon* (1975) – contains some useful suggestions in this area for the future.[17]

From the point of view of the debate about the *Americanness* of the Western (a debate introduced by Bazin, but given more coherence by

Jean Wagner), *Sixguns and Society* can be strongly criticised for the summary way in which Wright deals with those 'top-grossing' Westerns made outside the United States. Two Italian Westerns, *For a Few Dollars More* (1965) and *The Good, the Bad, and the Ugly* (1967) are mentioned in his survey, and, in his attempt to make these films fit the expectations of *American* audiences alone, he tries to squeeze them into the category of 'the Professional Plot'. But as I have argued elsewhere, Sergio Leone's films simply do not 'fit' this category: perhaps Will Wright would have made more sociological sense of them if he had started by 'reading' the films in terms of the equivalent *Italian* social values.[18] Hidden beneath this structural study of the Western is the firm belief (always assumed, never 'shown') that there is something distinctively *American* about the Western – that the folk-myth only functions for American society: this unstated belief, which may owe something to the neo-realists (of all people), perhaps explains why Wright never asks the question posed by Wilfred Sheed: 'Which of these myths rang bells in Europe, and which clinked? The success of, say, Eddie Constantine in France suggests that the lonesome, alienated hero is even more doted upon there than here, not because of any frontier, but because of the lack of one.'[19] A film like *The Magnificent Seven* (a 'professional plot, if ever there was one) made much more money in Europe than in America: and that can't be just because the 'profession' was originally that of samurai rather than gunslinger.

Discussing Will Wright's adaptation of Vladimir Propp, and, specifically, the narrative 'functions' Wright lists to define his 'Classical Plot', Frederic Jameson has this to say about potential criticisms of the book: 'At this point, no doubt, there will be room for useful and productive disagreement about the precise functions Mr Wright has defined: his final sequence (society accepts hero, who loses his special status) will certainly be questioned by other students of the Western'. Jameson is here referring to the radically different interpretations of the final sequence in *Shane*, presented by Wright and John G. Cawelti. Both consider that George Stevens's film is *the* most perfect embodiment of the 'classical' Western: yet, for Cawelti, at the end of the film Shane remains a gunfighter who is no longer part of the community, and his ride off into the mountains symbolises the impossibility of his ever living in that community (as it clearly does in the original novel); for Wright, Shane could easily stay in the valley to enjoy his justly-earned reward, or bask in the gratitude of the farmers, and this *possibility* suggests that he has really given up his status as a gunfighter (that he '*chooses instead* the dark night and cold mountains'). In other words, the two critics disagree about the final 'function' of the Classical Plot, if *Shane* may be taken as the most characteristic example of that plot. And Wright has the weaker case. Jameson continues: 'But to understand disagreement over various interpretations as an objection to Wright's method itself is to misconceive the very use of models in general. The reproach that the 'functions' are inaccurate would carry more weight against Propp than against Wright's modification of him, for the Russian theorist posited but a single sequence of functions for the fairy-tale in general. The use of his model thus encourages a primarily typological or classificatory activity, matching a given tale against the basic function to see whether it may be considered a folk-tale or not. Wright, however has used the concept of a sequence of functions to propose four fundamental variants. For him, therefore, deviation from a given sequence is meaningful and can only lead to further analytical activity, where for Propp it is simply 'noise' and an aberration, something which cannot be accommodated by his system. In other words, since Wright is discussing a series of permutations, his scheme can cope with conformity and variation alike: since Propp is simply dealing with a mode of classification, important variations could prove fatal to his scheme; in the former case, deviations will prove productive, in the latter, they will be destructive. (The problem with this, of course, is that exceptions can always be 'explained away' by the simple expedient of adapting Wright's major variants *ad infinitum*: in this way, his schema can *always* be made impervious to 'factual' criticism – in theory at least.) But Jameson is here pointing to a disagreement about a film *within the genre*. *Shane* may have a 'classical' plot, or the ending of the film may place it in the transition category: either way, there is plenty of room for the movie in one of Wright's four main variants. When Wright claims that at the end of *Stagecoach* Ringo does finally give up his vengeance (a claim which is essential, if the film is to fit his 'vengeance variation'), he cannot be writing about the same film as I have seen, in which John Wayne shoots all the baddies he set out to shoot: to worry about such a 'deviation' on a question of detail may very well be to 'misconceive the very use of models in general'.

Even if an entire sub-genre, such as the Italian Western, fails to fit his model – a criticism which seems to me to go well beyond 'mere nit picking' – it is conceivable that the model could be adapted to accommodate the noise, perhaps with the invention of an 'Italian Plot' as part of the 'transition'. But a more crucial disagreement would be about whether or not similar patterns of change are detectable in other formula genres, and in particular those which have traditionally been associated with Americanness, such as the gangster movie. Frederic Jameson has suggested that

we rewrite the history of the gangster film in terms of the formal evolution described in *Sixguns and Society*: the early 30s film of Robinson and Cagney, in which the gangster is seen as a lone psychopath, would be dependent on an opposition of hero to society analogous to that of Wright's classical plot. The great tragic gangster films of the 1940s – Bogart's in particular – would then correspond to the vengeance or transition periods. Finally, the ethnic gangster film reinvents the professional collectively of ghetto life and 'organised crime'.

Intuitively, this description is correct. The parallels between the Western and the gangster film, between rural and urban myth, Jesse James and Legs Diamond, have often been pointed out: indeed, one could argue that, in terms of dominating procedures, these are the only two types of Hollywood narrative cinema which can possibly benefit from a strictly generic analysis. So, on the face of it, Wright's analysis should be directly transferable from *Sixguns and Society* to Submachineguns and Society, to 'fit' the transition from the gangster-as-hero (1930s), via the gangster-as-soulless-killer-who-has-problems (1940s) to the gangster-as-part-of-the-organisation (1960s and 1970s). Give or take a few parodies (*Some Like It Hot* (1959)), spin-offs from Western successes (*The Sting* (1973)) and self-reflective movies about movies (*Bonnie and Clyde* (1967)), the model seems at first sight to work. Unfortunately, the sources do not entirely confirm the hypothesis. In the 1930s, *Little Caesar* (1930) and *Bullets or Ballots* (1936) did make it into the four million dollar category – as did *The Thomas Crown Affair* (1968) in the 1960s, and *The Godfather* (1972), *The Getaway* (1972) and *The Sting* in the 1970s. But, in between the 'Classical' and 'Professional' phases, no gangster plots which can be categorised as 'transitional' or 'vengeance' (with the possible exception of *Key Largo* (1948) appear to have made the grade. Quite apart from the problems raised by labelling *Little Caesar* a 'Classical' plot (to what extent does the film *depend* on 'an opposition of hero to society'. . .?), the quantum leap from Rico Badillo to Mario Puzo's Don needs rather more explanation than the data can support. And in the meantime, *Guys and Dolls* (1956), *Some Like It Hot* (1959) and *Oceans 11* (1960) did make the grade – while *Yankee Doodle Dandy* (1942) made much more money than any of Cagney's 'lone psychopath' movies: their success would seem to require a very different kind of analysis to that provided by Wright, one which takes into account the importance of musicals and *parodies* of genre pictures in Hollywood's marketing policy. *Blazing Saddles* (1974), *Paint Your Wagon* (1969) and *Cat Ballou* (1965) made more money at the box office than almost all of the Westerns listed by Wright, *Blazing Saddles* being the second most successful 'Western' of all time. During the years of Wright's 'transitional' phase, *Annie Get Your Gun* (1950) and *Seven Brides for Seven Brothers* (1954) were the horse operas which *really* had them queueing at the box office.

If the steady transition from 'Classical' to 'Professional' cannot be detected in the gangster film, from 1939 to 1969, it is unlikely that it can be detected in other genres, such as the musical or the horror film: for example, it would be a little far-fetched to argue that the shift from monster-outside-society (1930s) via monster-as-scientific-problem (1950s) to monster-in-the-family (1970s) was deeply significant. But perhaps it is unjust to criticise Will Wright for a claim which has been made on his behalf: after all, if the Western 'myth' *is* peculiarly American, as Wright believes, then perhaps his structural approach is peculiarly suited to it alone. A detailed study of other genres would in any case require a more differentiated analysis of American audiences than he provides. More telling criticisms of his model for *Sixguns and Society* (in addition to those mentioned already) might be suggested. There is no *prima facie* reason why the starting date of his history (the advent of the sound film) should coincide with any social or ideological change, or even with a significant change in 'forms of reasoning' about everyday life. Wright's model seems to change its purpose at some stage during the transition from the 'Classical' to the 'Professional' plot – whereas the 'Classical' plot is said to 'resolve', through story-telling, an ideological contradiction (in essence, a concept of individualism which is in the process of becoming outmoded by developments in socio-economic organisations), the 'Professional' plot is said to perform two very different functions. In the first instance, this narrative variant undertakes to 'present' a new ideology ('technocracy'), and, since that ideology is not yet felt to be contradictory, the variant then proceeds to 'reflect' or 'illustrate' both the new ideology and the new stage of social organisation which underpins it (the 'Classical' plot, we are told, 'corresponds' to one conception of society, the 'vengeance variation' begins to 'reflect' another, while the 'Professional' plot 'reveals' all). The sources on which Wright relies for his social history (to test the 'hidden history' he first discovers in the Westerns) are not, perhaps, the most happy choices – MacPherson (for 'possessive individualism'), Galbraith (for the 'corporate economy'), Reisman (for 'the lonely crowd') and, at the last minute, Habermas (for 'rationality' – brought in, as the author says, 'to the rescue' like the Seventh Cavalry) – and there is no sustained discussion of the model of historical development contained within these sources. Since Wright is primarily concerned with 'the internal dynamics of superstructures' (narratives, 'structures of feeling'), he rather prematurely (and without adequate theoretical justification) attempts to relate these 'dynamics' to social and economic infrastructures, in the process having to fall back on precisely those terms ('reflection', 'correspondence', 'parallel') he seems to have set out to avoid. Finally, Wright is *too* dismissive of the psychological approach to the Western myth (an approach he interprets as *necessarily* 'static' and 'ahistorical').

One of the key problems raised by Wright's analysis (and it is not, of course, confined to film studies) is how to analyse artefacts such as Westerns *symptomatically* (to use the current term), while at the same time treating them as artefacts. The decipherment process this entails should in principle involve looking at films as ideological *productions* (with that emphasis), rather than as purveyors of raw ideology. Of course, unless one adopts a crudely 'reflectionist' position (looking at plots in isolation, as direct 'reflections' of social and political structures), the problems of studying performance, 'style', images, production values and so on within this context, are immense. But if one ignores these problems one cannot hope to do justice to the films in question. Barry King has suggested one possible line of approach.[20] He argues that Wright's attempt to connect genre change with social change is perfunctory and mechanical to the point of mere juxtaposition': this is, he adds, because Wright leaves most of the important questions unanswered.

Given that American capitalism has changed (or rather popular awareness of its form has changed) and that the Western has changed, it is still necessary to show how Hollywood mediates this change and why. But since Wright argues a consumer sovereignity thesis, the influences of Hollywood must accordingly be played down. Apart from the circularity of claiming that box office Westerns are popular because they have a plot structure Wright detects, there is the practical evidence of Hollywood's efforts to influence popular opinion.

Since the change in American society from a market economy to a corporate economy did *not*, of course, take place during the brief forty-year period (1930–70) with which Wright is concerned (and since generalisations about 'popular awareness' of this change would require a great deal more proof than Wright offers), it might have been more useful to relate the shifting values he isolates to changes within *Hollywood*: 'In the period in question, it is Hollywood – not American capitalism – that moves from an individual (star, director, etc.) versus society (studio) opposition to a conflict between teams (independent production company) and society (distribution finance).'

To dismiss the 'culture industry' from an explanatory model simply because its effects cannot always be predicted with accuracy is, from a perspective such as King's, to sidestep the issue: many other factors, apart from audience expectations, come into play when a commodity such as a large-budget film is produced, marketed and consumed. A folk-tale which is told and retold does not emerge from an industrial context, is not disseminated through an elaborate distribution system, and does not have monetary exchange value: the effects of the differences between a folk-tale and a Hollywood movie may well be determining. In other words, where the 'mythic' function of film is concerned, the commodity which sells the best need not *necessarily* be the one which does the most efficient job.

But even if we agree that, at some level, what an audience is offered depends on what it has previously accepted, one evidential problem is not sufficiently noted by Wright: how can this 'acceptance' be empirically tested? Where the 'genre itself' is concerned, the raw data must either be all the films produced in a given historical period, or else only the most commercially successful films. Wright opts for the second alternative, and reckons that the best index of it is the list of 'top grossers' published annually in *Motion Picture Herald* and *Variety*, from which he extracts his 64 hit Westerns. Unfortunately for any film researcher, this list needs to be treated with the utmost caution. In the first place, it indicates *rental fees* in the USA and Canada, rather than actual box-office grosses (of which there is no reliable record): many of these rental fees were estimated in advance by the studios, and thus represent, at best, an educated guess. As a rule, re-issues do not appear on the list: long-term profits are impossible to calculate from the evidence. And, since Wright uses the magic figure of 4 million dollars as the basis for his selection, he does not allow either for changes in the value of money, or for changes in Hollywood's marketing policy, both of which are 'hidden' in his hit parade: 21 Westerns achieved 'top grossing status' in the twenty years from 1931 to 1951, while over twice that number made the grade during the following twenty-year period: clearly, Hollywood's emphasis on 'blockbusting' tactics from the early 1950s onwards helps explain the discrepancy. If *Stagecoach* (1939) made 4 million dollars, that would constitute a handsome rate of profit: if *Butch Cassidy* (1970) made the same 4 million figure, that would constitute an ugly rate of loss, but Wright is only interested in whether or not the films made 4 million dollars. Of *Variety's* top twenty-five 'All-Time Box-Office Champions', twenty-two were released after 1960; seventeen after 1970. And only one of them is a Wright Western. So there are problems about interpreting the only accessible evidence. But even this does not explain why Wright omits so many Westerns which do, in fact, feature on the list, and includes several which do not.

Top-grossing Westerns omitted by Wright
1938–9	Jesse James
1939–40	Drums Along the Mohawk
1952	Distant Drums
1958	Raintree County
	The Big Country (categorised 'a financial disaster' by Wright)
1959	Horse Soldiers
1962	Liberty Valance
1965	Shenandoah
1968	Bandolero
1970	A Man Called Horse

Top-grossing films, with Western associations, omitted by Wright
1937	The Girl of the Golden West
1948	Paleface
1950	Annie Get Your Gun
1952	Son of Paleface
1954	Seven Brides for Seven Brothers
1962	Sergeants Three
1965	Cat Ballou
1969	Paint Your Wagon

Westerns included by Wright, which did not in fact gross over $4 million
1948	Fort Apache
1950	Colt 45
1953	Naked Spur
1954	Johnny Guitar

1962   *The Commancheros*

Sources: *Motion Picture Herald*; *Variety*

These eight top-grossing films 'with Western associations' were probably omitted because they do not conform to Wright's definition of what constitutes 'a Western'. Of the ten others omitted by Wright, three are films which are centrally concerned with Indians, three with the American Civil War – precisely those aspects of the genre which *Sixguns and Society* has been criticised for neglecting, by Philip French among others. If we add all these omitted films to the thirteen Westerns for which Wright admits he has difficulty in finding 'distinguishing labels', then we discover that over thirty 'top-grossers' in the period 1931–72 do not 'fit', or are absent from, his analysis. To argue a consumer sovereignty thesis from such limited or problematic data is, as Wright might have said, to enter the gunfight with a half-empty revolver.

Despite all these criticisms, *Sixguns and Society* has in fact been underestimated as a contribution to the debate about the American Western and its American audience. Before the book was written, most serious studies of the problem were concerned with whether or not the Western is 'historically authentic', to what extent the genre is dependent on things called 'foundation myths', and the relative merits of *auteurs* such as John Ford and Howard Hawks – many of whose films were seen by remarkably few people. If the social implications were mentioned at all, they were usually read into a random selection of films in an arbitrary, if amusing, way. In this chapter I have attempted to outline Will Wright's uncompromising thesis, and the major criticisms of it, in the hope that these criticisms can only 'lead to further analytical activity'. Certainly, the book has stimulated discussion of some key issues: the limits of formalism, and the need to adapt Propp's schema to incorporate 'value-laden categories' ('before fitting a measure to a film, we must be alert both to what it measures and why we are measuring it'); the question of how films convey meaning, and what role 'formulas' have in this process (must 'film language', 'style' and even 'complex characterisation' be suppressed from a model which claims to be structuralist?); the adequacy of a theory which stresses the 'quasi-narrative' function of ideology; the more specific assumption that the Western is, at base, peculiarly American; the related assumption that Hollywood movies can be analysed in the same way as a structural anthropologist studies 'myth' (where do the 'binary oppositions' come from?); the urgent need to differentiate specific 'audiences' or 'viewing publics'; the dismissal of a psychological approach to 'film and society' on the grounds that it is necessarily 'static' and 'unhistorical'; the extent to which consumers decide about the films they are going to see; the empirical problem of how to select the 'most commercially successful' films over a given period of time, and whether it is best to measure 'success' as rate of profit, or as total dollars earned in rentals; the question 'does it matter if a film made money?'; and, most important of all, the limitations of any analysis which does not take account of the 'culture industry' ('it is still necessary to show how Hollywood mediates change, and why'). The American Western has been treated as part of a 'given' folk culture, to the exclusion of other possibilities, for too long – by auteurists, *auteur*-structuralists, literary critics, film historians, and sociologists of film: it is time to treat it as part of an entrepreneurial culture as well.

That one book should have encouraged discussion of all these issues – some technical, some theoretical – is quite an achievement in itself. To dismiss *Sixguns and Society* as the work of an academic who is taking it all far too seriously is to evade the issue: future analysts of the relationship between the American Western and American society will have, at some level, to take account of Will Wright.

Notes

1　See André Bazin, *What is Cinema?*, vol. 2 (Paris, 1961; California, 1971); J.-L. Rieupeyrout, *La Grande Aventure du Western* (Paris, 1964), esp. pp. 11–12, 35–49, 429–33; and Jean Wagner, *Le Western, l'Histoire et l'Actualité* (in *Le Western*, ed. Agel (Paris, 1961), pp. 252–63). An interesting survey of the neo-realist contribution is contained in Alan Lovell, 'The Western' (*Screen Education* (September/October, 1967), pp. 94–7).

2   George Fenin and William Everson, *The Western* (New York, 1962), esp. pp. 3–23; and Kevin Brownlow, *The War, the West and the Wilderness* (London, 1979), esp. pp. 223–99.

3   Jim Kitses, *Horizons West* (London, 1969), esp. pp. 7–27; and John G. Cawelti, *The Six-gun Mystique* (Bowling Green, Ohio, 1971), esp. pp. 66–86.

4   See Richard Collins, 'Genre', *Screen*, vol. 11, Nos. 4/5 (1970), pp. 66–75).

5   Will Wright, *Sixguns and Society* (Berkeley, Cal., 1975) and 'The Sun Sinks Slowly on the Western', *New Society* (6 May 1976). My account of the critical debate about Wright's thesis is based on articles by Frederic Jameson (*Theory and Society* (winter 1977), pp. 543–59); John Fell, (*Film Quarterly* (spring 1977), pp. 19–28); Janey Place (*Jump Cut*, 18 (August 1978), pp. 26–8); Demetrius Kitses (*Quarterly Review of Film Studies* (summer 1978)), as well as the articles by Michael Wood, Philip French and Barry King cited below. The empirical data for my survey come from *Variety*, *Motion Picture Herald*, and Cobbett Steinberg's *Reel Facts* (New York, 1978) pp. 326–54.

6   Andrew Bergman, *We're in the Money* (New York, 1971), esp. pp xi–xvii, 88–91.

7   Michael Wood, *America in the Movies* (London, 1975), esp. pp. 3–23, 75–96.

8   Michael Wood's critique of *Sixguns and Society*, *New York Review of Books* (July 1976).

9   Wilfrid Sheed's critique of *America in the Movies*, *New York Review of Books* (April 1976).

10   Philip French, *Westerns* (London, 1973), pp. 12–47; *Westerns* (revised ed. London, 1977), pp. 197–9; and critique of *Sixguns and Society* in *Sight and Sound* (spring 1976).

11   For a discussion of this problem, see the *Screen Education* reader on Ford's *The Searchers* (winter 1975/6), and especially the article by John Caughie, 'Teaching through Authorship' (pp. 3–13). I am grateful to Ian Green for sharing his ideas on authorship with me.

12   *Cahiers* collective text on Ford's *Young Mr Lincoln*, translated in *Screen Reader* 1 (London, 1977), pp. 113–70, with a discussion.

13   Vladimir Propp, *Morphology of the Folktale* (2nd ed., Austin, Tex.,

1968), esp. pp. 19–65.

14 See Ralph and Donna Brauer, *The Horse, the Gun and the Piece of Property* (Bowling Green, Ohio, 1975), esp. pp. 1–5, 9–22.

15 Peter Wollen, *North by Northwest: a Morphological Analysis, Film Forum* (spring 1976).

16 Philip Simpson, 'Directions to Ealing, *Screen Education* (autumn, 1977), pp. 5–16. Although this review article deals with the output of an English studio, Ealing, it raises some theoretical issues which are very relevant to our discussion.

17 Frederic Jameson, '*Dog Day Afternoon* as a political film', *Screen Education* (spring 1979), pp. 75–92.

18 See Christopher Frayling, *Spaghetti Westerns* (London, 1980).

19 Sheed, p. 34.

20 Barry King, critique of *Sixguns and Society, British Journal of Sociology* (June 1977).

Leonard Quart and Albert Auster

The working class
goes to Hollywood

Hollywood's treatment of the working class in American society has never been noted for its realism. Even in the 1930s when unemployment and poverty made class divisions intense and hard to avoid, there was always a tendency for the movies to patronise and trivialise the working class. Even the best of Hollywood's films about the working class – Warner's social conscience epics – never got beyond depicting workers as a mixture of urban ethnics, taxi-drivers, bellhops and chorus girls, all looking for the main chance – a world of elegance that was epitomised by a snap brim hat, a double-breasted suit and a diamond pinky ring. Nor did the screwball comedies of Frank Capra and other directors do much to clear up that image. The hobo-aristocrats like *My Man Godfrey* (1936) and the Cinderellas and 'ordinary Joes' from the working class who married the boss or his daughter never provided an authentic portrait of class in American society.

   In the 1950s, despite some interesting attempts like *Marty* (1955) and *On the Waterfront* (1954) to bring the working class and its world back into focus, the film industry's major pre-occupation was a non-ethnic middle class (e.g. Doris Day). However, with the success of *The Godfather* (1972), its more formally and intellectually venturesome sequel, *The Godfather II* (1974), and the critical success of *Mean Streets* (1973), Hollywood began to see profit in films which at least touched on class and social reality. These films, albeit within the confines of traditional melodramatic and violent Hollywood genre conventions, opened up questions of ethnicity, working-class mobility, family life, male—female roles, and the relationship of the working class to the American Dream. *The Godfathers* were just the opening wedge, and with the phenomenal box-office success of *Rocky* (1976) the trend took off into solid hits like *Saturday Night Fever* (1977) less commercially successful films like *F.I.S.T.* (1978), *Blue Collar* (1978), *Bloodbrothers* (1978) and *Norma Rae* (1979), all of which highlight working-class characters and situations. And even the Academy-Award-winning *Deer Hunter* (1978) with its controversial and sensational treatment of the war in Vietnam, is immersed in a working-class milieu and rituals.

When one looks at this trend a number of questions come to mind. First, why has Hollywood so suddenly become interested in the working class again? Second, what has made the American audience receptive to films about the working class? Finally, what are some of the major themes that have emerged from these films?

The first question – the sudden Hollywood interest in the working class – is perhaps the easiest to answer. In fact, it can be done in one word: television. Ever since the late 1960s when the film industry learned to live with television instead of fighting it, a major symbolic and profitable relationship has developed. One of its major achievements has been the transfer of big screen products to the small screen (e.g. situation comedies like *M*A*S*H* and *Alice*). As for working-class characters, these go back to Norman Lear's inspired decision to rush in on working-class resentment of 1960s protest movements with *All in the Family*. The success of that series, coupled with Fred Silverman's transformation of ABC-TV into a highly rated working class ghetto (*Laverne and Shirley, Welcome Back Kotter, Barney Miller* and *Fish*) paved the way for *Rocky* (1976), a broken-down pug whose speech and life style put him squarely in the working class (albeit on the margin).

Rocky was the turning point for Hollywood's treatment of the working class – it made ethnicity and the working class hero fashionable again. The fairy-tale dimensions of its story were equalled, if not eclipsed, by the Horatio Alger leap to fame of its writer–star, Sylvester Stallone, and its box-office bonanza (over $200 million gross world-wide). This clearly was enough profit to convince the film industry that there was gold in mining the working-class lode. So when British producer Robert Stigwood hired John Avildsen, the director of *Rocky* (subsequently fired), to do *Saturday Night Fever*, a loose adaptation of Nik Cohn's *New York Magazine* article about the sexual and social rituals of working-class kids in Brooklyn's Bay Ridge, a phenomenon had come of age.

While it isn't difficult to trace *Rocky*'s commercial origins and the film industry's interest in the working class, the answer to the second question – why have audiences responded to the films the way they have? – is a lot less clear. Certainly *Rocky*'s affirmation of the ideals of hard work, perseverance, and honesty had a lot to do with it; for Americans Rocky was some pre-psychoanalytic being – a man who could invoke nostalgia for a purer past. These were the same virtues that people responded to in the presidential election of that year, 1976. Its upbeat ending also hit a sensitive chord in an audience alienated by the downbeat quality of so many contemporary films. Similarly, *Saturday Night Fever* struck the same chords and added to them the macho sexuality of John Travolta and the falsetto romanticism of the Bee Gees. However, it is also important to underscore that the audience was also reacting to the first positive figure from the working class to come along since the benevolent but somewhat melancholy figure of *Marty* turned into the hippie-killing, reactionary *Joe*. It's possible that working-class lives had become for the American public a preserve of spontaneity, violence, warmth and vulgarity – noble and ignoble savages.

Although the audience had not turned its back on the middle class, it was clearly now more willing to accept films with themes dealing with the working class. The reason for this change lies less with the films themselves than with the political, economic and social changes that the working class experienced in the previous decade. This includes a series of events that saw parts of the working class become the vanguard of the Nixon–Agnew silent majority, with the resulting change in image from strike-fomenting disrupters of the public equilibrium to upholders of the public order.

What also stimulated working-class awareness (and this goes back to the black movement of the 1950s and 1960s) was the decline of the melting-pot ideal and the rise in ethnic consciousness, often of the pop variety. So if 'Kiss me, I'm Italian, Irish, Puerto Rican, etc.' wasn't on everybody's lapel button, it did fit on the agenda of America's ethnic and racial minorities. What is more, it made them realise that even beyond assimilation they had problems with real poverty despite presumably being beneficiaries of the American Dream.

Along with this came an economic decline which made the 1950s promise that there would be more of everything, even if there wasn't going to be a real redistribution of wealth and power, a faded dream. The financial pinch of the 1970s combined with a rising awareness of ethnicity may not have promoted class consciousness among many working-class Americans, but it did bring out a feeling that the social ladder might be a lot more like a greasy pole. On one level, the sense of economic frustration and anxiety could have been the factor that induced people to accept the second chance daydreams of *Saturday Night Fever* and *Rocky*. On the other hand, for those who found it impossible to embrace the pieties of those films, others like *Blue Collar* and *F.I.S.T.* could portray the root of evil as the betrayal and perfidy of the labour movement.

In these films, the idealism that once made unarmed men and women defy armed company goons had soured and union officials had turned into fat cats lolling around hotel poolsides who were quite willing and able to put the muscle on their own members. Union corruption thus became the catch-all for what went wrong with the dream.

However, as one watches films like *Blue Collar* and *F.I.S.T.* one increasingly gets the feeling of images drawn from 1930s Warners social melodrama, harnessed to the ideology of the 1950s, and used to explain the malaise of the 1970s. Perhaps the most revealing evidence of that is the way both of these films have been compared by reviewers to *On the Waterfront*. Vincent Canby, the film critic of the *New York Times*, called *Blue Collar* 'a poor man's *On the Waterfront*', and the reviewer for the *Wall Street Journal* said that 'one gets the sneaky suspicion that had there not been an *On the Waterfront* there might not have been a

Sylvester Stallone'. In *On the Waterfront* the theme of union corruption was used in part as a rationalisation for both liberal anti-communism and an implicit anti-populism. Squealing was okay as long as it exposed evil (a reference to friendly witnesses before HUAC like Kazan); and the working class needed charismatic leaders like Terry Malloy (Marlon Brando) since they themselves didn't have the courage or cohesion to initiate action against 'the boss'. But, for the 1970s, it seems totally lame to explain working-class anxiety and resentment by the existence of union corruption. For instance, the racism that eventually divides the workers in *Blue Collar* and the alienation they feel on the job cannot be pinned on union graft, nor can the decline of the idealism that once motivated labour unions be made a function of the Mafia's ominous presence.

In depicting the moral decline of a militant union organiser, Johnny Kovak–Jimmy Hoffa (Sylvester Stallone), *F.I.S.T.* places most of the onus on union corruption, though unconsciously suggesting that there may be more complex reasons for the loss of working class idealism. The first half of the film invokes the pop myth of a soft-focused, sepia-toned 1930s (the film's imagery is static and theatrical, lacking in both vitality and some sign of a directorial sensibility), where workers are hungry, fearful and comradely. The workers' leader, Kovak, supposedly has all the virtues of a 'people's hero' – courage, integrity and charisma. However, Stallone's mumbling, Rocky-like affability conveys neither charisma nor the tough, calculating ambition of his model, Jimmy Hoffa. What we get is a cocky slum kid with a heart of gold, who merely stumbles into an alliance with organised crime.

There is a scene early on in the film which prefigures Kovak's decline from 'people's hero' to union boss. When Johnny Kovak calls a spontaneous work stoppage, the men huddle democratically to decide on the management's offer. However, it's almost the last gasp of participatory democracy, for Johnny becomes a union organiser, and success and power replace solidarity and justice as ideas to live by.

One doesn't have to be an anarcho-syndicalist (preaching doctrines of anti-bureaucratisation and spontaneous class war at the work place) to get the idea that Johnny and the union movement lost out not when he sells out to organised crime, but when he stops consulting the men and starts representing the union, an organisation whose only ideals are higher wages and better working conditions. Perhaps it's this commitment to business unionism that is the snare and the delusion, rather than the dallying with criminals. In fact, the movie later shows us it is not so much Stallone's physical presence, or the clout of his three million plus union membership, or for that matter his Mafia ties, that wither management bosses in negotiations as much as Johnny's sneering 'I thought you were good businessmen'. He then goes on to make a deal sacrificing the right to strike in return for an eight per cent rise. The union has finally achieved its goal – it has become a corporation.

Moreover, the film also tells us that the union members are just as cynical as Johnny. They cheer him lustily whenever he's in sight, and, in a bad imitation of runner John Carlos at the Mexico City Olympics, give the *F.I.S.T.* salute. Johnny may be a robber baron, but he's their robber baron. Finally, to make the cycle complete, there is a crusading, headline-hunting, power-seeking US Senator, played by Rod Steiger, who rounds out a world of cynicism epitomised by Johnny's comment 'Ain't nobody clean'. And since there is nobody who is pure, with the possible exception of Johnny's old friend, the increasingly ineffectual Abe Belkin (David Huffman), it seems that the best place to point the finger of guilt is at the union movement.

The same bleak, pessimistic picture is repeated in *Blue Collar*. The film succeeds in capturing some of the oppression and alienation of the assembly-line – a goading, abusive foreman, deafening sound and pounding pace and rhythm. It also tells us that our consumer culture is a product of exhausting, dehumanising work, and not a gift delivered from the heavens. However, it fails to evoke the social and psychological texture of the workplace – a real feeling for how blacks and whites interact and any sense of workers who are any more individuated and complex than easily recognisable social types. Schrader does provide us with a witty and insightful portrait of an apathetic, complacent union meeting. In that scene, the petulant and manic Zeke (Richard Pryor, whose routines sometimes interrupt the film's narrative and emotional flow) provides an analysis that perceives the plant as 'just short for plantation' and then, without really being able to articulate his rage, falls back on the demand that the union should do something about his broken locker. For a moment, Zeke has a real perception into the nature of capitalism. However, instead of allowing it to provide him with real historical or even self-knowledge, he indulges in what novelist Henry Miller, the so-called 'minnesinger of the lumpen proletariat', has called the 'I don't want it when I'm dead, I want it now' attitude of the working class.

Nevertheless, instead of pursuing this insight – the fact that forty per cent of all auto workers are now aged under thirty and will not accept the same facts of work-life as the Depression generation that built the union – or even taking on the real issues of the sources of alienation and racism, *Blue Collar* shifts gears and lays the blame on the union. As a matter of fact, after Pryor and his two friends rob their union, it is the union that becomes the ultimate source of terror and coercion. This prompts the smartest of the three, Smokey (Yaphet Kotto), to invoke the Brechtian 'Everything *they* do – the way *they* pit the lifer against the new boy, the old against the young, the black against the white – is meant to keep us in our places' (emphasis ours).

Of course, by this time, after trying to scare Jerry (Harvey Keitel), killing Smokey and bribing Zeke with a shop steward's job, 'they' is clearly the union. In case there are any doubts as to who could possibly comprise the unholy 'they', both the company and the government have been left off the hook. In fact, a company rep who mediates a three-way conflict involving Zeke seems positively benevolent, as does an FBI man. *Blue Collar* has finally found a replacement for the Mafia as Hollywood's prime bogeyman: the United Automobile Workers.

Certainly there is nothing wrong with portraying union corruption, as indeed some unions have been and are corrupt. However the UAW has been in the American context one of the more democratic unions, with hundreds of caucuses and rank-and-file organisations which can send delegates to conventions without getting shot. The UAW is also the union that in the 1940s, in the name of social unity, broke the wildcat strikes that its white workers initiated to prevent the hiring of blacks. There is also something wrong with making corruption the central cause of what may have gone wrong with the unions, and ultimately why the American Dream has turned sour for so many workers. What is even more insidious is that films like *Blue Collar* and *F.I.S.T.* give hints that they might truly know what went wrong and where some of the skeletons are hidden. However, instead of working this insight through, they raise the issues as window-dressing and then sidestep them altogether in favour of easy solutions and melodramatic formulas. The films never work through the idea that the racketeering may be a natural consequence of a union movement permeated with no more elevated a vision than economism, or that the capitalist ethos has shaped and dominated the character and consciousness of American unions and the working class.

What is even more spurious is that when Hollywood gives us some of the other reasons for the disintegration of the Dream-alienating dead-end jobs, decaying neighbourhoods, oppressive family life and a culture built primarily on manufactured pop fantasies – it is always with a second chance tacked on. *Rocky* is the most striking and exhilarating of the second-chance films. The saintly pug, Rocky, has his moment of consciousness: a despairing sense of life going nowhere as either a boxer or an errand boy for a loan shark; but the film allows him magically to transcend it. For Rocky is allowed to cheat his fate and dispense with his loser's image. He finds a girl to love and some fairy godfathers in the form of Bicentennial merchandisers who package his Dionysian struggle against the heavyweight champion Apollo Creed. Rocky is a modern-day Horatio Alger who tells us the Dream is still there, if only you are kind, generous and hard-working.

Saturday Night Fever also offers the second chance. Tony Manero (John Travolta) is the lustily applauded and adulated king of the local disco, but his dancing is unable to lead him out of his Bay Ridge wasteland. Tony's world consists of a mother and father who feed his self-hatred and continually whack and shout at each other; a soiled-priest brother, who is off to live his own, secular life; a pill-popping, gang-banging, oafish group of friends; and a job without a future as a clerk in a hardware store.

There are suggestions that the film genuinely understands both Tony and the significance of social class. There are close-ups of an alienated Tony who is tired of his friends' empty ranking rituals and talk of big cars, 'spics' and gays. Tony is more sensitive, decent and perceptive than his friends, but Travolta avoids turning him into another saintly Rocky. He beautifully catches the mixture of Tony's crude street humour, macho posturing and self-absorption (he can use and dismiss friends without much consciousness of their existence) with his embarrassed awkwardness and blatant insecurity. And the film does convey the profound sense of inadequacy working-class people feel when they enter or relate to the world of upper-middle-class power and culture.

Though *Saturday Night Fever* is on the surface an exploitative and commercial film, it suggestively evokes (without much development) working-class sexism, frustration and rage, and how working-class people can be intimidated by the cultural allusions and rituals (e.g. Shakespeare and ordering in posh restaurants) which are part of the cultural baggage of the upper middle class. The coffee-shop scene between Karen Gorney (Stephanie Mangano) and John Travolta (Tony Manero) goes beyond viewing their relationship solely in terms of individual psychology, but conveys the suggestion that social class is an important dimension in American life. Stephanie is a working-class girl from Bay Ridge, who has uneasily picked up some of the cultural references and styles from Manhattan singles' life. She drops names (e.g. Laurence Olivier), self-consciously puts on an affected accent, and indulges in malapropisms. As she talks you can feel her tension and insecurity, but it is clear that Tony is nonplussed and overwhelmed by her. Despite her awkwardness, she is unique and distant enough to make him feel clumsy and foolish. She is somebody he can romanticise and idealise, a girl outside the narrow confines of his world who can transcend the good-girl–whore dichotomy. The other girls at the disco are treated with derision or contempt – they're either sexual objects or absurd, panting fans. However, Stephanie has that patina of 'class' and sophistication which both threatens and seduces Tony (a paradigm for the American working-class relationship to middle-class life).

The film throws in additional intimations of significance by using the symbology of the two New York bridges – the Brooklyn and the Verrazano. The Brooklyn, of course, is the old Hart Crane/Thomas Wolfe avenue of American success, possibility and power. The Verrazano has a less defined image except that its clean, beautiful, functional outlines connect two working-class communities, and its construction can be seen as a product of working-class creativity. Tony's daydreams are filled with images of the Verrazano whose beauty makes his own life seem even more meaningless than it is.

Nevertheless, most of the film prefers to keep its eyes averted from these realities, and concentrate on the dance floor where Tony's undulating energy and dynamism reign. These scenes are brilliantly executed, the camera dollying, zooming and panning from every angle, with multi-coloured filters and flashing lights capturing the electricity of the whole scene. And the film offers only one way out for Tony – flight from his destructive neighbourhood and a relationship with Stephanie. She is a frail reed to hang one's hopes on, but it is Stephanie who provides a second chance – the repudiation of one's class for upward mobility and supposedly a more humane existence in Manhattan.

Unlike *Blue Collar* and *F.I.S.T.*, which sidestep issues, find convenient scapegoats, or just lapse into despair, *Rocky* and *Saturday Night Fever* are determined to hang on to their Dream, no matter what. Needless to say, it is sheer will power that does it. But while this tenacity might be commendable, it ignores reality. There are bleak realities inherent in working-class life that cannot be wished away or ignored. It is as if the film industry, forced to go beyond television's portrayal of the working class as a stereotypical mumble and leather jacket, is still trying to keep the lid on Pandora's Box. But it remains to be seen how long real attitudes and emotional states like sexism, racism and alienation, and institutions like the family, the neighbourhood, the workplace, the church and friends can be straightjacketed by old Hollywood conventions. For the old melodramatic formulas (e.g. the robbery in *Blue Collar*), clichés (e.g. the gang war in *Saturday Night Fever*) and images straight out of 1930s Warner Brothers (e.g. the workers picturesquely singing on the steps in *F.I.S.T.*) have not been dispensed with.

The same unwillingness to confront the realities of working-class life can be seen in Michael Cimino's *The Deer Hunter*. The central figures in this epic are three young steelworkers, who go unhesitatingly off to fight in Vietnam, only to return physically or spiritually maimed or dead. These are men who are linked to each other and to their ethnic community not by words or ideology but by a number of visible and invisible strands of ritual and memory.

Cimino is in love with ritual and turns every experience, both mundane and grand, from rock songs to Russian roulette, into an elaborate ceremony. The food and beer fights, the bowling and drinking, and the impromptu drag races — activities which contain both adolescent and male chauvinist elements — are treated without condescension or criticism. Cimino is more interested in exaltation than in analysis — more concerned with evolving stunning images, of a warm, working-class community and the rich texture of its ritual, than in illuminating the social structure and culture of that world. In fact, his major characters barely have any familial relationships, existing more as ritual participants and working-class aristocrats (Robert de Niro as the taciturn, romantic, heroic deer hunter) than as actual members of a community.

Cimino's steel mill and factory town are in beautiful harmony with his vision. The steel mill is neither a monstrous pollutor of a virginal landscape nor a 'dark satanic mill' filled with alienated or resentful workers. It is elegantly outlined and framed in long shots, a stark monolith, night and day billowing aesthetically shaped smoke into the sky. The interior of the factory is enveloped in powerful furnace flame and sweating, sooty workers labour there with gusto and even pleasure. There is no union militancy or job resentment tarnishing this idyllic work situation. The night lights of the town seductively beckon, a home about which the film's protagonists express no criticism or ambivalence. As the camera tracks the streets, you get a closer look at a town devoid of grace or grandeur, but resonating with communal intactness and camaraderie.

In *The Deer Hunter*, Cimino is paying homage to a traditional working-class life, an ethic that may have existed only in myth and nostalgia. It's a life without dissatisfaction, anger or restlessness – a working class that has no hunger for success or mobility but is totally satisfied and complacent about both the virtues and limitations of life. The apotheosis of Cimino's homage to traditional working-class life is the ethnic wedding sequence. In this lovingly-detailed but overextended scene, we get a full view of the ornate, mosaic and saint-laden Russian Orthodox church and lengthy footage of the film's major characters singing, dancing and brawling. The sequence succeeds in evoking communal joy, but the camera fails to do more than convey the colour and vitality of the world – its surfaces rather than its essence. The scene tells us nothing about the structure of the community – the relationship between generations or the significance of family life.

The Deer Hunter is a film more interested in constructing powerful images and emotions than in providing a coherent vision of the working class. Cimino never tries to get an intellectual hold on the nature of his working-class community. He affirms rather than dissects their communal warmth and rituals – ceremonies which seem capable of submerging all one's private agony in their wake. His workers live in a time warp, politically unconscious and passive men and women who, except for the terrible intrusion of the Vietnam war, supposedly could have gone on forever working hard in the steel mill, drinking beer in the local saloon and for a 'high' going up to the mountains to rough-house and hunt.

Of course, Hollywood's working-class films are still commercial works which can only venture to suggest rather than illuminate the psycho-sexual, political and social depths of working-class life. They are not prepared to model themselves after Italian Marxist films like Elio Petri's *The Working Class Goes to Heaven* (1971) or German films like Fassbinder's *Fear Eats the Soul* (1973), which powerfully and dialectically evoke the way in which working-class alienation, resentment and racism is shaped by and helps shape the capitalist ethos.

Nor are they willing to emulate the more polemical left-wing films from the American independent cinema, like *Harlan County, USA* (1976) and *Union Maids* (1976), which show men and women whose idealism and commitment remain strong after years of struggle and defeat. And though these films tend to simplify reality (edging towards the creation of counter stereotypes and mythology), they do show a working class with a culture and identity that is both alive and able to fight its own battles without organised crime or charismatic heroes to aid them. These workers still believe in a dream, one that stresses collective decency, democracy and egalitarianism. Their ideology may be vague, but their *praxis* is strong.

Of course, one could ask if these exemplary souls are the real working class, or are the boys at the disco more authentic and representative? We suspect neither set of images tells the whole story. The working class is a complex phenomenon, rife with diversity, contradiction and historical ironies. However, one is fearful that in Hollywood's taking up with the working class, it will merely do, on a larger budget, what black exploitation films did for black life – use, abuse and betray. Certainly, if nothing more than a *F.I.S.T.* is produced, we will see only an echoing of Louis-Ferdinand Céline's warning to the working class: 'I tell you little people, life's riff-raff, forever, fleeced, beaten and sweating. I warn you that when the great people of the world start loving you, it means they are going to make sausage meat of you.'

Mary Ellison

Blacks in American film

In the black past things are rarely what they seem. Superficially slavery and segregation fulfilled their aims in that they did enslave and segregate, but at a deeper level they failed to crush the spirit of black independence or the dynamics of black culture. Indeed it was this very separation of the races that fostered the development of a black cultural identity that had its roots in Africa but drew its sustenance and acquired characteristics from the American soil and air. The strength of this culture manifested itself most clearly in a music that proved especially black and specifically American. One of the special features of this music was that it expressed more honestly than words alone the reactions of black Americans to the world within and around them. It was so powerful a sound that it invaded the world of white Americans and made them aware that blacks had something of irresistible value to offer. This music was absorbed into the fabric of American life and became one of the two original cultural contributions America has made to the world. Film was the other great art form to emerge from the experience of the United States, but here blacks were rarely initiators. Rather they were for the most part misrepresented subjects to be exploited by the new medium. Whereas music sometimes seemed to forecast, or promote shifts in political and social attitudes, film has mainly just reflected existing convictions about race. It has appeared necessary for change first to take place within the political system or society at large so that the screen can then act as a mirror. At times the screen has predicated against progress by fixing certain concepts and stereotypes in the public mind and artificially reinforcing the notion of their continuing usefulness. Time can stand still in a movie. I. C. Jarvie has put it succinctly: 'Films not only reflect society in its own image, they can cause society to create itself in the image of the films.'[1]

There is little doubt that films can influence the way in which an individual structures his world.[2] It is the kind and quality of the influence which can be disturbing since, as Hortense Powdermaker has said: 'Movies have a surface realism which tends to disguise fantasy and make it seem true.'[3] Sadly, it is both genuine realism and creative fantasy that the depiction of blacks in film has too often ignored. The superficial stereotypes that had begun in the era of staged blackface were continued into motion pictures.[4] More unreal characters were added and they were put in either unbelievable or segregated situations. Yet just as blacks had not only survived slavery but had carried out of it a vital and vibrant culture, they began to transform unpromising film situations into cinematic gold. It is a dramatic understatement to say that it was unfortunate that the first film to show that the motion picture could be great art was also undeniably racist. Such black stereotypes as shuffling Sambos, tragic mulattoes, available wenches and stoic mammies had already been smeared across the screen, but here these and even more dangerous false images were frozen into 'the frame of the greatest film then made'. D. W. Griffiths's *Birth of a Nation* (1915) has become the earliest movie 'which critics could now agree to discuss without patronage or condescension'.[5] At the same time, Griffiths purveyed the deepest of racist fears and obsessions with the utmost skill. His revolutionary style was oddly mated with the most conservative of societal views. His reactionary Southern view of Reconstruction is strengthened by employing 'every bigoted syndrome of characterisation and imagery that had been popularised throughout the previous series of Southern romance films – only he did so more obsessively, with outstanding and venemous conviction. Here, racist myths came into full bloom.'[6] He locked misconceptions about race into a technologically innovative movie that gripped viewers with its new ability to convey the full flavour of events and feelings. His greatest disservice to American blacks was to build an unforgettable picture of the savage, stupid and selfish black.[7] To *The Chicago Defender* it was the supreme example of vicious and harmful propaganda.[8] Simultaneously it restored Southern pride and assuaged Northern guilt.[9] It became widely regarded as both a piece of cinematic genius and a politically unacceptable blow to black self-respect.[10]

Major Hollywood producers became suspicious of so contentious an area and only black film companies such as those run by Oscar Micheaux and the Noble brothers made any widespread use of black actors until the late 1920s. Most of the black-produced films did little to foster a true racial perspective: too many were simply black versions of popular white movie themes, but there were notable exceptions such as Micheaux's *Body and Soul* (1924) in which Paul Robeson made his debut and a disturbing attempt was made to deal with the problem of racial identity.

The Hollywood mistrust of using blacks in any but minor, usually servant, roles in this period did have one notable exception in the *Our Gang* series of films that began in 1918 and was to go on into the 1930s. The films recorded the comic adventures of a group of children and were unique for their time in that there seemed to be no racial bias in the roles allotted to the black children. There was an ease in the relationship of all the participants that ignored racial rules and the black children were allowed to be bright as well as funny and leaders as well as followers. Indeed *Our Gang* has been called 'one of Hollywood's few contributions to better Negro–white relations'.[11] But such tolerance was only possible where children were involved.

Far more ambivalent was the impact of the first two Hollywood all-black talking pictures. In celebration of the coming of sound, both were musicals and both were set in the rural South; both attracted contradictory critical evaluation. *Hearts in Dixie* and *Hallelujah* came out in 1929 and within a few months the black writers Sterling Brown and Alain Locke had decided that '*Hearts in Dixie* is the truest pictorialisation of Negro life to date'. They glow with enthusiasm over Clarence Muse's humour and pathos, Stepin Fetchit's true and 'vital projection of the folk manner', and 'thrilling glimpses of the folk spirit'.

They have no such accolades for *Hallelujah*. Only the singing 'is so good that it makes one reflect rather bitterly on the forfeited possibilities of the whole picture'.[12] Modern writers have often reversed the judgements, calling *Hearts in Dixie* stereotyped, 'trite' and 'condescending', and *Hallelujah* a successful demonstration of sophisticated techniques being applied, by King Vidor, to viable racial imagery.[13] Despite a considerable number of brilliant performances in both films, the character that was to endure and be repeated endlessly was that of the lethargic, shiftless Gummy played by Stepin Fetchit in *Hearts in Dixie*:

To militant first sight, Stepin Fetchit's routines – all cringe and excessive devotion – seem racially self-destructive in the rankest way, and his very name can be a term of abuse. And yet, in looking at his performances . . . cooler second sight must admit that Stepin Fetchit was an artist, and that his art consisted precisely in mocking and caricaturing the white man's vision of the black; his sly contortions, his surly and exaggerated subservience can now be seen as a secret weapon in the long racial struggle.[14]

In quite a different way, a female stereotype was to be lifted into the realms of great performances by that most inimitable of blues singers, Bessie Smith. In 1929 she made a short film with an adequate, hackneyed story in which she was yet another black woman wronged by a double-dealing man. Her brilliance imbued the film with magic as she sang the anguish and loneliness of rejection. She expressed not just her own misery but the distilled essence of all black pain. 'The film swayed and resounded to her great ache. She remains as well the most sensual woman ever to have been turned loose in an American movie.'[15]

She belonged to an era when there was an explosion of black literary skill pouring out from the pens of writers such as Langston Hughes, Claude McKay and Jean Toomer, but their stories were not put on film. She was a contemporary of black orators and political spokesmen like W. E. B. DuBois and Marcus Garvey; but their speeches were too advanced for the screen at that time. They did not fit the stereotypes. A decade later black actors and actresses were still having to be content with making either the most or a mockery of the stereotypes they were given to play. In 1939 Hattie McDaniel won the Academy Award for best supporting actress for her role in *Gone with the Wind*, an indubitably racist film that was redeemed somewhat for blacks by the 'self-righteous grandeur' and total lack of any sense of inferiority that she brought to the part. She was supposed to be a typical mammy but she and other supporting actors such as Eddie 'Rochester' Anderson, Mantan Moreland, Bill Robinson and Louise Beavers played their types but played against them in film after film.[16] 'They built and molded themselves into what film critic Andrew Sarris might call nondirectorial *auteurs*. With their own brand of outrageousness the blacks created comic worlds all their own in which the servant often outshone the master.'[17] Singers, dancers and musicians were often deprived of the chance of twisting a stereotype when they were slotted into films where their roles were not crucial and could be cut out for screenings to Southern audiences. Only in all-black musicals such as *Cabin in the Sky* (1943) and *Stormy Weather* (1943) would black artists be sure that their contributions could not be tactfully dispensed with. Here their consummate artistry was celebrated as a tribute to the primitivism which had acquired a fashionable appeal. Both films were sentimental and naive and employed almost every existing black stereotype but had an enormous vitality and style.[18] Once again black talent had transformed its medium. *Stormy Weather* was almost the life story of Bill 'Bojangles' Robinson. He had had years of training in films such as *The Littlest Rebel* (1936) in twisting his material until he had a firm grip on it. He stormed through the musical and was aided by Lena Horne and musicians such as Cab Calloway in creating a film that was memorable for the quality of the performances and the music rather than the content of the story. Yet such quality in films as successful as *Stormy Weather* and *Cabin in the Sky* did not guarantee future employment in the cinema. Lena Horne starred in both but despite her scintillating acting she, with her unacceptably light skin, found herself only 'pasted to a pillar to sing my song'.[19]

Lena Horne was one of the few black Hollywood actors or actresses who openly complained about the treatment they received. Paul Robeson had been almost the only other active black protestor who had earned star status in the public eye and he too, with a few exceptions such as *Emperor Jones* (1933), had found it difficult to get parts suited to his talents. It was from a sense of outrage rather than from any political commitment that Lena Horne made an outspoken statement in 1943 that perfectly summed up black cinematic needs: 'All we ask is that the Negro be portrayed as a normal person. Let's see the Negro as a worker at union meetings, as a voter at the polls, as a civil service worker or elected official.'[20] The essential reasonableness of this plea was, of course, muted by the very simple fact that many blacks were still in reality unable to get jobs on equal terms, unable to join unions, unable to vote or become an elected official. It was only a few years since Philip Randolph had begun to pave the way for the era of non-violent direct action when he threatened in 1941 to lead a march of a hundred thousand blacks on Washington seeking job equality. The Fair Employment Practices Commission, set up to avert the march, hardly affected the general pattern of employment discrimination. To have seen a black elected official on the screen would have seemed a reflection of an almost bizarre fantasy. Even in the North, black Congressional representation was given only token symbolism by Adam Clayton Powell and there were to be no black mayors until 1968. In the South there were no elected officials or Congressional representatives who were black and most blacks were debarred from voting at all by one devious ploy or another. This political impotence was a symptom and effect of the economic and social stranglehold that white Southerners had put on the ex-slaves during the Reconstruction period. The arm of oppression was not to be lifted in any perceptible way until it was raised in anger at the non-violent activists led by Martin Luther King in the 1950s and 1960s. Any aberrant films that did demonstrate a spirit of racial equality at this stage could be thought to be either ahead of their time or a reflection of the more liberal feelings that did exist in parts of America.

Stereotypes were abandoned in one of the best films of the 1940s, *The Ox-Bow Incident* (1943).[21] Here it is a black man, Sparks, who is the voice of reason and compassion during a lynching.[22] Sparks has been called a 'silent, grieving witness to the abomination, the rustic Christian conscience who accepts sin in man, but who in the pacific strength of his own piety, can do little more than pray for the victims . . . he has gone by choice to act as the mob's conscience . . .'[23] Leigh Whipper portrays Sparks not as a grinning or shuffling Uncle Tom but as a sincerely moral man whose quiet dignity exposes the senselessness of unjust violence.[24]

A few films made in the same decade struck further blows at the basis of discrimination. *The Quiet One* (1948) shows black youths as intelligent and sensitive; it is their environment rather than the boys themselves that is seen to be inadequate and it becomes a human rather than a black problem.[25] A year later *Intruder in the Dust* (1949) appeared as 'not only one of the best films of the year but one of the most significant films on a racial theme to come out of Hollywood.'[26] It made two crucial statements when it demonstrated that there was no inherent justice for a black man in the South and when it portrayed a black man capable of invincible dignity. Juano Hernandez gave a fine and commanding performance and made the personality he conveyed far more significant than the way in which he was saved from a lynch mob, or the gallows, by the actions of an old lady and a boy.

The next decade opened with a film that signified as much for Northern blacks as *Intruder in the Dust* did for those in the South. *No Way Out* (1950) marked the debut of Sidney Poitier and also of the notion that blacks could attain excellence in America's most respected professions – basically a continuation into film of the idea originally expounded by the black political writer W. E. B. DuBois that a talented tenth of blacks could prove that black Americans deserved political and social equality. In *No Way Out* Poitier plays a young and brilliant doctor who is the vindicated victim of racist attacks by a psychotic white criminal. The film also showed that race riots would be the likely outcome of unchecked racial discrimination. He himself eschews violence however aggressive the provocation: he is the ideal herald of the era of non-violent black activism. Poitier was to carry on playing strong, talented, intelligent and compassionate men for the rest of the decade in films as different as *Blackboard Jungle* (1955), and *A Man is Ten Feet Tall*, also known as *Edge of the City* (1957), where his nobility led to his death.[27] In 1958 in *The Defiant Ones* black audiences thought that the character played by Poitier took compassion too far when he allows friendship for the white convict he escaped with to destroy his chance of freedom. Yet in this he was stating what he believed to be an American truth – that the future of black Americans was inextricably interwoven with that of its whites, and a way of living together on equal and integrated terms had to be found. The message of *Odds Against Tomorrow* (1959) a contemporaneous Harry Belafonte movie, was even stronger in that it clearly suggested that racial prejudice would lead to explosive violence and mutual destruction.

This faith in integration did not, however, go to its logical conclusion and condone interracial marriages. Female mulattoes in films such as *Pinky* (1949), *Carmen Jones* (1954) and the Douglas Sirk remake of *Imitation of Life* (1959) are still tragically disorientated and unhappy and any suggestion of impending interracial union soon meets a doomed end in *Pinky* and *Island in the Sun* (1957).[28] Even John Cassavetes's *Shadows* (1960), though subtle and beautiful, sees only pain for the light-skinned mulatto mixing sexually with whites. Not until the 1960s could a film like *One Potato, Two Potato* (1964) be made with an honest and moving unfolding of the realities of a fully developed black–white marriage and this, too, has to be soured by the legal decision to take the woman's white children away from their mother solely because she is married to a black man.

An allegorical use of the Western was often seen as a safer theme. In the mythical untamed West of so many frontier movies, the red and the black have long been taken to symbolise savage and alien threats to the encroaching white civilisation. The immutable social order reflected in the average Western has been splendidly described in a short story by Ted Poston. In 'Pat Joiner routs the clan' he reconstructs the fantasies that the black children of Hopkinsville, Kentucky weave around Buffalo Pete, the only black cowboy they have ever seen on the screen. He was to them a hero through their own hopes and anticipations rather than his incredible adventures on the screen because as one cynical boy observed one day: 'They don't never let him kill none of them white mens, no matter how evil they is. Oh yeah, they let him knock off a Indian every now and then. But only Bronco Billy kills them white bad mens.'[29] As Tonto is to the Lone Ranger, Buffalo Pete is nothing more than a faithful sidekick to the white hero, Bronco Billy. Progress has been made by the 1960s with John Ford's *Sergeant Rutledge* (1960) in that it presents a black man, played superbly by Woody Strode, as a fully developed personality. Ford in this film attacks the rampant and insidious racism that predisposes men who respected Rutledge as an individual to assume that his colour makes him capable of rape and murder. After the vindicating trial, his pride and his humanity are intact and the racism of his friends has been explored and, in some cases, undermined. Ford is attempting here to win his credentials as a supporter of civil rights. The whites are shown in the unflattering reflection of their racism and only the misjudged black is presented as truly honourable and selfless. In *Sergeant Rutledge*, Ford understands that racism is based on irrational fears that spring most of all from feelings of insecurity or confusion about sex. He dealt in other films with white reaction to sex between Indians and whites but is fully aware that 'it is far more potentially explosive to deal with the sexual nature of racism with regard to blacks than Indians'. The film basically attempts to show that a black hero can rise above sexual impulses and be stronger, braver and better than white men. In this it succeeds.[30] It is a film that is 'highly influenced by the civil rights milieu'.[31]

The neglect that the cinema had once bestowed on the role of black soldiers in winning the West and fighting the Indians is again redressed, but with far less style, in *Rio Conchos* (1964). This time it is Jim Brown who plays an army sergeant who is chasing Apaches. The most interesting aspect of this essentially weak film is that Brown, as Sergeant Franklyn, regards himself as far more humane than the Apaches and is very insistent that there should be no retaliation for brutality endured at the hands of the Indians.[32] Brown is a fair and high minded sheriff in *100 Rifles* (1969) and he gets Raquel Welch, but only at the cost of her being an Indian and dying. In both films it is a black man who again personifies the conscience of the West. In *Duel at Diablo* (1966) the

Apaches are this time hounded by an ex-cavalry sergeant who, as a black man, has considerable sympathy for the deceived and ill-treated Indians but still feels that he has to come to the aid of the army which protects the settlers against their hostility. Sidney Poitier plays Toller as an aloof, mysterious, and very independent dandy whose sophistication goes far beyond his clothes. Toller left the army in order to be able to exercise his freedom and individuality as a successful horse trader who gives rather than takes orders. The aid that he gives to the army in their confrontation with the Apaches is crucial because he is more sensitive both to the likely actions of the Indians and to the needs of the moment; he is also resourceful, intelligent and a good shot.

A better film on a related theme is *The Scalphunters* (1968) in which Ossie Davis plays Joseph Winfield Lee, a fugitive slave who has been captured first by some Indians and traded with a white trapper, Joe Bass (Burt Lancaster). Lee may be a slave but he is in no way servile. Rather is he clearly intelligent, forceful, spirited and opinionated, using his talents to try and persuade Bass to give him his freedom, and the two men jostle for dominance until by the end of the film they have established mutual dependence and respect. Sidney Pollack here mixes excitement with comedy and effectively reverses conventional situations. "Ossie Davis does not play a Western hero who happens to have black skin. He is not what we expect of a hero and the fact that he is black is pointedly emphasised.[33]

Buck and the Preacher (1972) is a black Western about a group of ex-slaves fleeing from Southern peonage in the wake of the Civil War and has Indians giving invaluable support to the blacks in defeating the evil whites who are attempting to drag them back South for use as cheap labour. This tense and witty film starred Ruby Dee, Harry Belafonte and Sidney Poitier, who also directed it, and the production team was made up of an unusually large percentage of black as well as some Indian technicians. Wit is also the strength of *Blazing Saddles* (1974). Mel Brooks directs Cleavon Little as a modern black hipster sherrif taking all his audiences for a ride.

Meanwhile, back in more accustomed settings, blacks in the cinema did clearly benefit from the civil rights activities and legislation of the 1960s and 1970s. Shirley Clarke's *Cool World* (1963) reflected without distortion the street ethos of young people in Harlem, and Ossie Davis' *Gone are the Days* (1963) satirised the black past with humour and dignity. *Nothing But a Man* (1964) was a film filled with hope for the future and brought alive by an inspired performance from Ivan Dixon; it was an 'heroic affirmation . . . by two people bent on making it, even with the baggage of stark deprivation with which they were encumbered'.[34] Poitier appeared to be coasting on the path he had already forged but there was a new 'subtlety and understanding' in the improvised visual and intonational ironies he brought to both *Lilies of the Field* (1964) for which he won an Oscar, and *In the Heat of the Night* (1967) where he is supercool and flaunts his intellectual superiority.[35] He is nobody's 'nigger' now. In *The Lost Man* (1969) Poitier actually risks and gets a failure when he embraces the causes of revolutionary change and interacial sex on film. With films such as this and *Uptight* (1968), where the choices for blacks were shown to be violent resistance or oppression, Andrew Sarris commented that now, at last, 'movies seemed to become more attuned to black ghetto audiences'.[36]

As the 1960s blended into the 1970s it is actually quite possible to say that more progress was made by blacks in the film industry than in real life. Genuine advances in black life were disappointingly small. There had certainly been a sudden upsurge in civil rights legislation, in the number of black elected officials and political representatives, but these could do surprisingly little to improve the lot of the black masses. Certainly more Southern black children now went to school with white children but economic deprivation had actually grown comparatively worse and blatant tokenism was seen as a substitute for genuine equality. At least on film there was an increasing tendency to show the true depth and breadth of black life, a tendency that should not be shrouded by the heavy cloud of blaxploitation movies that settled over the industry. 'One thing black cinema can achieve and is already achieving is the neutralisation of stereotypes.'[37]

Gordon Parks's career as a black Hollywood director may be best remembered for *Shaft* (1971), but his first film – and it was also the first for any black director in Hollywood – was his own warm and beautifully-filmed autobiography, *The Learning Tree* (1969). Ossie Davis, who directed the funny and fresh, if exaggerated, *Cotton Comes to Harlem*, also made the movingly realistic and painfully honest *Black Girl* (1972). Davis himself said about *Black Girl*: 'it is a serious film about a Black family for those who want some real information about ourselves as a way of understanding who we are and to use that understanding to protect and defend ourselves as a community'.[38] The drug-pushing, criminal world of films such as *Superfly* (1972) is offset by the compassion, tenderness and resilience shown in *Sounder* (1972), where family love was shown as stronger and more enduring than white discrimination, and *Five on the Black Hand Side* (1974) where pertinent political criticism is given impact by honesty and style. Even the most outrageous film of the early 1970s had within it both blaxploitative and totally true and important elements. Melvin Van Peebles wrote, directed and starred in *Sweet Sweetback's Baadasssss Song* (1971) and projected a new image of a black hero: 'of all the ways we've been exploited by the Man', he writes 'the most damaging is the way he destroyed our self image. The message of *Sweetback* is that, if you can get it together and stand up to the Man, you can win.'[39] The film was an enormous box-office success and has been called 'profane, profound, flashy and brutally candid'.[40] It showed a fast-talking, sexually aggressive ghetto black whose immorality does not stand in the way of his developing political awareness.[41] Black Panther leader Huey Newton urged the black community to see it and see it more than once since it attempts 'to communicate some crucial ideas and motivates us to a deeper understanding and then action based on that understanding'.[42] It was no coincidence that Newton led a group that relied on a combination of ghetto self-help and resistance with revolutionary ideology and awareness.

Throughout this period the most revolutionary force in black American life had been music. Music had fostered and reinforced black pride and had been the most articulate medium for black responses and demands. Just as music was an integral and essential part of black life, it became in the 1970s the most important element in many black films. There were films that were basically concerts like *Save the Children* (1973) in which the Reverend Jesse Jackson, the leader of Operation Breadbasket and PUSH, stressed that black film-makers could go beyond producing *Shaft* and *Superfly* to put the very best of black musicianship on film with the explicit aim of trying to help provide a better future for black children. The film became a document of black talent and a testament to black hopes.[43] In other instances it was a brilliant film score that made memorable such films as *Trouble Man* (1972) with Marvin Gaye, *Across 110th Street* (1972) with Bobby Womack, *Black Caesar* (1973) with James Brown, *Willie Dynamite* (1973) with J. J. Johnson and Martha Reeves, *Tough Guys* (1974) with Isaac Hayes, *Cooley High* (1975) with a marvellous selection of Motown or *Thank God It's Friday* (1978) with Donna Summer, The Commodores and Thelma Houston.[44] Between them, Gladys Knight and Curtis Mayfield have raised an enormous number of films to the level of sensationally-delivered, socially relevant art. They collaborated on the score of *Claudine* (1974) and the accurate depiction of the struggle fought by black Americans against inordinate prejudice and poverty was immensely strengthened by songs such as 'Mr Welfare Man' and 'To be invisible'.[45] *Pipedreams* (1976) was a fine film debut by Gladys Knight, transformed into one of lyrical beauty by her own score, while *Short Eyes* (1977) in its truthful capturing of the conflict between the violence of desparation and the power of hope is given depth by Mayfield's stunning music.[46] The humour, ebullience and joy of *Carwash* (1976) were made incandescent by its shimmering score, sung by Rose Royce, and without its pleasing songs *The Wiz* (1978) would have been only a little short of a catastrophe.[47] 'As a Matter of Fact', writes black actress and essayist Ellen Holly, 'the one consistent star to emerge from "black" movies in general is Black Music. Again and again, from one film to the next, by the beat, funk, and vitality of their music the Marvin Gayes, Isaac Hayeses and Curtis Mayfields have pumped life into what would otherwise be thoroughly mediocre footage.'[48]

There was possibly some strange kind of perversity at work when it emerged that the score of *Lady Sings the Blues* (1972) was one of the less successful aspects of that film. The music was too much Billie Holliday's and the voice too little. Diana Ross proved she could act but the story she had to tell was not the reality of the greatest jazz singer America has ever produced. A more successful biopic was *Greased Lightning* (1977) in which Richard Pryor brilliantly showed how Wendell Scott won success in the most unlikely of sports against the toughest racial opposition. The significance of his triumph is emphasised by cutting at one point to newsreel of the Southern I AM A MAN campaign.[49] The year before Richard Pryor had hilariously put over the character of a jive-ass thief in *Silver Streak* (1976). Equally ridiculous were the effective parodies of both the black superstud and Cleopatra Jones stereotypes in *Kentucky Fried Movie* (1978). Here the effect was ludicrous and laughable and maybe even therapeutic. Humour is a release from tension and here could provide a way out of the confines of the stereotypes which were affecting not just the black screen image but the pattern of everyday existence. Reality was still tough enough without new false images being thrust on to already laden shoulders by the cinema.

It is almost fifteen years since Malcolm X died believing that the battle of the poor against the rich was more significant than that of black against white. Since then many prominent black nationalists have become socialists or Marxists and a fundamental change in the political, economic and social system has been sought. Race is now regarded as an oppressive way of dividing the oppressed. In films such as John Carpenter's *Assault on Precinct 13* (1978) this awareness is faintly reflected. A bored teenage gang has mixed black and white membership and they kill a child and hound her father into the local precinct. The officer-in-charge is black (Austin Stoker) but this is only relevant in that he is one black who made it up out of this area into a position of authority. The film is a kind of urban Western where blacks are both Indians and symbols of white authority. In a similar way the film version of Sol Yurick's book *The Warriors* (1979) is anti-racist. Whereas the gangs in the book had clear racial components, in the film they are mixed. The Coney Island gang around which the film centres has a black leader who is killed, upon which the blacks in the group easily accept the authority of the white who succeeds him, whereas in the book the leader was white and merely gets injured. The film's most interesting moment from a political point of view comes early when Cyrus, the black leader of New York's chief gang, proposes that all the gangs, whatever their racial composition, should combine and take over the city. In the book no one takes him seriously, but in the film the incredulous silence gives way to support and affirmation. He is then shot and the possibility of harmony is ended.[50] *Blue Collar* (1978) is as clearly bound up in the class struggle but not as indelibly anti-racist. Two black workers do combine with one white to try and beat the system that sets black against white but only succeed in being bought off or destroyed by those who have power, in the form of a corrupt union, and the FBI. Despite strong performances, it is a warped, fatalistic film in which the Marxist conclusion seems false — 'It's a class struggle picture thought up in a fancy office, or maybe beside some Beverley Hills swimming pool.'[51]

It can be claimed that the failure to portray real black men and women on the screen has begun to be rectified now that full citizenship has become an actuality rather than a legal artifice. But the failure still exists. John Killens has exaggeratedly accused Hollywood of 'creating the image of black inferiority' and 'of being the most anti-negro influence in this nation in the 20th century'.[52] Jim Brown has recently and bitterly echoed this: 'Hollywood is the way it is in Mississippi. We've retreated to a new plantation.'[53] It has been suggested that 'Putting the image of black Americans into the hands of other Americans is like asking management to paint a flattering portrait of workers on strike'.[54] Yet not all black film-makers have been innocent of exploitation and distortion and many of the least racist films have been made by whites. Nevertheless, it is essential that black film-makers be given the scope to express the ideas they wish to convey and that the image of black people should be projected with truth and insight, whether it is done by black or by white directors. New stereotypes have gone on replacing the old ones for quite long enough and among these shadows there have been enough glimmerings of real characters in genuine situations for there to be hope for change. Hollywood is gradually becoming more sensitive to social and political change.[55] It is even possible to conceive of an imaginative, experimental art-form thrusting ahead of the grindingly slow machinery of government. It is certainly feasible to believe that a committed and brilliant film director could perceive a more productive way of looking at race than many a trammelled politician would be capable of. The cinema could throw into relief the true political choices that seem to face black Americans. While no film could positively demonstrate whether full absorption into the political mainstream is likely or if it would provide greater opportunities than some form of revolutionary change, such questions could be tested on the screen more fully than has happened so far. Film is a medium of enormous potency, and some of its strength and energy might yet push forward the cause of black equality. Entertainment may be the basic aim of the cinema but there need be no conflict between truth and entertainment.

Notes

1   I. C. Jarvie, *Towards a Sociology of the Cinema: a Comparative Essay on the Structure and Functioning of a Major Entertainment Industry* (London, 1970), p. 197.

2   F. Fearing, 'Influence of the Movies on Attitudes and Behaviour', *Annals of the American Academy of Political and Social Science*, (1947), pp. 70–9.

3   Hortense Powdermaker, *Hollywood: the Dream Factory* (Boston, Mass., 1950), p. 14.

4   Thomas Cripps, 'The Movie Jew as an Image of Assimilation, 1903–27', *Journal of Popular Film*, vol. IV, No. 3 (1975), p. 195.

5   V. F. Perkins, *Film as Film: Understanding and Judging Movies* (Harmondsworth, 1972), p. 10.

6   Jim Pines, *Blacks in Films: a Survey of Racial Themes and Images in the American Film* (London, 1975), pp. 11–12.

7   Jack Temple Kirby, 'D. W. Griffith's Racial Portraiture', *Phylon*, vol. XXXIX, No. 2 (summer 1978).

8   Edward Mapp, *Blacks in American Films: Today and Yesterday* (Metuchen, New York, 1972), p. 19.

9   Donald Bogle, *Toms, Coons, Mulattoes, Mammies & Bucks: an Interpretive History of Blacks in American Films* (New York, 1973), p. 20.

10 Paul O'Dell, *Griffith and the Rise of Hollywood* (New York, 1970), p. 11; Lewis Jacobs, *The Rise of American Film* (New York, 1939), p. 177.

11 Lawrence Reddick, 'Of Motion Pictures', in *Black Films and Filmmakers*, ed. Lindsay Patterson (New York, 1975), p. 9.

12 Alain Locke and Sterling A. Brown, 'Folk Values in a New Medium', in *Black Films and Filmmakers*, pp. 26–8.

13 Pines, *Blacks in Films*, pp. 22–7; Daniel J. Leab, *From Sambo to Superspade: the Black Experience in Motion Pictures* (London, 1975), p. 86; Lee Edward Stern, *The Movie Musical: a Pyramid Illustrated History of the Movies* (New York, 1974), pp. 27–8; King Vidor, *A Tree is a Tree* (London, 1954), pp. 119–28.

14 Joseph McBride, 'Stepin Fetchit Talks Back', *Film Quarterly*, vol. XXIV, No. 4 (summer 1971), p. 20; see also Robert Benchley, 'Hearts in Dixie', in *Black Films and Filmmakers*, p. 85, and Eileen Landay, *Black Film Stars* (New York, 1973), p. 43.

15 Bogle, *Toms, Coons, Mulattoes, Mammies & Bucks*, p. 45.

16 Alex Barris, *Hollywood's Other Women* (New York, 1975), p. 164.

17 Lawrence Reddick, 'Of Motion Pictures', p. 17; Bogle, *Toms, Coons, Mulattoes, Mammies and Bucks*, pp. 125, 49.

18 Bosley Crowther, 'Cleaving the color line', in *The Black Man on Film: Racial Stereotyping*, ed. Richard A. Maynard (Rochelle Park, N.J., 1974), p. 56.

19 Lena Horne and Richard Schickel, *Lena* (London, 1966), p. 140.

20 Lawrence Reddick, 'Of Motion Pictures', p. 23n.

21 David M. White and Richard Averson, *The Celluloid Weapon: Social Comment in American Film* (Boston, Mass., 1972), p. 99.

22 George Bluestone, *Novels in Film* (Baltimore, Md., 1957), p. 195.

23 Bluestone, *Novels in Film*, pp. 171–8.

24 Pines, *Blacks in Films*, pp. 60–1.

25 Walter Rosenblum, '*The Quiet One*: a Milestone', in *The Documentary Tradition: From Nanook to Woodstock*, ed. Lewis Jacobs (New York, 1971), p. 245.

26 Gary Null, *Black Hollywood: the Negro in Motion Pictures* (Secausus, N.J., 1975), p. 126.

27 Alvin H. Marill, *The Films of Sidney Poitier* (Secausus, N.J., 1975), pp.

20–2, 46, 72–5; Andrew Dowdy, *The Films of the Fifties* (New York, 1975), p. 143.

28 Albert Johnson, 'Beige, Brown or Black', *Film Quarterly*, vol. XIII (fall 1959), pp. 39–43; Lindsay Anderson, '*Lost Boundaries, Pinky, Home of the Brave*', *Sequence* (January 1950), pp. 179–83; Jon Halliday, *Sirk on Sirk* (London, 1971), pp. 129–30.

29 Ted Poston, 'Pat Joiner routs the clan', in *Soon, One Morning*, ed. Herbert Hill (New York, 1969), p. 380.

30 J. A. Place, *The Western Films of John Ford* (Secausus, N.J., 1974), pp. 174–196.

31 Pines, *Blacks in Films*, p. 92.

32 Mapp, *Blacks in American Films*, p. 86.

33 Jenni Calder, *There Must Be a Lone Ranger: the Myth and Reality of the American Wild West* (London, 1974), p. 36.

34 Otto Lindenmeyer, *Of Black America: Black History: Lost, Stolen or Strayed* (New York, 1970), p. 197.

35 Albert Johnson, 'The Negro in American Films: Some Recent Works', *Film Quarterly*, vol. XVIII (summer 1965), p. 17; Pearl Bowser, 'Film: History Lesson: the Boom is Really an Echo', *Black Creation*, vol. IV (winter 1973), p. 35.

36 Andrew Sarris, *Politics and Cinema* (New York, 1978), p. 191.

37 James P. Murray, *To Find an Image: Black Films From Uncle Tom to Superfly* (Indianapolis, Ind., 1973), p. 59.

38 Laura T. Hurd, 'Film: director Ossie Davis talks about *Black Girl*', *Black Creation*, vol. IV (winter 1973), p. 39.

39 Charles Peavy, 'Black Consciousness and the Contemporary Cinema', in *Popular Culture and the Expanding Consciousness*, ed. Ray Browne (New York, 1973), p. 197.

40 Horace W. Coleman, 'Melvin Van Peebles', *Journal of Popular Culture*, vol. V, No. 2 (fall 1971), p. 369.

41 Thomas Cripps, *Black Film as Genre* (Bloomington, Ind., 1978), pp. 128–40; Pauline Kael, *Reeling* (Boston, 1974), p. 62.

42 Murray, *To Find an Image*, p. 77; Pines, *Blacks in Film*, p. 122.

43 Cannonball Adderley, Sammy Davis Jr., Roberta Flack, Marvin Gaye, Gladys Knight, Curtis Mayfield, the O'Jays, Bill Withers *et al.*, *Save the Children* (Motown M800R2).

44 Marvin Gaye, *Trouble Man* (Tamla T322L); Bobby Womack, *Across 110th Street* (UAS 5225); J. J. Johnson, *Willie Dynamite* (MCA 393); James Brown, *Black Caesar* (Polydor 2490117); Isaac Hayes,

Tough Guys (ENS 7504); Diana Ross, Stevie Wonder, *et al.*, *Cooley High* (Motown STML1204); Donna Summer, *et al.*, *Thank God It's Friday* (Columbia TG1F 100).

45 Gladys Knight and the Pips, *Claudine* (BDS 5602 ST). Ellen Holly, 'Where are the Films about Real Black Men and Women', *New York Times* (2 June 1974), reprinted in *Freedomways* (third quarter 1974), p. 270.

46 Gladys Knight and the Pips, *Pipe Dreams* (BDLH 5017); Curtis Mayfield, *Short Eyes* (Custom K56430).

47 Rose Royce, *Carwash* (MCA MCSP278); Diana Ross, *et al.*, *The Wiz* (Quincy Jones MCSP 287).

48 Holly, 'Where are the Films about Real Black Men and Women', p. 271.

49 Richard Schickel, 'Vroomy movie', *Time* (15 August 1977), p. 41.

50 Sol Yurick, *The Warriors* (London, 1967), pp. 13–19, 44, 147.

51 Tom Dowling, 'The Marxist Dilemma, as Viewed at Poolside, Seen in a Straight Jacket', *Washington Star* (24 March 1978), p. B.11; Richard Combs, '*Blue Collar*', *Sight and Sound* (winter 1978–9), p. 60; Leonard Quart and Albert Auster, 'The working class Goes to Hollywood', elsewhere in this volume.

52 John O. Killens, 'Hollywood is Black and White', in *Black America's Images in Conflict*, eds. P. M. Banks and V. M. Burke (Indianapolis, Ind., 1970), p. 31.

53 Jim Brown, 'On the record', *Time* (11 June 1979), p. 45.

54 Clayton Riley quoted in Alfred E. Opubur and Adebayo Ogunbi, 'Ooga Booga: the African Image in American Films', in *Other Voices, Other Views: An International Collection of Essays for the Bicentennial*, ed. Robin Winks (Westport, Conn., 1978), p. 357.

55 Null, *Black Hollywood*, p. 230; Landay, *Black Film Stars*, p. 189. See also Philip Davies, 'A Growing Independence', elsewhere in this volume, for a discussion of the extent of, and limitations on alterations in the motion picture industry's sensitivity to social and political change.

Robert Reiner

Keystone to Kojak:
the Hollywood cop

Crime and law enforcement have been central themes of the movies from their inception. One of the earliest American story films, Edwin S. Porter's *The Great Train Robbery* (1903) is usually cited as the precursor of the Western genre. But this is to classify it in terms of the generic taxonomies of a later period. When Porter's film was shot in wild and woolly New Jersey, Butch Cassidy and the Sundance Kid were still robbing trains and Wyatt Earp still active. *The Great Train Robbery* must have been regarded then as a tale of *contemporary* crime and law enforcement, not one set in a mythical old West. Law and order have remained staple movie concerns ever since, although the legacy of Porter's film has bifurcated into the alternative generic traditions of the frontier lawman *v.* outlaws, and the detective *v.* the urban criminal.

A lot has been written about the Western and the crime film. However, much less attention has been paid to the way the movies have depicted the law-enforcer. In particular, Hollywood's treatment of the *cop*, as opposed to the *private* investigator has been neglected. Partly this is because there have been relatively few films with cops as central characters, and these cannot be seen as constituting a distinctive genre, i.e. a set of 'patterns/forms/styles/structures which transcend individual art products, and which supervise both their construction by artists and their reading by audiences'.[1] Westerns, gangster films and private eye movies all represent abiding traditions recognised by both the industry and the audience. Cop movies do not form a comparable generic pattern. At most, there has been a handful of relatively short cycles of movies about cops which for a time have staked out a discourse with a common set of themes, references and questions. I would recognise four such sub-genres: the 'G' Man films of the late 1930s; the police procedural cycle of the late 1940s; the bent cop films of the 1950s; and the superhero cops of the late 1960s and early 1970s. As will be apparent when I examine these cycles in greater detail, they do not contain any uniting patterns or characteristics which could constitute a single genre, other than the extrinsic property of having professional policemen as heroes.[2]

Thus the problematic of this paper, to trace the changing images of the Hollywood policeman, is one where the uniting question is given by an externally defined object, rather than the analysis of a common mythic pattern found in a genre of films. But the movie treatment of the police is important in at least two ways. First, as a case-study of how Hollywood's handling of a major social institution has changed over time, and the explanation and implications of these vicissitudes. Second, because the image of the police projected by Hollywood, world capital of the consciousness industry for the last seven decades, is of considerable social and political significance. The contribution of the police to the maintenance of order is accomplished at least as much by their symbolic role as guardians of public morality as by any concrete achievements in catching crooks.[3] The media are clearly crucial to the propagation of this police image, as police sensitivity to their treatment indicates.

The implicit model which informs my account of changing treatments of the police is set out in Ryall's study of the gangster film.[4] Attention must be paid to the immediate social relations of production, including the artistic sensibilities of both film-makers and audience, and those located within the network of social practices constituting both the industry and the wider social formation (a conceptualisation which avoids the reified and consensual connotations of the term 'society'). All these elements are needed for an understanding of Hollywood's treatment of the police, although the salience of different factors in different conjunctures varies. The remainder of this chapter will sketch out the changing image of the Hollywood cop, and the reasons for these changes.

Do detectives think?

In 1926 Laurel and Hardy made a two-reel short, *Do Detectives Think?*, a rhetorical question which sums up the then prevailing image of the cop in Hollywood movies (and indeed crime fiction more generally). Policemen were incensed by their clownish screen portrayal, epitomised by the Keystone Cops, especially when this was contrasted with the more romantic presentation of criminals in early gangster movies. In 1910 the International Association of Chiefs of Police adopted a resolution condemning Hollywood's treatment of the police. Association president Richard Sylvester complained that 'in moving pictures the police are sometimes made to appear ridiculous, and in view of the large number of young people, children, who attend these moving picture shows, it gives them an improper idea of the policeman'. These protests are the start of a perennual police anxiety, occasionally amounting to paranoia, about their screen image.

Perhaps what really hurt was that the movie idea of the policeman was not as 'improper' as Sylvester would have wished. A number of contemporary commissions which investigated the police described a state of inefficiency and bungling, as well as corruption. The domination of police forces by political machines led to selection of police officers on the basis of partisanship not competence. One enquiry found that 'some recruits were overweight, undersize and over-age; others were illiterate, alcoholic and syphilitic, still others had outstanding debts and criminal records; and one Kansas City patrolman had a wooden leg'. Even Keystone could not have capped that!

Apart from the comedy cop, in the silent film the police appeared mainly as subsidiary figures in other genres, notably detective and gangster movies, and in the shape of the Western lawman. In the late 1920s there were several important and successful gangster films, notably von Sternberg's *Underworld* (1927) featuring George Bancroft as a sympathetic mobster. As in many later examples of the genre, the police appear primarily as the nemesis necessary to instil the then inevitable 'crime doesn't pay' message.

This is true by default in the classic trinity of early sound gangster films. The police are shown as incapable of containing the activities of gangsters. In *Little Caesar* they do finally gun down the hero whose rise and fall has been charted. But there is no implication of an end to gangsterism or the triumph of law and order. The *parvenu* is crushed, but more as a result of his own hubris than police efficiency. The 'Big Boy' survives to carry on the rackets. In *Public Enemy* the police are conspicuous by their absence. It is rival gangsters who dump Cagney's mummified corpse on mummy. Paul Muni in *Scarface* was killed by the police, but his downfall owed more to his tortured, incestuous jealousy over his sister's marriage. There is evidence that the ending which has him being killed by the police was the result of censorship pressure, and certainly it was the New York censor board which insisted that the sub-title *Shame of a Nation* be tacked on.

A lesser-known gangster film of 1931, *The Secret Six*, most explicitly drew the moral that the regular police were incapable of fighting crime. The eponymous sextet, a group of masked businessmen and civic leaders, employ tough reporters Clark Gable and John Mack Brown to investigate Wallace Beery's bootlegging operations. As Rosow states: '*The Secret Six* was one of the earlier films to suggest vigilante action as a means of dealing with gangsters. The masked vigilante businessmen are particularly sinister, a precursor of the various crime-fighting superheroes who appeared at the end of the decade.'[5] Gary Cooper, the hero of *City Streets* (1931), summed up the attitude to the police which was prevalent in the early gangster cycle when he was asked to join the beer rackets. 'Beer? I'd as soon be a cop as that.' Bergman rightly comments that this was 'the worst of comparisons in 1931: a flatfoot'.[6]

The other crime movie genre which dominated the early 1930s was the classical private detective story. Gentlemen sleuth mysteries have not generally flourished in Hollywood. Stories concentrating on Labyrinthine plots with the emphasis on ratiocination rather than action or characterisation are not easily translatable into cinema. But the 1930s were the 'golden age' of the classic detective story, before the withering fictional onslaught of the more uncouth private eye. Partly reflecting their literary popularity, and partly the suitability of early sound technology to sets confined to the drawing-room or library of an English country house, many of the best-known grey-celled wizards appeared in series during the 1930s.[7]

It seems paradoxical that two such dramatically contrasting perspectives on crime should flourish in the same period. 'Mayhem in parva',[8] gentlemen killed in their studies with ancient Chinese daggers by their gentlemen's gentlemen, is a world away from smoky gambling-joints, seedy diners and garish speakeasies, the ambience of the Little Caesars and Public Enemies.

The gangster movies clearly reflect the peculiar tensions of working-class existence in Depression America. The contradictory pressures of a materialistic society with a 'rags-to-riches' mythology, in a context of mass unemployment, are manifested in these rise-and-fall sagas. The 'crime doesn't pay' conclusions pointed working-class audiences to a choice between short-lived success and a longer life of dull poverty, while also making the films acceptable to respectable middle-class viewers.

The classic detective-story, on the other hand, in its literary form, appealed in the first place to the upper class.[9] In movie form their interest lies less in the puzzle element than in the evocation of a lifestyle of indolent luxury and froth. The world of the gentleman sleuth was that of other 1930s escapist entertainments like the Astaire–Rogers musicals, with a tone of nostalgia for a never-existent present, inhabited by high IQ versions of Bertie Wooster. The police in these films, as in their literary counter-parts, are plodding, dimwitted and unimaginative, as contrasted to the remorseless professionals of the gangster movies or the corrupt brutes of the private-eye story. They are essentially foils to highlight the brilliance of the gentleman amateur. What is expressed in social terms is upper-class snobbery and disdain for the working-class cop.

While in these ways early 1930s gangster and detective films appealed to different concerns in different parts of the audience, they also shared certain common elements. Both implied the impotence of professional law enforcement agencies to combat crime. In the detective story, crime is an individual rupture in an otherwise tight-knit social fabric. The world is a predictable place, a presupposition of the 'clue' – the deduction of identity or suspiciousness on the basis of observed, taken-for-granted regularities of habit. At the end of the day the detective restores the shattered order (until the next time he is invited to weekend in a country house). But the solution of crime is attributable to individual genius not deliberate social policy or organisation, and the essentially vigilante activities of the detective are approved. The gangster movie displays a similar view of the futility of police organisation, but attributes it to the remorselessly criminogenic character of society, not the intellectual deficiencies of the bureaucratic employee as opposed to the enthusiastic amateur.

Don't shoot, G-Men!

In 1935 the film image of the policeman was dramatically transformed with the advent of the 'G-Man' cycle, the first time the professional cop achieved star status. The film which inaugurated the cycle was William Keighley's *G-Men*, which had James Cagney switching his guns to the right side of the law.[10] It is seldom that a new movie cycle can be traced so clearly to overt political pressure (although this is not the whole story).

As mentioned above, police spokesmen had been concerned about Hollywood's denigration of their dignity for some decades. The gangster cycle of the early 1930s redoubled their protests, as well as those of civic groups. In 1934 the Hays Code, with its strict rules about the way crime could be presented in the movies, began to be rigorously enforced. Finally, 1934 marked a peak in the FBI's rise to prominence as the nation's Public Defender number one. It was the most publicity-conscious law-enforcement agency in history. Under the directorship of J. Edgar Hoover, since 1924 the Bureau had transformed itself from its origins as a relatively obscure agency of the Department of Justice.[11] In 1930 it achieved an important controlling role *vis-à-vis* local police forces when it became the national clearing house for the Uniform Crime Reports system, thus monopolising the main measuring rod of police success. In 1933–4 various headline-grabbing crimes, notably the Lindbergh kidnapping and the wave of Mid-Western bank-robberies carried out by such legendary names as Bonnie Parker and Clyde Barrow, 'Pretty Boy' Floyd, and above all John Dillinger, led to a considerable expansion of the FBI's jurisdiction, and the granting of power for agents to carry arms. In September 1934 the FBI scored a much-touted success when agents killed Dillinger, Public Enemy No. 1, as he emerged from a Chicago cinema having seen *Manhattan Melodrama*, a new gangster pic.

Hoover had become adept at gaining maximum publicity for his bureau's coups (and for himself – Melvin Purvis, the agent who tracked down Dillinger was seldom mentioned). Following Dillinger's death, Hoover was prevailed upon by Jack Warner to relent on his previous non-cooperation with Hollywood and permit a film about his agency. So pleased was Hoover with the result that *G-Men* was subsequently re-issued in 1949 to celebrate the twenty-fifth anniversary of the FBI (more precisely, the twenty-fifth anniversary of Hoover's appointment as Director, but he glossed over the difference).

Despite little touches of verisimilitude – reference to the Lindbergh law and the legislation arming the FBI, documentary-style scenes of FBI training and forensic methods – *G-Men* and the subsequent law-enforcement cycle it spawned are crime melodramas in strictly traditional, Hollywood style. None the less they were warmly welcomed by police spokesmen and civic groups.[12]

G-Men was quickly followed by other Warners films with cop heroes, all embodying the essential iconography of their earlier gangster pictures – screeching tyres, wailing sirens, chattering tommy guns – but now the central character was a law-enforcer. The most important of these was William Keighley's *Bullets or Ballots* (1936), with Edward G. Robinson as cop Johnny Blake. Both *G-Men* and *Bullets or Ballots* are remarkable in the way the plots allow for the essential elements of the Cagney and Robinson gangster persona despite their police roles. It is not just a question of personal styles of aggressive, violent energy. In *G-Men*, Cagney grows up amongst hoods before training as a lawyer at the expense of a kindly paternalistic old mobster. *Bullets or Ballots* has Robinson apparently kicked off the force. Secretly he is working for the crime commission which is trying to discover the identity of the 'Big Boys' behind the rackets. He joins the gang run by Barton MacLane and Humphrey Bogart, and, in sequences which are virtually a reprise of *Little Caesar*, works his way to the top. The populist sentiments of the early gangster films are carried over in the revelation that the 'Big Boys' are a group of wealthy, apparently respectable bankers. Robinson is mortally wounded as he kills Bogart in the final shootout, but dies happy because he has preserved 'a world where every punk will still tip his hat to a cop'.

The most disturbing aspect of the G-Man cycle was their unashamedly vigilante spirit. All encouragement was given to violations of due process and contempt for the law by the supposed enforcers. This is encapsulated in some titles: *Let 'Em Have It, Muss 'Em Up, Don't Turn 'Em Loose, Show Them No Mercy*. The fascist ethos of such pictures was noted by contemporary critic Milton Meyer: 'It is the spirit that seeks order at the expense of justice. It advocates "treating 'em rough", whether 'em' are labourers on strike, Communists at talk, or criminals in flight. It embraces the creation of a police army to fight crime, with the general view that police armies may be put to a number of uses.'[13]

The G-Man cycle was not merely a response to police and civic pressure. After all, protests had not prevented the earlier gangster cycle, and the few films starring racket-busting policemen in the early 1930s (like the 1932 *Beast of the City* with Walter Huston as a tough cop, which was warmly welcomed by the League of Decency) were commercially unsuccessful. The G-Man films chimed in with a change in public consciousness. As Bergman notes, they coincided with a general adulation of benevolent Federal government which pervaded many movie genres following the New Deal. 'Along with the renaissance of the western hero and the elevation of the federal government into a virtual leading man in Warner Brothers' topical films . . . it [the G-Man film] brought that law and that government into a strong position in the culture.'[14] More specifically, the G-Man pictures reflected the need for a scapegoat for the Depression. As Milton Meyer noted at the time: 'Beneath the enthusiasm for the war on crime lay, after four years of national panic, the public's desperate need for a bogeyman. This is an old and inveterate failing of society beset by economic straits. In most of present-day Europe, the bogeyman is a political or religious minority; in this country he has taken the form of a moral minority – the criminal.'[15]

The advent of a real bogeyman in the shape of Hitler killed the G-Man cycle. Hollywood turned its resources to the war effort, producing escapist entertainments, and putting Nazi villains into all its action genres.[16] The submersion of domestic conflicts in the face of the common enemy is epitomised by *All Through The Night* (Warners, 1942) which stars Bogart as racketeer Gloves Donahue leading his gang against Nazi spies.

Mean Streets

In 1941 John Huston's *The Maltese Falcon* heralded a new kind of screen detective. The private eye, owning only 'a coat, a hat and a gun', fought the mean city's corruption with integrity, pride and a hard head for blows, booze and broads. The gumshoe, not the policeman, was the crime-fighting hero of the mid-1940s, with a string of Raymond Chandler movies – *Farewell, My Lovely* (1944), *The Big Sleep* (1946) etc. – and other private eye films, like *The Dark Corner* (1946). All these movies are pervaded by the characteristic postwar tone of *film noir* – 'sombre, claustrophobic, deadpan and paranoid. In the shaded lights and raining night it is often just a little difficult to tell one character from another.'[17] The private eye makes his hopeless little moral gestures, but even if he clears up a specific case, this is a Canute-like holding operation against the relentlessly flowing tide of corruption. The cops in these movies are mainly brutal, dishonest or just plain shabby. Even the honest ones are demoralised by the futility of their endeavours. The image of the cop and his role is best summed up by Marlowe in *The Long Goodbye*:

'Cops are like a doctor that gives you aspirin for a brain tumor, except that the cop would rather cure it with a blackjack.'[18]

In some *films noirs*, for example *Crossfire* (1947), a central character is a police detective. The policemen in these films exhibit some integrity and even idealism, but these qualities are subordinated to the downbeat moral and psychological bleakness and confusion of the neon-punctuated blackness they walk through. The tone seems attributable to a mood of disenchantment among returning soldiers not finding a home fit for heroes (explicitly portrayed in *Crossfire*), as well as stylistic imports from Europe via the emigré directors responsible for many examples of *film noir*, such as Siodmak, Preminger, Lang, Wilder. Other contributory factors are increasing interest in psychological exploration (encouraged by the impact of psychoanalysis and a switching of attention inwards from the social problems of the 1930s, and the number of liberal directors (like Dmytryk and Dassin) then in Hollywood, following the years in which Fascism was the enemy and prior to the McCarthyite onslaught.

Just give me the facts, ma'am

In 1948 Jules Dassin's *Naked City* began a new cycle of films with policemen in the lead. The keynote of these was an attempt to project a realistic, deglamourised portrait of police procedure, with its tedious, sole-destroying routines of enquiry. The main assets of the heroes, ordinary guys just doing a job, were not fists but fingerprints, forensic labs. and solid footwear. The style was neo-documentary, owing much to Louis de Rochemont's pre-war *March of Time* series, with the use of outdoor city locations, narrative voice-overs giving facts and figures ('there are eight million stories in the naked city. This has been one of them'), and loving attention to the details of police paraphernalia and technology.

The police procedural cycle diverged from the G-Men films in featuring ordinary police, not FBI, special agents or other élite investigators. Nor was there any encouragement of police vigilantism.

The influence of this neo-documentary style is reflected in such films as Kazan's *Boomerang* (1947), *T-Men* (1947), and *White Heat* (1949). The police procedural was relegated to 'B' feature status in the 1950s, but achieved more lasting success on TV, with the long-running *Dragnet* and its derivatives like *Highway Patrol*. *Dragnet* with its relentless insistence on 'authenticity' ('just give me the facts, ma'am') marked a new high for the policeman's status in Hollywood, and stars Jack Webb and Ben Alexander were much sought-after speakers at police conventions. The procedural had its swan-song in the late 1950s and early 1960s with *The FBI Story* (1959), essentially a Hoover whitewash.

Freudian fuzz and rogue cops

The cynical tone and psychological brooding of the *film noir* combined with the interest in police work engendered by the procedurals to generate a mini-cycle of movies in the early 1950s concerned with probing the psyche of the policeman and/or exposing police wrong-doing. The two are connected, in that the source of brutality and dishonesty was often explained psychologically rather than in terms of social processes. The penchant for psychologising was a widespread phenomenon of 1950s films, producing such fashions as the 'adult' Western. The theme of civic corruption was also prevalent in the early 1950s, most notably in *On the Waterfront* (1954) and other more minor gangster exposes such as *Hoodlum Empire* (1952). The immediate inspiration was clearly the Kefauver and other crime commissions of the time.

Outstanding examples of the disturbed/brutal/corrupt cop cycle were Wyler's *Detective Story* (1951), Lang's *The Big Heat* (1953), and Welles's *Touch of Evil* (1958). The central issue in these films is the perennial police dilemma in a democratic society of how to maintain order without violating the rules of due process of law. In the 1930s such problems of the liberal conscience were not allowed to inhibit the enthusiasm of the gangbusters. But a central figure in the 1950s is the tough, no-holds barred cop (like Glenn Ford in *The Big Heat* – 'a corn-stepper by instinct') whose unrelenting pursuit of criminals leads to brutality and illegal methods. The vigilante cop is viewed sympathetically with the aim of understanding (albeit in crude, pop psychoanalytic terms), but his actions are questioned if not deplored.[19] The overall implication of this cycle is summed up by crook Victor Mature's comment to Assistant DA Brian Donlevy in *Kiss of Death*: 'Your side of the fence is almost as dirty as mine.'[20]

Detective Story is of particular interest in attempting a realistic portrayal of a day in a New York precinct house. Kirk Douglas plays a characteristic figure of this cycle. He is a tough and authoritarian detective crusading for order, who obtains confessions by beating suspects. When he discovers his wife is unable to have a child because she once had an abortion (carried out by a man he hates), he cannot forgive her. He commits suicide by allowing himself to be killed by a prisoner attempting to escape. Douglas's unbending authoritarianism is traced back to the childhood trauma of having a dishonest and brutal father who drove his mother to insanity.

The last of this cycle, Welles's *Touch of Evil*, embodies all its quintessential themes. It contrasts Charlton Heston (as an idealistic Mexican policeman, honeymooning in an American border town) with Orson Welles as the gross and shabby local police chief. Heston is drawn into investigating the explosion which opens the film. He encounters racial prejudice and professional antagonism. He discovers not only that Welles is on the take from the local hoods, but that he has acquired his reputation by fabricating evidence against countless suspects. Heston pressures Welles' assistant Joseph Calleia to plant a bug on him and tapes a confession. Welles discovers the bug and dies in a final shootout. Welles's vendetta against criminals is psychologically explained (by the earlier murder of his wife). But his vigilantism also reflects a certain sense of justice, for he only framed men he felt were guilty and would otherwise escape. Even the suspect he framed for the opening explosion turns out to be guilty after all. The upright Heston can only get the goods on Welles by underhand tactics echoing those he condemns.

Whatever his motives, however, Welles's violations of legal rules, his touch of evil, brings about an inexorable moral decay, reflected Dorian Gray-like in his physical degeneration. None the less his complex and twisted character is far more riveting than Heston's rather colourless Mr Clean. As Marlene Dietrich remarks over Welles' corpse, 'he was some kind of a man'.

The new blue films

These themes were explored more fully in the late 1960s, when the cop achieved superstardom, and movie and TV screens were dominated by sirens and flashing blue lights. The new wave began in 1967–8 with such films as *In The Heat of the Night* (1967), *The Detective* (1968), and *Madigan* (1968). The thematic concerns of the cycle are already evident in these examples. The films revolved around two central tensions: law versus order, and the professional versus bureaucracy. The law/order contradiction was foreshadowed in the earlier 1950s cycle. However, whereas in the 1950s the dilemma was presented as a universal metaphysical or psychological problem, in the 1960s the issue is much more concretely rooted in the specific social conflicts of the time. The films are peppered with explicit references and allusions to contemporary events. The films in the cop cycle divide into those with liberal and those with conservative or reactionary stances on the law and order issue.

However, at another level the cop cycle is united in the position taken on the professional versus bureaucracy question. This theme is one which pervaded many other genres at that time, and thus clearly connected with more fundamental social concerns than the specific law *v.* order debate. It is the basis, for example, of what Will Wright calls the 'professional' plot which characterised Westerns of the period. This itself is a variant of the more general individual/society tension, which Wright sees as the concern of the classical Western too. The resolution of the contradiction in the classical Western, Wright argues, doesn't work in a period dominated by the large-scale, bureaucratic organisations of monopoly capitalism. The 'professional' Westerns, such as *The Wild*

Bunch, no longer aim to reconcile the strong, resourceful individual to a peaceful, settled civilisation. Society is dominated by faceless, lifeless minions of impersonal corporations (like the 'superposse' in *Butch Cassidy*). The only point of identity and meaning is the exercise of skills within a professional group – the code and camaraderie for their own sakes, not any ultimate social purpose such as building a land fit for families to be raised in. This tension pervades the police cycle too, uniting films which divide at the more superficial level of the law *v.* order issue. In almost all the cop movies of the 1960s and 1970s the hero is a lone-wolf, lower-rank policeman (occasionally with one partner), working *against* the organisational hierarchy. Unlike the rogue cop movies of the 1950s, it is the loner with whom we are meant to sympathise.

The cop cycle can be divided into four kinds of movies, according to their location on the two axes: law *v.* order and professional *v.* bureaucracy. Virtually none of the 1960s or 1970s movies fits the bureaucratic category (with the possible exception of *Magnum Force*). The 1950s rogue cops are behaviourally analogous to the order/professional heroes, but their actions are not unreservedly approved by the films.

	Law	*Order*
Professional	The liberal cop, e.g. Frank Sinatra in *The Detective*	The police vigilante, e.g. *Dirty Harry* (also the 1950s rogue cops)
Bureaucracy	The organisation man, e.g. the TV cops from *Dragnet* to *Ironside* and *Kojak* (and the earlier police procedurals)	*Magnum Force* (also, the G-Men of the 1930s)

It could be that the movies with different ideological positions on the law *v.* order issue appealed to different social groups. It is likely, however, that the films worked in such a way that even groups who in political practice opposed specific policies would support them in the context of the movie. The professional/bureaucracy theme transcended particular social conflicts and interests. That it was the latter, even more than the law and order issue, which was the basis of the cycle's appeal was recognised by Clint Eastwood himself. He once remarked: 'In the complications of society as we know it today, sometimes a person who can cut through the bureaucracy, and red tape . . . a person who thinks on that level is a hero.'[21]

Although the ultimate weight of the cycle was politically reactionary, supporting hard-line 'law and order' policies, the first few examples were all liberal. Penn's *The Chase* (1966) had Brando as Sheriff of a small Texan town vainly fighting bigotry, corruption and lynch-law. The enormously successful *In The Heat of the Night* (1967) echoed *Touch of Evil* in its portrayal of the conflict between the black, highly-trained and skilled Northern detective Virgil Tibbs (Sidney Poitier), and Rod Steiger as the prejudiced, vigilante-style sheriff of Sparta, Mississippi. True to the liberalism of the film, Steiger comes to realise the superior power of the college degree over the third degree (unlike the more ambiguous ending of *Touch of Evil* where there is no clear implication that legal methods are necessarily also more effective). It is noteworthy that in both *The Chase* and *In The Heat of the Night* the law/order conflict is located in a rural Southern context. This superimposed a kind of urban disdain for yokelish bigotry and backwardness on the anti-vigilantism theme. (The imagery was reversed in the ultra-reactionary 1973 *Walking Tall*, where the corruption and decadence represented by the city threaten the law and order efforts of good ol' country boy Sheriff Buford Pusser.)

The only *urban* film of this period to take a liberal stand on the law/order issue was *The Detective* (1968). Sinatra played Joe Leland, a dedicated, skilled and honest cop whom we see graduating from uniform to detective status. He is loyal to 'the department' as an abstract symbol and tradition. (He joined the force because his father was a cop and 'it's the most useful thing I can be'.) He is not a bureaucrat, however, but a professional. He 'could go all the way to the top' as his boss keeps reminding him, but keeps endangering his chances because he won't 'kiss ass'. He is liberal in his views and fair in his methods. When a colleague harasses gays he takes him behind a car and punches him. When a patrolman kills a black, and his boss and buddies are considering ways of protecting him and the department from protestors, Sinatra says 'If internal affairs don't get you, and the civil rights people don't get you, watch out for me!' As these examples show, Sinatra's playing it by the book is limited by his own sense of justice. At the end of the film he even burgles an office in order to uncover civic corruption. The general import of the film, however, is that brutality and illegal methods are not just wrong but also counter-productive. Under pressure to crack a case to protect the department (and also secure his promotion) Sinatra psychologically torments a suspect into confessing (after stopping his colleagues beating him up). Later the man turns out to have been innocent, and Sinatra resigns from the police. (This is also necessitated by his reluctance to drop investigations into the corrupt city planning department, responsible for the ghettos and poverty that he sees as the real cause of crime in the social dustbin which it is the police task 'to keep the lid on'.) Sinatra is the ideal, liberal policeman that all the Presidential Commissions of the 1960s sought to produce by a combination of organisational reforms and college education.

Madigan and *Bullitt* (both 1968) mark a transition from the liberal ethos of the previous cop films (which reflected the 'Great Society' aspirations of the Johnson era) to the hard 'law and order' line which prevailed in the Nixon years. Steve McQueen's *Bullitt* is an essentially ambiguous character, summed up by the enigmatic look he takes at himself in the mirror in the film's last shot. He wastes cars, buildings and people with abandon to get the job done, but seems not to relish it. Violence is an unfortunate necessity. 'That's where half of it's at – you can't walk away from it', he tells his protesting girlfriend, Jacqueline Bisset. Robert Vaughn, the smooth, politically opportunist DA, is shown sporting a 'support your local police' sticker on his car, and the implication is that this slogan (short-hand for 'support the right-wing backlash' as a *Nation* editorial commented in 1966) is as irrelevant to effective policing as Bisset's squeamish pacifism.

Don Siegel's *Madigan* does essentially side with the tough, no-nonsense methods of Richard Widmark as Dan Madigan, a street-wise cop. But the liberal, rule-book-following Commissioner played by Henry Fonda is viewed sympathetically, even if his values are ultimately shown as untenable. However, Madigan's are not much more successful. He gets his man with his strong-arm tactics, but dies in the process. The picture is of the city as a jungle where toughness is the only viable response even if it ultimately solves nothing.

The city-as-jungle theme is continued in Siegel's 1969 *Coogan's Bluff*, Clint Eastwood's debut as a contemporary law enforcer. The film shows the moral and physical confusion and decay of New York City through the eyes of Eastwood as an Arizona deputy tracking down a lost prisoner. Eastwood brings his cowboy persona ('a man's gotta do what a man's gotta do' as city cop Lee J. Cobb mocks him) to the role of Coogan, and the film makes explicit the connection between the traditional Western hero and the new image of the police. The extent to which the cop had replaced the cowboy as folk-hero was emphasised when John Wayne (who had originally turned down the part of *Dirty Harry*) was forced to jump on the paddy-wagon in *McQ* (1974) and *Brannigan* (1975).

The 'order before law' position of *Madigan* and *Coogan's Bluff* became most explicit in *Dirty Harry*, the next Eastwood–Siegel cop collaboration, which was enormously successful in 1971. *Dirty Harry*, with its explicit condemnation of the due process requirements laid down by the Supreme Court, clearly supports the reactionary demands of police organisations and right-wing politicians who saw the law as 'hand-cuffing' the cops. The film chimes in with the grass-roots 'police rebellion' against liberal chiefs, lawyers and politicians which exploded in the late 1960s.[22] But it is important to note that the message works within the context of the movie in such a way as to win the support of audience groups who would normally support civil liberties. The film achieves this by postulating that the law primarily protects the rights of an insane psychopath, whereas in reality the majority of suspects are poor, inarticulate and ignorant petty criminals open to police bamboozlement. *Dirty Harry*, like most policemen, justifies his contempt for civil liberties by a 'victim' oriented perspective. This is made explicit in the last of the trilogy, *The Enforcer* (1976). Harry is hauled over the coals by his Captain after he has driven his car through a store window to save some hostages, and put three criminals in hospital. 'For your information the minority community of this city has just about had it with this kind of police work.' Harry replies: 'By minority community I take it you mean the hoods?' 'It so happens they're American citizens too. They happen to have rights.' 'So does that old lady who had a sawed-off shotgun in her ear. Or doesn't she count any more? What the hell is going on around here? What kind of department are we running when we're more concerned with the rights of the criminals than of the people we're supposed to be protecting?' A British policeman I interviewed put it almost identically: 'We need more power ... The only persons you'd be oppressing are the law-breakers and speaking from a policeman's point of view it doesn't give a damn, because they're oppressors in their own right.'[23]

Magnum Force (1973), the second Dirty Harry movie, is perplexingly confused ideologically. In it Harry tracks down the killers of a number of known and vicious hoods about whom the police could do nothing. He finds that the murderers are a group of uniform cops led by the clean-cut David Soul (of Hutch fame), organised by Harry's apparently liberal superior. (The idea mirrors the real-life activities of police vigilante death squads in Brazil at that time.) What is perplexing is why Harry objects to behaviour not unlike his own in *Dirty Harry*. His explanation clearly points to the professional *v.* organisation dichotomy. The vigilante cop tells him: 'What the hell do you know about the law? You're a great cop, Harry. You've got a chance to join the team but you'd rather stick with the system.' 'Briggs, I hate the goddammed system, but until someone comes along with some changes that make sense I'll stick with it.' Harry is here arguing that vigilantism, the pursuit of order at the cost of law, is acceptable but only if it is organisationally sanctioned (the *system*) not maverick action (the *team*).

The French Connection, the other big cop success of 1971, presents an equally bleak (if more ambiguous) message. Gene Hackman plays Popeye Doyle (based on real-life cop Eddie Egan, who appears in the film in a small part) as a brutal, boorish bully, but one who gets results. However, as Pauline Kael has pointed out, the film's cynicism is such that the pursuit of the heroin (which is the central plot) appears meaningless, an obsessive chase for its own sake, rather than socially useful. The film can be read in different ways by audiences with different sympathies. For example, 'when Popeye walks into a bar and harasses blacks, part of the audience can say, "That's a real pig", and another part of the audience can say, "That's the only way to deal with those people. Waltz around with them and you get nowhere".'[24] Nor is it clear whether we are meant to see Popeye's ruthlessness as justified by his success in getting the job done. At the end we are told that all the dealers received ludicrously light sentences.

Following these hugely successful movies, an army of cop heroes flooded the screen in such films as *Badge 373* (1973), *The Stone-killer* (1973), and *French Connection II* (1975). Police series also became omnipresent on TV in the early 1970s, the heyday of *Kojak* and *Columbo*.

However, this love-affair with the cops was only one side of Hollywood's treatment in these years. In other genres the police appeared less favourably. The counter-culture movies of the late 1960s, such as *Easy Rider*, showed the cops as brutal pigs, an image echoed in the contemporary cowboy, driver and trucker cycles of the 1970s, like *J. W. Coop* (1972), *Vanishing Point* (1971), and more recently, *Convoy* (1978). By contrast, a student demonstration (and/or a ghetto riot) was almost *de rigueur* in the cop movies, allowing the working-class hero to exhibit contemptuous disdain for such spoilt brats. Interestingly, student radicals were never portrayed as more than a nuisance. In *McQ*, for example, Big John kicks them around, but when his bureaucratic boss

Eddie Albert suspects student militants of being behind the killing of policemen, Wayne senses the hand of the Syndicate.

The cop films treated above are all superficially mystery/detective/crime stories, albeit with professional police heroes. Contrasted with earlier cop cycles, however, there are several innovations, notably a greater emphasis on internal police relationships. Indeed in many of the films these are more important than the ostensible crime plot, the real enemy being the bureaucratic establishment who handcuff the police. Furthermore, an element of 'realism' is conveyed by suggesting that the detective cannot concentrate on only one case at a time. Harry has only to go for a hamburger to happen on a holdup or hijacking, which implies both that he is a resourceful guy who can handle an emergency and that the cops are an undermanned thin blue line in an urban jungle.

A handful of films treated the police without the conventional framework of the crime story. *Serpico* (1973) tells of the hounding of the eponymous hero by colleagues and superiors as he tries to expose corruption within the force. The film is based on the real-life cop whose revelations stimulated the 1972 Knapp Commission Report on the wholesale corruption of the New York City Police Department.

Electra Glide in Blue (1973) was a probing exploration of the psychological roots of police machismo. Robert Blake played John Wintergreen, a short motorcycle cop who boasts of being the same height as Alan Ladd. Shown lovingly donning his boots and uniform, Wintergreen dreams of becoming a stetsoned detective like his idol, Harve Pool, a star investigator who is obsessed in a paranoid way with an imagined conspiracy to commit police genocide. Temporarily assigned to assist Poole, Wintergreen is returned to uniform after showing him up. He beats Poole to the solution of a murder, and hears his mistress drunkenly reveal Poole's impotence. Back on motor cycle patrol, Wintergreen is gratuitously killed by some hippies to whom he is trying to return a driving licence (a reversal of *Easy Rider*). The last shot shows him slumped in the middle of Monument Valley (of John Ford fame), the end of all American dreams, from the traditional Westerner to the Easy Riders and the saint cops.

In a class of their own are the films derived from the novels of Joseph Wambaugh. Wambaugh was a thirty-four-year-old Los Angeles police sergeant (and nightschool graduate in English literature) when he published the 1971 hit novel, *The New Centurions*. Wambaugh himself epitomises the dedicated cop, seeing his job as a mission. Despite fame and fortune he continued to work the beat until a couple of years ago, when he claims it became impossible because so many fans came to gawk. To date, three of his books have been filmed: *The New Centurions* (1972 – called *Precinct 45, Los Angeles Police* in Britain); *The Blue Knight* (1973) and *The Choirboys* (1978). (His work has also inspired two TV series: *The Blue Knight* and *Police Story*.) The Wambaugh-derived movies are not crime stories or law-and-order homilies. There is no question of actually containing the crime or misery the cop sees all around him. His struggle is to preserve some minimum integrity and decency in an irredeemably savage and amoral world. The films are picaresque tales depicting the routine phases of police work: rounding up prostitutes, spying on gays, rescuing suicides or battered babies, sorting out domestic disputes, as well as shooting it up with liquor store robbers. The central quest which holds the episodes together is not solving a crime but saving the policeman's soul. Will the cop be able to mature and develop as a man, despite the degradation he is immersed in, as the *New Centurions* do, or will he surrender to the vicious cynicism of Roscoe Rules, the most foul-mouthed and bigoted of *The Choirboys*? As Wambaugh himself has emphasised, the danger facing a policeman is not so much physical as spiritual. His cops *do* risk violent attack (Stacy Keach in *The New Centurions* survives a stomach wound only to be killed in a domestic dispute call). But as Wambaugh stresses, many occupations are *more* exposed to physical risk than the police. In all these stories the real threat is to the policeman's humanity of spirit, the tip of the iceberg being the high suicide, mental and marital breakdown rates of the police.

The ideology of the Wambaugh-derived movies cannot readily be classified as either conservative or liberal. Wambaugh is certainly not in the law-and-order camp. His good policeman is not the sharpshooter, but the man who can talk a hysterical, junkie mother into handing over her battered baby, or, when asked to evict some poor Chicano tenants who cannot pay their rent, turns on the slum landlord who called the police in the first place (as George C. Scott does in *The New Cenurions*). But at the same time, the policeman has a tragic vision and deep pessimism which precludes any hope of social change.

The Choirboys is the least successful of the three movies. It centres on 'choir practices', the after-hours orgies the police hold in McArthur Park with cop groupies like Ora Lee Tingle. The book is a black comedy showing the policemen ground between the dual pressures of a soul-destroying job and an oppressive bureaucratic hierarchy. 'Choir practice' is their safety-valve, but leads to the choristers' moral destruction. During the revelry a passing gay is accidentally shot, and the book's hero, an old street-wise cop Spermwhale Whalen, is broken by the threat of losing his pension and confesses to the authorities. The film translates this into a series of tasteless scatological jokes, and tacks on an unconvincing 'happy' ending with Whalen getting the better of the bureaucrats during his interrogation.[25]

Although not sharing the law and order concern with other cop movies, the Wambaugh films do deal with the professional/bureaucracy issue, taking the grass-roots police viewpoint. The police are pitted against not only civilian 'ass-holes', but their own bosses. Senior officers are dishonest dictators like Lieutenant Hardass Grimsley of *The Choirboys*, who grafted their way to the top, or incompetent and naive penpushers (like Lieutenant Finque) with no street savvy. They hamstring real police work by emphasising spit, polish, and the rule-book. The men fight back in their own way. Lieutenant Grimsley in *The Choirboys* is set up with a black prostitute in a motel, and Spermwhale and his partner burst in at the pre-arranged signal from the girl: 'Oh honey! You got balls like an elephant and a whang like an ox!' Thus the anti-bureaucracy theme unites the whole cop cycle, although the films differ on the law-and-order issue.

The last couple of years seem to have witnessed the demise of the cop sub-genre. *The Choirboys* apart, there have been only two major movies featuring policemen: Clint Eastwood's *The Gauntlet* and John Carpenter's *Assault on Precinct 13* (both 1978). While they are interesting and important films, neither fits into the cop cycle. *The Gauntlet* does echo the old theme of honest policeman *v.* corrupt hierarchy. But essentially it aims to debunk the previous Clint Eastwood mythology. His lone-cop, machismo mystique suffers some rude blows. Proud of being selected for a mission to bring back an important witness, a prostitute, it transpires he has been chosen precisely because he is the most incompetent cop on the force, and his bosses want him and the witness killed before she can testify. They survive only because the erstwhile loner is continuously helped by the advice of the wise and wise-cracking girl he is meant to protect and ends up depending upon. The mythology of solving problems by gun-play is shattered by two elaborately constructed scenes. First, the police literally shoot to pieces a house Eastwood is hiding in, but he escapes. Second, in the climax Eastwood and the girl run the gauntlet of the whole Phoenix City police force emptying their guns into their hastily armoured bus, but are unscathed.

Assault on Precinct 13 is concerned with none of the themes of the previous cop movies. It is essentially a reprise of the old Indian-fighting Western in an urban setting. A father shoots down one of two young punks who have killed his little girl during a robbery. He is chased to a police station in a derelict part of town which is to be closed down the next day. Also holed-up there is a bus taking some prisoners, including a notorious killer, to jail. The station is attacked by a seemingly endless horde of anonymous, wierdly painted youth gangs who pick them off one by one and close in on the building. Finally, the last few survivors are rescued by other police. The plot echoes that of many Westerns featuring a stagecoach or fort besieged by Indians, but saved in the nick of time by the cavalry. This is not to say that the film is ideologically innocent, any more than was the traditional Hollywood portrait of the savage redskins. But the image of the threatening and faceless teenage gangs is subordinated to the generation of suspense.

The decline of the cop cycle is not surprising. The Watergate

revelations have made unabashed support of police vigilantism harder
for conservatives, while liberals have more weighty targets than routine
police practice. However, the cop will not disappear from the screen. As
Marlowe said in the closing words of *The Long Goodbye*: 'I never saw
any of them again – except the cops. No way has yet been invented to
say good-bye to them.'

Notes

1   Tom Ryall, *The Gangster Film* (London, 1979), p. 2.
2   Stanley J. Solomon, *Beyond Formula: American Film Genres* (New York,
    1976), Ch. 5, 'The Search for Clues', does suggest that there is an
    abiding genre of detection films with distinct sub-categories of police
    or private detective heroes. To cope with films like *The New Centurions*
    (1972) or *Detective Story* (1951) where the central concern is
    manifestly not with criminal investigation, he postulates a third,
    smaller category: 'police life' films. Solomon is correct to discern
    common patterns in the private detective tradition, although he tends
    to neglect the important differences between the hard-boiled private-
    eye and gentlemanly amateur sleuth genres. However, I would not
    accept the argument that there is a common generic pattern
    encompassing the various cycles of films with police heroes
    (Solomon's examples are actually all drawn from the 40s *policiers* or
    the 1960s–1970s supercops). Solomon's attempt to discern such a
    pattern neglects crucial differences. For example, he claims 'The
    sources of motivation in the detective film do not constitute an area of
    interest . . . in virtually all police films and all but a few private eye
    films the motivation proceeds from the standardised, unquestioned
    elements of the milieu. Briefly stated, all detectives hate crime and
    criminals' (p. 204). While this is true of many films in the earlier cop
    cycles, it is certainly not true of the more recent examples which I
    discuss below as 'the new blue films'. The concern of these movies is as
    much with the character and motivations of policemen and police
    work (which Solomon would see only as the theme of the 'police life'
    category) as with crime detection.
3   This is the conclusion of much recent historical and sociological work on
    the police, for example Peter Manning, *Police Work: the Social
    Organisation of Policing* (Cambridge, Mass., 1977).

4   Ryall, *The Gangster Film*, esp. p. 23.

5   Eugene Rosow, *Born to Lose: the Gangster Film in America* (New York, 1978), p. 388.

6   Andrew Bergman, *We're In the Money: Depression America and its Films* (New York, 1971), p. 14.

7   For informative histories of cinema detective series see William Everson, *The Detective in Film* (New York, 1972), and Jon Tuska, *The Detective in Hollywood* (New York, 1978).

8   Colin Watson's memorable phrase from *Snobbery With Violence* (London, 1971).

9   'The values put forward by the detective story . . . are those of a class in society that felt it had everything to lose by social change', as Julian Symons puts it in *Bloody Murder* (London, 1974), p. 16. It was *de rigueur* for apologists to stress that this apparently trivial and 'cheap' form of literature was avidly read by 'top' people. 'It is a familar fact that many famous men have found in this kind of reading their favourite recreation, and that it is consumed with pleasure, and even enthusiasm, by many learned and intellectual men', as R. Austin Freeman put it in his 1924 'The Art of the Detective Story', reprinted in *The Art of the Mystery Story*, ed. Howard Haycroft (New York, 1946), p. 8. For all the pretensions of paraphernalia like the oath of the Detection Club and Ellery Queen's 'challenge to the reader', the appeal of the detective story probably lay less in the intellectual puzzle element, than the twin factors titled by Colin Watson: *Snobbery with Violence*.

10 The irony was stressed by the advertising copy: ' "Public Enemy" Becomes Soldier of the Law'.

11 See Carlos Clarens, 'The Hollywood G-Man 1934–1945', *Film Comment*, vol. XIII, No. 3 (May–June 1977), pp. 10–16; and R. G. Powers, 'J. Edgar Hoover and the Detective Hero', *Journal of Popular Culture*, vol. IX, No. 2 (fall 1975), pp. 257–78.

12 Bergman, *We're In The Money*, pp. 84–5 cites several examples of the enthusiastic response from the guardians of the nation's morals.

13 Milton Meyer, 'The Myth of the G-Men', *The Forum* (September 1935), p. 145.

14 Bergman, *We're In The Money*, p. 88.

15 Quoted in Rosow, *Born to Lose*, p. 226.

16 The apotheosis of this trend was the appearance on the range of rustling Nazi or Japanese saboteurs trying to disrupt the US Army's supply of

livestock in such 'B' Westerns as *Cowboy Commandos* or *Texas to Bataan*.

17   Raymond Durgnat, 'The Family Tree of the *Film Noir*', *Cinema Cambridge* (1970), pp. 49–56.

18   Raymond Chandler, *The Long Goodbye* (London, 1959), p. 298.

19   There were, of course, films in this period which chimed in with the McCarthyite atmosphere and advocated no-holds-barred methods, especially against the 'Reds', Mickey Spillane providing a literary model for this. Andrew Dowdy, *The Films of the Fifties* (New York, 1973), Ch. 2 analyses the cycle of rabidly anti-communist G-Man films like *I Was A Communist for the F.B.I.* (1951). Mostly these were box-office fiascos, suggesting that McCarthyism couldn't fool all the people all the time.

20   Donlevy's optimistic reply 'the law only hurts bad people' is patently false in the context of these films.

21   Quoted in D. Downing and G. Herman, *Clint Eastwood: All-American Anti-Hero* (London, 1977), p. 63.

22   This police backlash is discussed more fully in Robert Reiner, 'Fuzzy Thoughts: the Police and Law and Order Politics', *Sociological Review* (May 1980).

23   Robert Reiner, *The Blue-Coated Worker* (Cambridge, 1978), p. 79.

24   Pauline Kael, 'Urban Gothic' in *Deeper into the Movies* (London, 1975), p. 318.

25   Wambaugh dissociated himself from the film and took out an injunction against the use of his name in publicity for it. Another film based on a Wambaugh book, *The Onion Field* (1979), has appeared since the time of writing.

Eric Mottram

Blood on the Nash Ambassador: Cars in American films

1

Decoding the automobile in American movies is part of the study of interactions between culture and technology, between the human body and its extensions in tools and machines, and their presentation in the 'multivocal and polysemous' structures of America or any society. The intervention of a new machine 'alters the sense ratios or patterns of perception' and restructures the environment and what Claude Bernard called the *milieu intérieur*, and Hans Selye translates as 'the internal environment'.[1] Cars are used for other purposes besides transport. The large black 1920s limousines in Roger Corman's *The St Valentine's Day Massacre* (1967) register the use of vehicles for submachine guns in the hands of agents of gangster leaders, and their violin cases did not protect violins (Billy Wilder had fun with this fact at the beginning of *Some Like It Hot*, 1959). The car as transport is parodied, just as the mob's boardroom meetings at large polished tables parody the gangster operations of corporation directors. As Michael Corleone explains to Tom Hagan in *Godfather II* (Coppola, 1974), 'all our people are businessmen'. In Corman's film Jason Robards's Al Capone is a Carnegie who stretches the law only a stage further than the 'legitimate' millionaire. In the interchange of cars and motorcycles, the police and the criminal share their violations within the elasticised interfaces of law and permission. In Peckinpah's *The Getaway* (1973), the car which harbours Steve McQueen and Ali McGraw parodies home as the only enclosure their love on the run is afforded – which in turn parodies the usual uses of the getaway car in gangster films. In these and related ways, the automobile's mobility frequently indicates the amorality and immorality of human needs in action and the sheer adjustability of American social codes to requirements of the thrusting self in a society which has hardly begun to consider seriously the nature of peaceful relationships between vertical personal projection and lateral community coherence. Expedient mobility evades rigid oedipal obediences as far as possible. Stanley Milgram's dramas in *Obedience to Authority*[2] are endlessly paralleled in American films since the 1929 Crash, the key event of disillusionment and patching recovery, overlaid with moral perfidy, in recent American history. The car has been a major instrument in the battle to establish levels of popular morality in an endlessly collapsing and recovering hegemony. Necessarily, American films have shown an insatiable appetite for this continual state of emergency.

The combined weaponry of car and gun dominates law, and thereby enables the challenge and response structure in Penn's *Bonnie and Clyde* (1967), the classic evasory movie of the South-east Asia War and domestic Civil Rights period, and in the elaborately timed attacks of Don Seigel's *The Killers* (1964). Technically, capers invariably parody free enterprise and warfare, the main occupations of official America; as Edward G. Robinson says in *The Biggest Bundle of Them All* (Annakin, 1966), 'Timing, planning and, above all, daring and it's ours'. So that there are few surprises in American films, outside cutting and editing effects. Recognition patterns dominate, generating an audience with, as William Gaddis puts it, 'the unhealthy expectancy of someone who has seen a number of American moving pictures'.[3] In the history of conventions in Hollywood 'situations are as recurrent in movies as the set themes of speeches in Seneca's plays'.[4] Even technology in science fiction films generates the unknown – a blob, a Thing, a gorilla, an ant – so that it can be dealt with in customary categories. It is the apes who use minimal technology rationally, playing the Houyhnhnms to astronauts in *Planet of the Apes* (Schaffner, 1968), not the technologically superior but emotional humans. Cool Buster Keaton never actually triumphs over the machine he is caught up with: it becomes instrumental, since *he* is the ape on the planet of *The General* and *The Navigator* (Keaton and Clyde

Bruckman, 1926; with Donald Crisp, 1924), surviving the train and the liner – and in other films the steamboat, camera, film-projector, car and motorcycle. But in doing so he becomes a machine himself, hence the emotionless mask, very nearly the mask of a 'bachelor machine':[5]

> . . . each 'meet' with Machine some 'sport' with larger and more emphatically playful Gods.
> The chronological trace of his whole careering shows Buster growing smaller and – finally tiny . . . insect-like – in relation Deus Ex Machines. They use him much as he Them. He has become a wildly flexible cog in Their Destination. He is an involution sizewise back thru the whole of childhood to himself as Cosmic Hero: Tom Thumb.[6]

In comparison Jerry Lewis appears as a surreal escaper – in *The Family Jewels* (Lewis, 1965) he comes on as the idiot who falls out of a plane and disarms a torpedo, a fantasy comic-strip character, an extension of Mack Sennett's escapers in cars, part of a world whose violence cannot violate or seriously injure. The Kid/Idiot triumphs through luck and rapid instinct rather than intelligence and understanding. It is Frank Sinatra's cop in *The Detective* (Douglas, 1968) who uses the car to think in, and the Joad family that escapes Dust Bowl extermination and makes for the orange groves of California in a Model T in *The Grapes of Wrath* (Ford, 1940) for a new life within the capitalist structure. The Joad trek is parodistically prefigured in the exodus of W. C. Fields and his family in *It's a Gift* (McLeod, 1934) and itself becomes the model for one kind of road-movie to come. Their battered jalopy became the archetype of American automobile usage during the Depression and later. Survival by car is a fixed motif in American films.

But the sparagmatic dismemberment or utter demolition of the car is equally obsessive, nowhere more so than in the Laurel and Hardy classic *Big Business* (Horne, 1929) where car demolition is paralleled by house-smashing. Brakhage takes its implications further: '. . . the subject is 'war' itself . . . Xmas in Los Angeles – that was a start! . . . a joke perhaps – along with a house that was due to be wrecked . . . a destructable prop'.[7]

But 'war' in Laurel and Hardy's scenario is virtually divided between the sheer fun of smashing a house and the sheer fun of competitive revenge through the vulnerability of a car's parts: a dream, in fact, of violence fulfilled within the limits of a dream movie. Cars, like any other familiar object, re-function in transformatory situations in dream and waking life alike. Hitchcock's car dream tells him a scene he can use: 'In one of my dreams I was standing on Sunset Boulevard, where the trees are, and I was waiting for a Yellow Cab to take me to lunch. But no Yellow Cab came by; all the automobiles that drove by me were of 1916 vintage. And I said to myself, 'It's no good standing here waiting for a Yellow Cab because this is a 1916 dream'. So I walked to lunch instead.'[8]

The eminent practicality of Hitchcock's films includes the treating of technology as apparatus for dream and murder. So that the sinking of the car in *Psycho* (1960) is not only Norman Bates's method of eliminating evidence against his 'mother'; the bubbling, sucking sound is the sound of traumatic experience, but also of the overcoming of any fetishistic clinging to cars. Car-owners in the audience for *Psycho* watch the type of their beloved, paid-for, intimate object being taken over, wastefully, by nature. Two years later Leslie Caron and David Niven escape from a swamp in which their 1957 Ford station-wagon is vanishing (*Guns of Darkness*, Asquith, 1962). Movies imitate the information processing of dreams in their semantics. The car's resurrection under the end-titles of *Psycho* adds to the perturbation, especially since it is so muddied. For those to whom the car is a partly vicious, partly lethal instrument the scenes afford peculiar satisfaction, ambivalently placed within the rest of the film's coding, leading to involvement in a certain poetry:

Whereas the instruments of poetic or philosophical communication are already extremely perfected, truly form a historically complex system which has reached its maturity, those of visual communication which is at the basis of cinematic language are altogether brute, instinctive. Indeed, gestures, the surrounding reality, as much as dreams and the mechanisms of memory, are of a virtually pre-human order, or at least at the limit of humanity – in any case pre-grammatical and even pre-morphological (dreams are unconscious phenomena, as are mnemonic mechanisms; the gesture is an altogether elementary sign, etc.).[9]

Hitchcock has once again involved us in re-enaction of secret desire. The decoded scene speaks volumes about the universal car situation, the conversion of transport into libidinous impulse. The accumulation of such effects is in fact the cinema: 'Each film is not only structural but structuring . . . The viewer is forming an equal and possibly more or less opposite "film" in his/her head, constantly anticipating, correcting, re-correcting – constantly intervening in the arena of confrontation with this given reality, i.e. the isolated chosen area of each film's work, of each film's production.'[10] Simplistic structuralist separations into natural and cultural, denotative image and connotative composition, primary and secondary 'levels' – as for example in Christian Metz[11] – weaken complex reception of the simultaneities in Hitchcock's vision, or indeed practically any car images crucially used in a film. For the director who understands film image, the sign is never, as the Saussure line insists, arbitrary; the object is never a metaphor; 'no symbols'.[12] Each film requires the kind of 'collective text' produced by the editors of *Cahiers du Cinema* for Ford's *Young Mr Lincoln* (No. 223, 1970), so that what Pasolini calls 'the profoundly oneiric nature of cinema, as also its absolutely and inevitably concrete nature' can be read. The oneiric and concrete constitute a poetics rather than a semantics: the artist's necessity precedes the parasitism of the theorist; the society of the audience precedes the critic's journalistic needs to hold his ego-column within whatever bit of the Press has afforded him a ledge. The relationship of image to reality – arbitrary terms since the reality is itself a construct – is usefully given by Umberto Eco as 'iconic sign' which reproduces 'some of the condition of perception, correlated with normal perceptive codes . . . we perceive the image a message referred to a given code, but this is the normal perceptive code which presides over every act of cognition'.[13] John Wayne big-game hunting by car in *Hatari* (Hawks, 1962) or W. C. Fields golfing from a 1930 Bantam called 'Spirit of Brooklyn' (*The 300 Yard Drive*, Monte Brice, 1930) set up complex systems of memory and anticipation.

2

Raymond Lee has provided us with excellent iconic information on Hollywood's absorption of the automobile from the beginning (in fact film, car and jazz grew together as a key twentieth-century triad for major interfaces).[14] But although cars are evident in very many movies, their use is often for other purposes than transport. Clara Bow, Joan Crawford and Jean Harlow were the first girls to have love scenes in cars, parallel to Bogart, Cagney and Robinson using cars as wheels for guns. Andy Hardy/Mickey Rooney fell in love with a car. Miss Bow took a California football team riding in the early hours in her Kessel. Valentino raced his Isotta Fraschini and Avion Voisin (1925). Miss Harlow vamped it up in her black V-12 Cadillac. Jackie Coogan kept two Rolls Royces, even if he had to maintain a kid-star image, and his father brought the first Rolls agency to Southern California. Dolores del Rio drove a Model A Ford. And so on, all the data still on record. But then Cecil B. DeMille mounted a camera on the back seat of a car; Hoot Gibson bulldogged a steer from a car; and back in 1910 or 1913 – reports vary – Mack Sennett quoted Ezekiel x. 10 – 'As if a wheel had been in the midst of a wheel' – and the Tin Lizzie became a star – chased, caught, chasing, and choreographed. Raymond Lee's stills and snaps tell the story of car–star–director interchange, with informative captions such as 'Adolphe Menjou tempts Constance Bennett with a 1930 Cadillac, which introduced the V-16 engine. The car, which cost over $8,000, is today considered a true classic' (a quarter of a century later Judy Holliday will realise her transport dreams of wealth in *The Solid Gold Cadillac* (Quine, 1956)), and of Cagney's wound in *Each Dawn I Die* (Keighley, 1939): 'The blood is being spilled on a 1930 Nash Ambassador.' The fantasising of cars occurs from the beginning of movies. Since both cars and movies were distributed throughout the class structure, fantasy proliferated according to class need. The car has never become entirely alien, even if it is a major energy waster, environment polluter, and is out of date by every known standard by 1960. The Keystone Model T Fords were gag instruments, implements of farce and the grotesque in national imagination, along with the police (in outsize uniforms which suited the destroyed fetish of the automobile *and* the sense that law-enforcement was acrobatics). As recently as 1968 the Model T is fantasised – Fred MacMurray flies in a 1915 version in *Son of Flubber* (Stevenson, 1963) – and cars are gag props in *The Great Race* (Blake Edwards, 1965), the exemplary parody of Grand Prix and road movie genres. Laurel and Hardy tore apart a 1919 Model T in *Two Tars* – and so did Harry Langdon and W. C. Fields (*It's the Old Army Game*, Edward Sutherland, 1926). James Dean drives a 1926 Ford pickup in *Giant* (Stevens, 1956), while the rich Texans own Rolls Royces and Lincolns, and Elizabeth Taylor seduces Dean in a 1932 Duesenberg. Dean's own Porsche Spyder came later and still exists in sacred fragments in various parts of America.

The Three Stooges used a Model T for fun, but in the 1930s cars began to bear the brunt of gangster action or were crashed for nemesis. The 1942 Ford Jeep came of age as a shield for Spencer Tracy in *Bad Day at Black Rock* (John Sturges, 1955) – although there had already been *Four Men in a Jeep* (Lindtberg, 1951), *Four Jills in a Jeep* (Seiter, 1944), and the Martin and Lewis vehicle *At War with the Army* (Hal Walker, 1950).

Cars on fire are standard joys, especially since colour tinged the screen: the examples are too numerous to mention. But among other uses can be cited John Wayne fighting off a rhinocerous from a 1948 Chevrolet truck in *Hatari!*, John Conte caught between a 1958 Thunderbird and a 1958 Mercedes in *Ocean's Eleven* (Milestone, 1960), and probably the first car to be driven into a shop – the 1914 Model T in a 1917 Keystone comedy (this is now a cliché of course). Drunken driving for fun is established in Chaplin's *City Lights* (1931 – the car is a Rolls Royce). W. C. Fields's driving in *The Bank Dick* (Eddie Cline, 1940) terrifies a bank bandit into a dead faint, while the gays polishing highly polished cars with swansdown puffs in *Kustom Kar Kommandos* (Anger, 1965) to the sound of Mick Jagger's 'Satisfaction' provide other sensuous pleasures (the film was started when Anger received a Ford grant).

Taxi Driver (Scorsese, 1976) is the most recent in a long taxi series exploiting the vulnerability and opportunities of the trade. Joan Crawford starred in *The Taxi Dancer* in 1927 and Cagney was a cabbie in *Taxi* (1932, Roy del Ruth). 'Follow that car!' is a command convention, and so is the private eye's friendly cabbie (notably in *The Maltese Falcon*, Huston, 1941). Scorsese's Travis Bickle investigates city life through his cab, and trains for moralistic vengeance with fetishistic guns, becoming a national hero by rescuing an under-age junkie hooker by slaughtering her pimp. His fellow taxi drivers either fantasise his sexual powers and his bravery in taking fares all over New York, or, like Wizard, offer a sham reputation for knowledge and insight. In fact he moves out, through his cab, into the alien world of Times Square and the political upper middle class. He works nights anywhere, as the opening scene makes clear, because he cannot sleep, the indication being that he fears masturbation and that this relates back to an experience with the Marines. His life lies between tablets and guns in a squalid bedsitter and the taxi, between an enclosed private life and social life dominated by the exigencies of taxi driving – so that the opening huge close-up of the yellow cab and the closing shot of the same cab in the same downtown streets is accurate. Travis is a male degenerate, loose on the night streets, a soldier fighting a myth of violence in an ignorance appalling in its rabid self-generation. *Taxi Driver* is a war film: Travis needs to intervene in other people's lives out of inadequate knowledge and a desire to dominate – hence the Cherokee haircut. His gun-ridden invasion and his subsequent heroism constitute an analysis of war and its glorification in a society which still refuses to understand its intervention in South-east Asia.

Between the city gangster and taxi films, and the road films, lies the major genre of the race movie. Examples are legion, from an early Christie Comedy, *Race Caper*, and the 1927 *Fast and Furious* (not Busby Berkeley's 1939 film of the same name) to Hawks's *The Crowd Roars* (1932), with Cagney as a racing driver and using an actual race track (as in *Devil on Wheels*, 1939), Clarence Brown's *To Please a Lady* (1950 – Clark Gable as a racing ace), and movies with titles like *The Green*

Helmet, Road Racers and *The Racers* (with Kirk Douglas) through to Corman's *The Young Racers* (1963). In Paul Newman's *Winning* (Goldstone, 1969) the hero is a victory maniac, and the work features footage of a seventeen-car smash-up on the Indianapolis track. Stars' personal involvement in racing is well documented. James Dean's morbid desire to race probably began with the making of Nicholas Ray's *Rebel Without a Cause* in 1955, conceived as 'a pool of information gathered from police, parents and kids'. The 'chickie run', in which Dean drove a 1946 Ford, records a commonplace challenge structure within the corrupt morality of competitive society:

[Irving] Shulman remembered a newspaper item about a 'chickie run' at night on Pacific Palisades. A group of adolescents had assembled in stolen cars on the clifftop plateau. Drivers were to race each other towards the edge. The first to jump clear before the rim of the cliff, the drop to the sea, was a 'chickie'. On this night one of the boys failed to jump in time. The 'chickie run' on the cliff replaced the original blind run through the tunnel.[15]

(*The Blind Run* had been considered as a script initially for a film on children and adolescents; Ray chose Shulman as his scriptwriter because he had been a high-school teacher and was deeply interested in sports cars.) Dean researched his role by mixing with teenagers and gangs modelling themselves on movies until the film became a personal responsibility, a deliberate counteraction to *The Wild One* (Benedek, 1953) – incidentally Marlon Brando contemplated narrating a documentary on Dean, 'maybe as a kind of expiation for some of my own sins. Like making *The Wild One.*'

Dean used cars for the risks of speed, as a philobat's need to draw near to death,[16] first driving an MG, two Porsches, and a Ford station wagon, and then racing cars in 1955, working on his own machine, reaching a level sufficient to be entered in the California Sports Car Club races: 'It's the only time I feel whole'. He also loved bullfighting, kept a Colt .45 on the film lot, entertained Aztec fantasies, posed in a coffin, kept a model gallows in his New York hotel room, was known – according to Kenneth Anger – as 'the human ashtray' for his sexual proclivities,[17] and used to repeat a line from Ray's *Knock On Any Door* (1949): 'Live fast, die young, and have a good-looking corpse'. He died at the wheel of his Porsche Spyder after being ticketed for driving at 65 in a 45 speed zone. He had driven into a Ford sedan which he could not avoid.

The car enabled Dean to be self-accountable, an extension of Emerson's cowboy self-reliance, which remains in control of the American male. In *Giant* his cowboy hat and old car exemplify his mobility. After his death, the James Dean Death Club lit candles, played Wagner, and discussed their cult centre. For fifty cents you could sit at the wheel of the wrecked Spyder, and bits of its metals were sold as relics. Frank O'Hara celebrated him twice as the sacrificed hubristic hero of the gods, 'racing towards your heights', and Dos Passos placed him as an age type in *Mid Century* in 1961, one of 'the Sinister Adolescents' who were 'box office'. And Dean features among the dedicatees of Kenneth Anger's *Scorpio Rising* (1966) and among the star devotees of bondage in Anger's *Hollywood Babylon*.[18]

Steve McQueen's less morbid involvement is documented in McCoy's biography.[19] After military service, he partly supported himself motorcycle racing, but in 1960 hung a sign on his bike reading 'The Mild One', in protest against his Hollywood reputation, and transferred his speed addiction to cars: 'speed rivals making love'. Facial plastic surgery, broken limbs and deafness were no obstacle. By 1965 he had gained a good reputation as a racing driver and owned a glittering stable of cars. He maintained that his dedication was without 'any death wish like Jimmy Dean'. For *Bullitt* (Peter Yates, 1968), he carried out his own stunts – under licence from a generously paid city – and his role as police lieutenant chasing criminals came second to the car smashing, reminiscent for him of 'the old Keystone Cops'. The over-rated speed sequences in *Bullitt* were followed by the dullness of *Le Mans* (Lee H. Katz, 1971) and the quieter pleasures of *The Reivers* (Mark Rydell, 1969), in which McQueen played Faulkner's Boon Hogganbeck, driving a 1905 Winston Flier. In *Junior Bonner* (Peckinpah, 1972), his old car and horse trailer take him round the dwindling rodeo circuit in an excess of nostalgia related to the car and plane killing of the last mustangs in *The Misfits*, with its receding dream of independent male life, free from wage-slavery (Huston, 1961).[20]

The difficulties of creating race movies without boring duplications of car scenes are only partly overcome in John Frankenheimer's *Grand Prix* (1966), in which cars are choreographed in pastoral and track scenes, presented in multiple screen images, with their engines orchestrated. But the aim is still to document speed leading to maiming, suicide and virtual murder in a bizarre macho drama. The drivers are junkies of speed hurtling towards ambivalent apocalypse.

For the car chase obsessions in *The French Connection* (Friedkin, 1971), city permission was again received to clear traffic and 'use real pedestrians and traffic'.[21] The director 'had members of the New York City tactical police force to help control' the streets, and maintained that 'murderous and illegal actions' were justified because they were those of 'an obsessive, self-righteous, driving, driven cop'.

Disaster dominates American films as much as it governs British news bulletins on radio and television. A wrecked or flaming car raises desire. The murder of Glenn Ford's wife by car explosion at the beginning of Lang's *The Big Heat* (1953) is therefore ambiguously moralised as the destruction of a police family unit by a crime–business syndicate (as Emmerich remarks in Huston's *The Asphalt Jungle*, 1950, 'after all, crime is only a lefthanded form of human endeavour'). To be uncertain is to be involved. Lang's skills depend on the fact – one of the reasons why Godard placed him centrally in *Le Mépris* (1963). If a police or syndicate car crashes, pleasure is unalloyed – a mainspring of, for instance, Brian de Palma's *The Fury* (1978), in which suprior scientific and occult information is hardly challenged by the old-fashioned technology of a police car. As McLuhan once observed in connection with 'our intensely technological and, therefore, narcotic culture', 'at the heart of the car industry there are men who know that the car is passing'.[22] Obsolescence must be speeded up. Simultaneously the junkie needs another vein. The choreographic film crash continues the dream of inevitable casual disaster on which the renewals of the State is based:

social and economic recovery is as inevitable as the Crash itself.

Films maintain the characteristic western confusion of human life with machine energy, a personal and social neurosis increasingly destructive of well-being in cultures dominated by engines and electronics. We are for ever putting on and plugging into machines and circuitry. Michel Carrouges's *Les Machines célibataires* identifies the typical networks of pleasure and pain. Men and women have always been connected to machines for torture, and *Grand Prix* invites to a feast of tortured pleasure for heroics, money, and the deadly limits of masculinity, auto-erotic and automatic games, 'the nuptial celebration' of a curious but accepted alliance which produces only 'intensive quantities ... to a point almost unbearable – a celibate misery and glory experienced to the fullest'.[23] By ecstatic example, *Grand Prix* increases death on the American roads by intensifying the desire to turn them into tracks of hallucinatory power whose final equilibrium is the production of stereotypical suicide and murder. *Bullitt* and *The French Connection* are also accessory. The human breaking point obsesses the twentieth century, and cars in films are frequently instruments for this process of testing and climax. *Grand Prix* and the rest indicate the tolerance level of gun and car violence quite as much as the more commonly cited *Rebel Without a Cause,* or *Bonnie and Clyde* (Penn, 1967) with its joyful getaways in a 1930 Model A Ford, a 1931 Plymouth, a 1931 Graham, and so on. 'The observation of aggression is more likely to induce hostile behaviour than to drain off aggressive inclinations' is Leonard Berkowitz's research conclusion.[24] The range of cars and stars in Blake Edwards's *The Great Race* (1964) is the exception to the rule – a film almost devoid of brutality and suicidal climax.

In *Bonnie and Clyde*, which combines the chase and road genres, violence results from using cars to violate the status quo, with the criminal pair as 'retaliators for the people' – the words of Arthur Penn, perpetrator of this ambivalently focused, if not muddled, film. The 1930s cars on country roads and in fields, parallel the pastoral effects in *Grand Prix* as the Barrow gang enters its civil war, backed by the jaunty banjo-picking sounds of Earl Scruggs' 'Foggy Mountain Breakdown'.

The Joads appear, as it were, in the form of a share-cropper family invited to fire at the expropriation notice the bank has placed on their old wooden house, and as Bonnie's family and the camp-site travellers who give C. W. Moss water towards the end of the trek. These are supposed to be the "poor folks" – Clyde's phrase – who justify robbery and murder. In fact the car wars focus a country-gangster movie, with the sheriff's posse of the Western in counter-cars. Certainly Penn's car-consciousness made the film:

At that time, there was no national police force: they were all state-confined police forces. When Ford made the V-8, which was sufficiently powerful to out-run the local police automobiles, gangs began to spring up. And that was literally the genesis of the Clyde and Bonnie gang. What happened was that they lived in their automobile – it was not unusual for them to drive seven or eight hundred miles in a night, in one of those old automobiles. They literally spent their lives in the confines of the car. It was really where they lived. Bonnie wrote her poetry in the car, they ate ginger snaps in the car, they played checkers in the car – that was their place of abode. In American Western mythology, the automobile replaced the horse in terms of the renegade figure. This was the transformation of the Western into the gangster.[25]

But *Bonnie and Clyde* spoke contemporaneously, since the car remains the American's second home – it is the plot gist of scores of films, and a reason why a work as critical of car usage as Godard's *Weekend* (1968) has been virtually impossible in America. Directors concentrate on car menace (Robert Mitchum in *Cape Fear*, J. Lee Thompson, 1961), car anxiety (classically in *Duel*, Spielberg, 1971), and the car as the centre of intense energy (*Point Blank*, Boorman, 1967; *Chinatown*, Polanski, 1974; and Barry Newman meeting death in a road block of dredger tractors in *Vanishing Point* (Richard C. Sarafian, 1971)). A major part of car effect emerges from the common identity of cars used by gangsters, diplomats, police, millionaires and mafia. But it is in *The Detective* (Gordon Douglas, 1968) that Sinatra's Joe Leland uses the car for private self-consideration, the only place he can be alone, think back, between the domestic apartment (the female) and the precinct building (the male job); driving in city streets is the arena of flashback. And it is only in Dreyer's accident prevention film, *They Came to a Ferry* (1948) that death actually appears as a car driver before the victim's moment of truth, as a fact in driving itself; and he steers, of course, an antique car. Nor is Guido's escape at the beginning of $8\frac{1}{2}$ (Fellini, 1963) American. In absolute silence, a shot of the back of his head as he sits in his car, traffic jammed in a low tunnel – then the camera pans out of darkness, over the cars, into over-exposed light, looking for an exit. Guido's nervous breathing breaks the silence as his car fills with steam. Other car people look dead. He pounds the window. One driver strokes a woman's breasts. Guido climbs out, *flies* from the tunnel, over the sea. Similarly, in another European's film, *Zabriskie Point* (Antonioni, 1970), Mark walks down a Los Angeles street to phone within a dense technological space, including cars. He escapes it by stolen plane, up into clear space. Beneath him, a middle-class camper driven through Death Valley is covered with tourist labels, signs of false mobility, limited change within the urban density. Bresson's *Le Diable probablement* (1977) reverses the action: suicide takes place within the technology of record player, phone, guns, river boats, television and cars.

3

In contrast, the car contest in *Rebel without a Cause*, the car versus train contest in *The French Connection* (Friedkin, 1971), the car chase in Siegel's *The Line Up* (1954), and the cars, helicopters, motorcycles and horses all entangled in the chase sequence of Arthur Marks's *Detroit 9000* (1973), accept the perverse exhilarations of technological density. American directors freely manipulate audiences' possessive affection for their cars. In *Castle Keep* (Sidney Pollack, 1969), Corporal Clearboy is deeply attached to a Volkswagen, one of the most popular cars in the world. He envisages VWs populating the Earth when men have died out, and when his fellow soldiers fail to sink his car ('it's just showing off'), one of them shouts 'Jesus Christ, it's still alive!' – and Clearboy says 'They're drowning her'. In Bogdanovitch's *The Last Picture Show* (1971) a car is given as a deeply felt gift between youngsters; it acts as a courting apparatus; and it is active as a major alleviation of drudgery, loneliness and isolation in rural America. Cars are courting and testing apparatus again in *American Graffiti* (Lucas, 1973) – the director has said: 'That was my life. I spent four years driving around the main street of Modesto, chasing girls. It was the mating ritual of my times, before it disappeared and everybody got into psychedelics and drugs.'[26] In the film itself cars function nostalgically, therefore, in a vision of a hardly existent uncorrupted America before rock went political. The cars are choreographed to the eras 45s – the age from Ike to JFK, the heyday of radio programmes, with mystic disc jockeys (here it is Wolfman Jack) playing minimal unseen guru and fixer for the kids. As in *The Last Picture Show*, this world has to be relinquished for manhood and the wars of America.

Lucas's soundtrack is mainly an acoustic environment of motors and radio songs. But the car sounds are repeatedly reduced to an over-all monotone, the sound of putting on cars like clothing. Cars are homes, once again; there are no scenes insides homes, and only two buildings are entered – a drive-in restaurant with waitresses on roller skates and the college hall with a commencement dance in progress. The film's style itself is steadily mobile, speeded up only for action against cops (a police car's back axle wrenched away) and a disastrous macho race at the end (much less solemnly stylised than in *Rebel Without a Cause* nearly twenty years earlier). The necessity of car to life is as accepted here as in Michael Pressman's *Boulevard Nights* (1979), with its work in cars and the burnt car as a personal violation.

In Lucas's *THX 1138* (1970), Americans have become technologised full zombies, reminiscent of the workers in *Metropolis* (only uniformed in white, not black). God is a televised picture (based on the blown-up reproduction of a Durer self-portrait). The accoustic environment is as white as the clothing and decor, dehumanised and electronic. Where Curt Henderson escapes small-town America by plane in Lucas's later film, here THX reverts to a racing car to avoid total enslavement; although it is a highly amplified future-car, it images sufficient nostalgia to suggest that the automobile never entirely died.

Even in *Close Encounters of the Third Kind* (Spielberg, 1977) roadside peasants react to early sightings of spacecraft with something like 'They can put rings round the moon but we sure as hell got 'em beat on the roads'.

So much attachment is culturally assumed that it must hurt when James Coburn's new car – a real sign of wealth in the 1930s – is smashed by a livid thug as a warning to pay his debts (*The Streetfighter*, Walter Hill, 1978); and the streetfighter himself expresses his detachment from corruption by refusing a car. The sheer retentiveness of car life began controlling vocabulary early in the twentieth century: in *Skateboard Kings* (Horace Ové, 1977), the cult design of clothing, pads, dance routines, and the defiance of gravity by skate-boarding in a desert water-pipe section, are contained in a spoken language drawn largely from car and bike – for example, movements are labelled grinder, front side-car, aerial edge, extreme tail top, and so on.

Film therefore reflects America as a nearly century-old car culture of remarkable tenacity. *Psycho* plays with the facts, a film dominated by women and cars. A car switch enables a sensual repentent thief from Phoenix, Arizona, with a bird's name – Marion Crane – to escape discovery. After her murder, Norman Bates sinks her getaway car to the same bubbling sounds we heard earlier in the shower as he cleaned up. Between the opening voyeuristic penetration of fugitive bedroom sex, to the retrieval of the muddied car, the film collects policemen, car salesman, private detective, Marion's boyfriend and Bates, like cars, to sink them. Marion is killed 'because' she acted male and trapped herself in Bates's male trap, a motel for car travellers, and victory is from the thrust of Marion's sister Lila and the woman in Bates. Back in 1932 *The Times* pointed up the ambiguities of car-obsession in *The Crowd Roars*: 'The various episodes of this romance of the American motor racing track are at least as painful as they are exciting . . . The ugly emotions of the crowd which delights in such disasters are represented with some accuracy, but it is not explained what we are to think of ourselves if we enjoy this film.' Years later Hitchcock tells Truffaut: "the placing of the images on the screen, in terms of what you're expressing, should never be dealt with in a factual manner". And as Lawrence Alloway observes, violence 'is still a matter of general taste, embodied elsewhere in the styling of American automobiles, which has not fundamentally altered during the same period. The annual style changes were sufficient to entertain us with a comedy of newness but not radical enough to disrupt continuity with earlier models'.[27] In his useful compilation on the 1950s, Jay Berman indicates the first climax of car culture in the United States:

> Automobiles boomed in the fifties. A combination of new found leisure time and money for luxuries created a demand for more elaborate and specialised vehicles; and production facilities, swollen by the defense jobs of World War II, shifted to fulfil the demand.
>
> The auto, formerly a mode of transportation, sought to be a total environment on wheels, rivaling home for comfort and luxury. The auto was heaped with adornment worn as a badge of status, and admired as a piece of jewelry. It filled those empty hours with a new activity, 'motoring'.[28]

Two-passenger sports cars designed for speed became popular in the same decade. Film language using cars has changed likewise. In *The Man on the Flying Trapeze* (Bruckman, 1935), Ambrose Wolfinger's need to drive quickly to the wrestling match is interrupted into stasis by a cop, a chauffeur and a runaway tyre, but that action is largely archaic for the 1960s and 1970s. So is the pessimism in Welles's *The Magnificent Ambersons* (1942), in which 'The Original Morgan Invincible' begins to undermine a bourgeois America founded in the horse city. But by then, as Colin McArthur shows, cars had become murder weapons in 'repeated patterns' which 'might be called the iconography of the genre ... the means whereby primary definitions are made'.[29] Once Sergeant Bannion's car is blown up in *The Big Heat*, repetition of the same scene instils anxiety – as Christian Metz says, 'the cinema is language, above and beyond any particular effect of montage' (although the five bathtub images reproduced in Monaco's *How to Read a Film* indicate the limitations of this idea).[30] Gangsters use city and industrial technology – guns, cars, phones – automatically (the Kojak series is dull because it repeats the genre like a doggerel of slick conservative morality, which a lollypop-sucking officer does nothing to modify). McArthur usefully quotes Andrew Sinclair – saying that the gun-cars 'created a satanic mythology of the automobile which bid fair to rival the domain of the saloon'. But it should be added that by the 1950s the car had become the lethal weapon of any 'average person', voluntarily or not. The gangster film's 'symbol of unbridled aggressiveness', so strong that 'characters may respond with fear to an automobile without seeing the men within it',[31] is repeated in general usage as much as in, say, the car images in *The New Centurions*, in which cars are used as if they were private weapons by men committed to law-enforcement and self-enforcement in a society structured for leadership and competition. The prowl car is a weapon on both sides of the law – if, indeed, that distinction still holds effective meaning. One effect of the Volstead Act of 1919, illegalising the manufacture and sale of alcoholic drinks except for medicine (hence the term 'medicine' for booze) not only gave crime its 1920s impulse, but brought death to the roads as a common daily occurence.

Changes in the sides of law are manifest in *Assault on Precinct 13* (Carpenter, 1978). By this time the car-hunt had become commonplace – revived effectively in, for instance, *The Savages* (Lee H. Katzin, 1974), in which Andy Griffith plays a lame sadist hunting a young guide through the desert. Hunter cars are casual in American action – in Reisz's *Who'll Stop the Rain* (or *The Dog Soldiers*, 1978) cars are used as thoughtlessly as helicopters and armoured vehicles in South-east Asian warfare, in an America given as a combat state in which FBI methods are indistinguishable from any other terrorist order. In Carpenter's film, cars are vehicles of attack by urban guerrillas terrorising a police station. Their prowl car parodies the police, and their siege parodies *Rio Bravo* (Hawks, 1959), pointing up changes as much as using nostalgia as technique. A small girl protests to the ice-cream man that she has the wrong flavour as she is gunned down from the prowl car. There are no innocent bystanders in America, 1978. And when Julie cries, 'Why would anybody shoot at a police station?', the audience knows exactly why. The black limousine besiegers are the 1970s equivalent of gangsters or, in Hawks's terms rustlers from out of town. Ethan Bishop, a black police lieutenant, is named after John Wayne's character in *Rio*

Bravo, but it is real blood that drips – not on to a Nash Ambassador but on to a police patrol car – from the murdered telephone linesman. This politics is, in fact, more distinct than Carpenter claims in interviews (for instance, in *Sight and Sound*, spring 1978).

In Walter Hill's *The Driver* (1978), the nature of the getaway driver is examined as professional for the first time. But Hill – who wrote the script for *The Getaway* – opposes Bruce Dern's obsessed cop to Ryan O'Neal's getaway man. Dern's lip-smiling cop admits to no difference between police and criminal except that he is better at his job; the scene is a game. O'Neal, homeless, girl-less, gun-toting maniac killer, poses as a cool, sane man at play in the only game, which is also his job. Having established these contemporary facts, Hill concentrates on the sound and accelerating rapidity of the car in the hands of a manic driver, the dream speedster in all automobile owners, with the same kind of abuse of technology that characterises *Targets* (Bogdanovich, 1967). Ostensibly, beginning with the opening printed examples of beserk murders, the film promotes enquiry into the uncontrolled ownership of firearms. But Bogdanovich lovingly shows us that the car boot is Bobby Thompson's arsenal of weapons with which he will pick off motorists on the highway and in a drive-in cinema. His target is the average secure American in his car home and movie seat. The film's strength is precisely this intersection of guns, cars and film at the point of maximum personal vulnerability, with Boris Karloff as the retiring horror movie actor understanding exactly what action has to be taken against a terrorist to disarm him.

The average car owner believes himself a secure citizen, as secure as the old lady nourishing herself on rape fantasies and obscene phone calls in the trailer park of *Charley Varick* (1973). But there is no privacy in the sacrificial combat state. Don Siegel plays variations on the city mafia extortion movie, but the genre scene is shifted to a small-change business played out in provincial trailer parks, and the action is filmed mostly in sunlit woods and fields. Like Rubber Duck and Dirty Lyle in *Convoy* (Peckinpah, 1978), Varrick is one more "Last of the Independents" – a crop-duster and small-town bank robber. He discovers that his stolen money is part of an out-of-state Mafia drop. In one scene Molly, the

Mafia hit-man, repossesses a car from a terrorised black family; so that Varrick's final victory over Molly is a vindication of the victimised – and it takes place in a huge used car dump, ironically re-used as a barricade against technology and terrorism. Varrick's independence, as well as his sidekick Harman's vulnerability, are exemplified by his trailer home – mobile and anonymous, a combination neatly exploited in Howard Zieff's *Slither* (1973). In this film, a collection of loosely moraled egoists battling for embezzled money are enclosed in a red car hauling a trailer, in which Peter Boyle's wife is permanently housed. And the trailer has been converted from a quarantine tank used by astronauts returning from the moon. They are followed by two huge black armoured vehicles, quasi-military trucks labelled for a children's camp, whose drivers are as invisible most of the time as the aggressive truck driver in Spielberg's *Duel* (1971), the classic road movie exemplifying driving as combat between temporary psychopaths.

In Hitchcock's *North by Northwest* (1959), Roger Thornhill is hunted by a crop-duster plane, across an empty stubble field, flown by a faceless assassin. In Richard Matheson's screenplay for *Duel*, Frankenstein's monster has become a 1970s truck, the road menace for millions of American – and British – drivers. But the work is more complex than the singularity of the action suggests. The exhaust stack of the tanker (labelled or named 'Flammable') pollutes the air stream in which the advertising executive David Mann is compelled to drive. Mann responds to the jungle demands of a male-dominated society. His car radio broadcasts part of a phone-in which includes a wife-dominated, impotent man attacking marriage, and, during a phone call, it is clear that Mann's wife believes he failed as a man in not challenging a man who, she alleges, "practically raped" her at a party. His sense of inferiority becomes pathologically obvious when confronted by working-class truckers in a road café. But it is the tanker which gives the broken-down school bus a helping push, and then, while attempting to kill Mann, wrecks an old lady's Snakerama. Mann accepts the unseen Goliath's challenge, but at the risk of burning his own car out (he failed to renew a damaged radiator hose). He sacrifices the car rather than himself, but the final shots show him whimpering and crying in hysteria while tossing stones down the cliff where the two vehicles lie grotesquely entangled. The blazing sun seems to emphasise the futility of the whole episode.

The police are not involved as they customarily are, in, for example, *Convoy*, and in Sarafian's *Vanishing Point* (1971) – a remarkable film in which the police-hunted driver this time is Kowalski, ex-Marine hero with an honourable discharge after fighting in the Vietnam War, ex-policeman (detective) hero with a dishonourable discharge (drugs and general attitude towards the force), and ex-racing biker who now delivers cars faster than anyone. Sarafian's hero is therefore a man involved in America's official law and technology, and now at large in the huge spaces of the South-west. Kowalski arrives in Denver urgently wishing to return to California; his contract entrusts him with a super-charged Dodge Challenger of exceptional performance. The ensuing chase is used to contain brief flashbacks of his life – a crash, a tender love affair, the rescue of a young girl from mauling narcotics cops, and so on – and to refer him to various people who attack or help him on the road, including the transmissions of Super Soul (Cleavon Little), a blind black disc-jockey operating from a local Colorado station with messages within rock and country music. Hostility comes largely from small town people and from various States' police, and the man-hunt is energised by helicopter and taken up by CB radio. Police bikes and cars duel with Kowalski (no Christian name is found by the police) on the roads of Colorado, Nevada and California; he is handed on from force to force with no explicit charge of crime except fast driving (in each crash he stops to see if the other driver is alive and walking). So that the main theme, as in *Convoy*, is official aggression on the roads – all these films are in fact analogues of American official aggression, both imperialist and domestic. Kowalski's friends are a black biker, a white biker and his stunningly lovely girl (motorbiking nude around their patch of ground in mid Nevada), and Super Soul, who informs of police action until his station is smashed (by local white thugs). To Super Soul, Kowalski is – like the heroes of so many of these road movies – in the hyped-up language of the DJ, "the last beautiful free soul on the planet", and he renames his station after him as it returns to the airwaves.

The internal plot of *Vanishing Point* (like that of Tennessee Williams's *The Fugitive Kind*, made by Lumet in 1959) concerns not only the flight of the independent but the possibilities of salvation – a revivalist group, police law, small-town aggression against a pair of homosexual men who fake a breakdown in their car and turn on Kowalski with a gun – or from forms of individualism: Kowalski himself, the lone snake-catcher in his broken down old car, Super Soul, and the two white hippies. Kowalski finally accepts defeat and crashes his car to explode in a police barricade of huge yellow clearage vehicles. He has used up his resources. There is no place for his courage, energy and driving skills. He takes his place with the men of *The Misfits, Convoy, Two Lane Blacktop* and *J. W. Coop*.

The road movie of the 1970s became a major vehicle for a main traditional American hero, translated from the West, the backwoods and the prospecting sites, and the battle fronts. Cliff Robertson's *J. W. Coop* (he starred in and directed his own script in 1971) copes with the same field as Junior Bonner but with less despair and more technique. After a ten-year sentence he resumes a rodeo career and challenges the reigning national champion, Billy Hawkins. The latter flies a Beachcraft to his rodeos, and Coop has to graduate from a 1949 Hudson to his own monoplane. Transport technology enables old-fashioned masculinity games to survive. Coop ends broken by a huge bull, but still lone and independent, and in addition rich and having had a love affair with an intelligent hippie, with whom he formed a core of value against the corrupt rodeo world and the 'silent majority' aggression, exemplified by a middle-aged farmer driving a Ford truck and a middle-aged driver of a colossal oil tanker, who both identify the enemy as the unions and the "commies".

The three drivers and the hippie girl in Monte Hellman's *Two Lane Blacktop* (1971) are nameless – the Driver, the Mechanic, G. T. O., and the Girl – and homeless, but the cars *are* named in the cast list – Chevrolet, Pontiac and so on. Human lives are dominated by the road, the characters travelling across America as if it were a plain with halts for gas, or an infinite race track. G. T. O., a dreamer and liar, a drifter, a car-proud speed-freak, meets the challenge he needs in the driver and mechanic (a certain class opposition is only identified in the cost of G. T. O.'s car). He races them to the futile end – beyond which the film itself burns out. Hellman creates a fable of expended energy in competition without end, the search for imagined and never achieved satisfactions and victories – and in fact the Girl sings 'Can't get no satisfaction' – once again – while playing a pinball machine. Behind the forlorn elegance of this elegiac film lies the car door banged endlessly on Stan Laurel's bandaged foot, Jackson Pollock photographed on the running board of his old Ford, the used car dump in William Wyler's last film, and scores of Westerns. *Two Lane Blacktop* is the penultimate parody of the core American movie. The ultimate is Peckinpah's effort to bring Rubber Duck and his woman through the obstacle race of *Convoy* (1978), without too much sentimentality and nose-thumbing.

The softness of Peckinpah's nostalgia can be contrasted with Spielberg's *Sugarland Express* (1973) and, more sharply, with Harvey Laidman's *Steel Cowboy* (1978). The former is based on an actual event: in 1969, in which a young Texan couple hijacked a police car, forcing the patrolman to drive them three hundred miles to Sugarland, where the girl is to reclaim her baby, taken by the State from his foster parents. The film is one long chase by a convoy of police cars over several days – the cars talk to each other by loudspeaker, the cops trying to protect their colleague from the inevitable final bullet. The humour is more corrosive and less good-natured than in the Peckinpah, but both films are nostalgic for independence against the State. *Convoy* is nearer in spirit to Raoul Walsh's *They Drive by Night* (1940), a rig melodrama in which two truckers (Bogart and Raft) fight for their money within the competitive violence of the trucking racket. But Peckinpah is more ambitious: 'the purpose of the convoy is to keep moving', says a leading trucker, and in fact this south-west road convoy is an allegorical procession, a process which deliberately collects the nation's problems of leadership, direction and law. 'Keep moving and the complaints will need no serious analysis' is the traditional motto built into this film. The status quo of combat is maintained in a traditional 'Western' equilibrium in which Dirty Lyle Wallace, the patrolman–sheriff claims: 'I represent the law' – against the truckers who actually dramatise themselves as cowboys. Mobility within conflict is the tradition, and it is the very substance of American capitalism. To maintain that order, the Army is introduced to crush the trucker leader, Rubber Duck: 'the State, its police, and its army form a gigantic enterprise of antiproduction'.[32] When, at one point, a police car increases mobility and charges over an embankment, the effect is dreamlike, as if it were an invention of the unconscious.

C. W. McCall's trucking ballad is used to manipulate the cowboy-law elements into a safety region, but the convoy music itself is military rather than country, emphasising combat leading to final confrontation. *Convoy* summarises trucker and road movies right down to a repeat of John Wayne's car being crushed between two trucks in *McQ* (Sturges, 1974). One trucker, observing Lyle's squeezing, remarks: 'They're making the sheriff into a sandwich!' But *Convoy* is as much a war film as *Who'll Stop the Rain* or *The Deerhunter*: the Army blow up Duck's high explosive tanker on a bridge in a scene duplicated and parodied from endless war movies. Borgnine's presence as Lyle ensures the stereotyping. Conflict between the trucker fraternity and the cops undermines the mutual individualist understanding between Lyle and Duck (the CB name of Martin Penwald). Pig Pen, Spider Mike, and the rest with CB code names, are finally trapped in the strict coding of American society, which they, like millions of others, believe supports independence rather than State intervention. Lyle easily obtains his bribes from the fraternity, which knows very well he will continue to demand more and that beating him up in the café makes no substantial difference. Lyle faces Duck with 'there aren't many of us left' – the Junior Bonner and J. W. Coop theme – but it is the racist issue that brings out the latent tension between law and cowboy. Smashing the jail with trucks to release a black comrade is a minimal chivalrous despair in this male, police-ridden world (in which women have babies, are seduced by casual male glances, are eminently beddable, or become themselves forcible truckers – like the fraternity member named the Black Widow).

Peckinpah's café brawl is violent and farcical, in line with his need to make the film a victorious comedy for Duck and the fashionable photographer Melissa. The absurdity of the angry situation and its parodies of macho confrontations is not lost on the director, but the convoy still has to contain the anarchic emotions, protests and frustrations of the south-west community and, by implication, 1970s America, as it keeps moving against police, politicians, and Teamsters' union alike. Governor Haskins proposes taking Duck's protest against police harrassment to Washington as a national cause, which will also help him politically. But Duck refuses because the immediate issue is Spider held in a Texas jail, a black trapped in the rigidities of American racism. The trucker breaks here with both Melissa and some members of the trucker fraternity in order to chase 'the Devil . . . Dirty Lyle', as the ballad has it. When Melissa asks, 'why do they follow you?', Duck replies: 'I'm just in front'. So the discrediting of American leaders will not be corrected from the independent loner. The politician panics when the people choose Duck as a popular hero – practically manufactured by the media, in fact – but the mobility plot is easily allowed to take over: it is the civil war story, without the élitist, samurai overtones of *The Magnificent Seven*. As in *Vanishing Point*, radio communication ambivalently aids the hero, although CB technology and code are devices cop and cowboy have to share. But, as in *Who'll Stop the Rain* and *The Deerhunter*, helicopters intervene, in an attempted arrest by air of the trucker leader on the road: as Duck leads the convoy through the police cars, "the bear in the air" extends the bear in the patrol car.

But Peckinpah's rescue of his independent is comic-strip stuff – no wonder he has Lyle laughing at Duck's escape! Once again sentimental anarchy wins in American fiction: law and army lose out to the miraculous resurrection of Duck from holocaust. Law is defied, but manic law has the last laugh, as extra-legal as it was in the old Keystone movies. America remains a perpetually destructive comic society – at least in its favourite myths. Peckinpah reassembles his dismembered hero and the film ends with an old couple in an old car left in the dust of the victorious convoy, gently kissing. Spider has presumably reached his wife. Melissa has Duck. The car and the truck have enabled Americans to refuse law, the will of the people, politics and the unions. Capra rides again. Peckinpah inherits the Mr Deeds hero, the man without dogma or scripture, and asks us to accept his equation of the laughing cop and the laughing cowboy driver. Americans repeat themselves – the nth time as farce: 'Like car-stylists, film-makers have to work for the satisfaction of a half-known future audience . . . This is one source of the extraordinary quality that films have of being topical while being at the same time conservative and folkloric. A successful film representing a mutation of a current convention will be imitated because it introduces vital information about previously unknown audience interests'.[33]

But a skillful director can put the realism back into a convention and cut the sentimentality. Laidman's *Steel Cowboy* modifies Walsh's 1940 simplifications while using at least some of the old myths. Clayton Pfanner's truck is called 'Outlaw', and both he and his partner K. W. ('I always wanted to be a cowboy') wear cowboy hats and speak in a south-west manner in a language layered with exotic images and, in K. W.'s case, literary instances ('You're harder to find than Richard the Third's horse'). Clayton's wife, Jesse, has an unfinished university degree course to return to; she is both beautiful and intelligent, and finally leaves the husband she loves because his cussed independence leaves them in constant financial anxiety. The increased 1970s cost of living is explicitly the context of Clayton's outlaw sense. When K. W. says 'we're about a week away from wearing uniforms' – company uniforms – Clayton responds as if his manhood is at stake. He drives across a picket line of strikers in order to drive through a payload, smashing through two parked cars outside the depot.

Laidman indulges in little of Peckinpah's fantasy and is concerned continually with the practical matter of living as a trucker, and with the loneliness of the trucker's wife: Jesse's response to her husband's plans for gaining an extra buck is 'And what am I?' Being steadily in debt in the 1970s is pointless; she might as well go back to college. The boss villain, Pinkie Pincus – pink shirt or, like Gatsby, pink suit, and pink custom-decorated car (with cattle horns) – offers fast money for cattle rustling by truck. K. W.'s scruples and his influence on Clayton are eliminated by Pinkie's hit men: he joins Western Trucking (wears a uniform) and is blown up with their truck carrying oil drums. K. W. had functioned as the male equivalent of Jesse's necessary normal perceptiveness of what the financial situation really is ('old Clint Eastwood didn't have to wait this long'). Clayton has to deny he ever had this buddy relationship in order to maintain his independence, but eventually and utterly alone, he can only assert independence by driving his Outlaw through Pinkie's house full of Meissen china, crystal glass, and other expensive knick-knacks – 'this is for you, K. W.!' – a scene in loving and, for once, justified slow motion. Clayton hands over his truck to a driver whose own has burnt out, and fades out of the movie by thumbing a truck lift and by a long shot of reunion with his wife – a touch of sentiment which does not weaken the treatment of transport cowboy independence at all, since Jesse is the point of realism rather than rear view mirror nostalgia.

The road saga will continue for the same reasons that America cannot solve its fuel-consumption greed: the automobile culture is coterminous with Americanism.[34] The process has been lengthy – at least from the smiling Cagney nursing a submachine gun in his limousine in *G-Men* (William Keighley, 1935) to the two neurotic cops of *The New Centurions* (Richard Fleischer, 1972) in a patrol car inscribed: 'to protect and to serve'. The pile-up of cop cars and bikes at the end of *Scarface* (Hawks, 1932), the car advancing on you in a blind alley, the face in the windscreen wipers, the exploding car – still lovingly exploited by Coppola – have long been stereotypes. The Joads of *The Grapes of Wrath* are relegated to the margins of *Bonnie and Clyde*, a film which attempts to make fun out of murder by reverting to Keystone Kop chase methods. The Sennett system made farce out of what Ivan Illich, years later, would dub 'industrial violence such as the speed of cars'.[35] The suicidal games continue to imitate Fields's drive to the maternity hospital – his car gets stuck in a fire-engine ladder. The Princess will continue to entice Orpheus to Hell in her Rolls Royce.

Notes

1   Marshall McLuhan, *Understanding Media* (London, 1964), p. 18; Victor Turner, *Myth and Cosmos* (New York, 1967), p. 269; Hans Selye, *Stress Without Distress* (London, 1977), p. 18.
2   Stanley Milgram, *Obedience to Authority* (New York, 1974).
3   William Gaddis, *The Recognitions* (New York, 1955), p. 844.
4   Lawrence Alloway, *Violent America: the Movies 1946–1964* (New York, 1971, p. 7.
5   Michel Carrouges, *Les Machines célibataires* (Paris, 1954).
6   Stan Brakhage, *Film Biographies* (Berkeley, Calif., 1977), p. 175.
7   Brakhage, *Film Biographies*, p. 155.
8   Francois Truffaut, *Hitchcock* (London, 1969), p. 324.
9   Pier Paolo Pasolini, 'The Cinema of Poetry', in *Movies and Methods*, ed. Bill Nichols (Berkeley, Calif., 1976), pp. 542–58.
10 Peter Gidal, *Structuralist Film Anthology* (London, 1976), p. 3.
11 Christian Metz, *Film Language* (New York, 1974).
12 Charles Olson, 'An Ode to Nativity', in *Archaeologist of Morning* (London, 1970).
13 Nichols, *Movies and Methods*, pp. 493–529, 545, 593–4; see also U. Eco, *A Theory of Semantics* (London, 1977); pp. 191ff.
14 Raymond Lee, *Fit for the Chase* (New York and London, 1969). For car industry information see, for example, James J. Fink, *America Adopts the Automobile, 1895–1910* (Cambridge, Mass., 1970); Joseph J. Schroeder, *The Wonderful World of Automobiles, 1895–1930* (Northfield, Ill., 1971).
15 Nicholas Ray, 'Story into Script', in *Hollywood Directors, 1941–1976*, ed. Richard Koszarski (Oxford and New York, 1977), pp. 244–56.
16 c.f. Michael Balint, *Thrills and Regressions* (New York, 1959).
17 David Dalton, *James Dean: the Mutant King* (New York, 1975), pp. 290, 358, 301.
18 Kenneth Anger, *Hollywood Babylon* (Phoenix, Ariz., 1965), p. 181; Jon Dos Passos, *Mid Century* (New York, 1961), pp. 468–75.
19 Malachy McCoy, *Steve McQueen* (London, 1974), from which the following information and quotations are derived.
20 James Goode, *The Story of the Misfits* (New York, 1963).
21 William Friedkin, 'Anatomy of a Chase', in *Hollywood Directors*, ed. Koszarski, pp. 392–403.
22 McLuhan, *Understanding Media*, pp. 42, 220.

23 Gilles Deleuze and Felix Guattari, *Anti-Oedipus* (New York, 1977), p. 18.

24 Leonard Berkowitz, 'The Effects of Observing Violence', *Scientific American* (February, 1964).

25 Arthur Penn, '*Bonnie and Clyde*: Private Morality and Public Violence', in *Hollywood Directors*, ed. Koszarski, pp. 360–4.

26 Cited in Michael Pye and Linda Myles, *The Movie Brats* (London, 1979).

27 Truffaut, *Hitchcock*, p. 331; Alloway, *Violent America*, p. 25.

28 Jay Berman, *The Fifties Book* (New York, 1974), pp. 76–7.

29 Colin McArthur, *Underworld USA* (London, 1972), p. 24.

30 Metz, *Film Language* (New York, 1974), p. 47.

31 McArthur, *Underworld USA*, pp. 30–2; James Monaco, *How To Read a Film* (New York, 1977), pp. 150–1.

32 Deleuze and Guattari, *Anti-Oedipus*, p. 235.

33 Alloway, *Violent America*, p. 15.

34 Antonio Gramsci, 'Americanism and Fordism', in *Selections from the Prison Notebooks,* ed. Q. Hoare and G. N. Smith (London, 1971), pp. 279–322.

35 Ivan Illich, *Tools for Conviviality* (London, 1973), p. 2.

The authors

Albert Auster is a Lecturer in History and Cinema at the City University of New York.

Philip Davies is a Lecturer in the Department of American Studies at the University of Manchester.

Mary Ellison is a Senior Lecturer in the Department of American Studies at the University of Keele.

Christopher Frayling is Professor of Cultural History at the Royal College of Art, London.

Richard Maltby is a Lecturer in American Film in the Department of American and Commonwealth Arts at Exeter University.

Philip Melling is a Lecturer in American Literature at the University College of Swansea.

Eric Mottram is a Reader in American Literature at the Institute of United States Studies, King's College, London.

Brian Neve is a Lecturer in the School of Humanities and Social Sciences at the University of Bath.

Leonard Quart is Assistant Professor of Cinema Studies at the City University of New York.

Robert Reiner is a Lecturer in Sociology at the University of Bristol.

Ralph Willett is a Lecturer in the Department of American Studies at the University of Hull.

Index of films

Directors and date are cited only if they are omitted in the text. The date given is intended to be the year in which the film was first shown.

General index